OUT ON FRATERNITY ROW

OUT ON FRATERNITY ROW

Personal Accounts
of Being Gay
in a College Fraternity

Edited by

Shane L. Windmeyer
and
Pamela W. Freeman

alyson
books

LOS ANGELES • NEW YORK

NOTICE

Quotation marks around the name of a person indicate the use of a pseudonym. All other names are the actual names of the individuals writing the story.

MANUFACTURED IN THE UNITED STATES OF AMERICA.

THIS TRADE PAPERBACK ORIGINAL IS PUBLISHED BY ALYSON PUBLICATIONS INC.,
P.O. BOX 4371, LOS ANGELES, CALIFORNIA 90078-4371.
DISTRIBUTION IN THE UNITED KINGDOM BY TURNAROUND PUBLISHER SERVICES LTD.,
UNIT 3 OLYMPIA TRADING ESTATE, COBURG ROAD, WOOD GREEN,
LONDON N22 6TZ ENGLAND.

FIRST EDITION: SEPTEMBER 1998

03 04 05 06   10 9 8 7 6 5 4

ISBN 1-555583-409-4

LIBRARY OF CONGRESS CATALOGING-IN-PUBLICATION DATA
    OUT ON FRATERNITY ROW : PERSONAL ACCOUNTS OF BEING GAY IN A COLLEGE
    FRATERNITY / EDITED BY SHANE L. WINDMEYER AND PAMELA W. FREEMAN.—1ST ED.
        A COLLECTION OF ESSAYS SOLICITED BY THE LAMBDA 10 PROJECT.
        ISBN 1-55583-409-4
        I. GREEK LETTER SOCIETIES—UNITED STATES. 2. GAY COLLEGE STUDENTS—UNITED
    STATES—BIOGRAPHY. 3. COLLEGE STUDENTS—UNITED STATES—CONDUCT OF LIFE.
    4. GAY COLLEGE STUDENTS—UNITED STATES—CONDUCT OF LIFE. I. WINDMEYER,
    SHANE L. II. FREEMAN, PAMELA W. III. LAMBDA 10 PROJECT.
    LJ51.088 1998
    378.1'98'55—DC2   98-8371 CIP

COVER PHOTOGRAPH BY WILBER OWENS.

Dedicated to my fraternity brother Jon Moore
and the many brothers of Phi Delta Theta who
gave me the courage to come out, the love to
accept myself, and brotherhood for a lifetime.

Yours In The Bond,

shamu #324

To do what ought to be done,

but would not have been done unless I did it,

I thought to be my duty.

—*Robert Morrison, a founding father of*

Phi Delta Theta, at Miami University, Oxford, Ohio, in 1849.

CONTENTS

PREFACE

INTRODUCTION

SILENCE

STRUGGLE, FEAR, AND ISOLATION

TRUTH AND HONESTY

CAMARADERIE AND BROTHERHOOD

A STRAIGHT BROTHER'S PERSPECTIVE

CONCLUSION

EDUCATIONAL INTERVENTIONS

L et it be said that fraternities are about what matters most: enduring friendships founded on shared principles and personal affinities; living out good lives, not just having good times; cordial laughter, delightful gaiety, robust merriment; the lively pleasures of good companions; the sustaining loyalty of old comrades through whatever fortune or adversity may appear; the settled conviction that lives are lived to the best effect when firmly secured by mutual bonds of deep affection, administration, and respect. In freedom, if wisely chosen, there is fraternity, and in fraternity, if rightly used, there is joy.

—Excerpt from the Baird's Manual of American College Fraternities, 1991

Acknowledgments

A great number of people and organizations have contributed to this anthology and the success of the Lambda 10 Project. First and foremost, we would like to thank the writers who shared their stories with the Lambda 10 Project, especially remembering those who were not included in the final anthology. All of the stories are what made this anthology possible. We thank each writer for his courage, his willingness, and his leadership in "breaking the cycle of invisibility." We would also like to thank Alyson Publications, especially Julie Trevelyan, Greg Constante, Dan Cullinane, Kevin Bentley, Gerry Kroll, and Tom Radko, for making this anthology a reality. Together the stories in this anthology will increase understanding about being gay in a college fraternity and provide an educational tool to counter homophobia in the Greek system.

Numerous organizations and individuals assisted with general support of the Lambda 10 Project and helped with promoting the call for writers in an effort to gather a wide, varied pool from which to select stories for the final anthology. Several organizations deserve special recognition, as follows: American College Personnel Association–Standing Committee on Lesbian, Gay, and Bisexual Awareness; Association of College Union International–Gay, Lesbian, Bisexual Concerns Committee; National Association for Student Personnel Administrators–Gay, Lesbian, and Bisexual Concerns Network; Association of Fraternity Advisors; National Inter-fraternity Conference; Indiana University FIRST STEPP; national office of Parents, Friends, and Families of Lesbians and Gays; *Windy City Times; Bay Area Reporter; The Washington Blade;* and the Center for the Study of the College Fraternity. Several individuals also deserve special recognition, as follows: Richard

McKaig, Mary Korte, Douglas Bauder, Douglas N. Case, Bill Shipton, Jeff Cufaude, Elizabeth Couch, Banu Berkem, Martha Gioia, Rueben Perez, Tony Ellis, Gerald Olson, Mark Guthier, Brett Perozzi, Julie Rowlas, Teri Hall, Karen Frane, Katrina Ross, Tom Jelke, Dale Masterson, Warren Blumenfeld, Mark Connolly, Jillian Kinzie, Jim Johnson, Barry Magee, Jeffrey Spahn, Roger Heineken, John Boyle, Brian Protheroe, Ronn Gifford, Matt Brillhart, Travis Wirtz, Carol Fischer, Sophie Shaaf, Kris Day, and Donovan Walling. We thank these organizations and individuals for their professional and personal support of the Lambda 10 Project.

We also give our thanks to Nita Allgood, Administrative Secretary, who always gave her heart and 110% to the Lambda 10 Project in her "extra" time. Such acknowledgment also is extended to the entire staff of the Office of Student Ethics and Anti-Harassment Programs as well as the Indiana Memorial Union Board at Indiana University. Without their support the Lambda 10 Project would not have been possible.

In addition, we acknowledge that the Gay, Lesbian, Bisexual Anti-Harassment Team and the Kansas Epsilon chapter of Phi Delta Theta provided the impetus for the Lambda 10 Project. The antiharassment team served as a continual reminder of the violence and harassment that gay college students face on campus, while the brothers of Phi Delta Theta gave hope that fraternities can foster brotherhood among gays and straights. Both of these groups served as the inspiration for the Lambda 10 Project and made clear the necessity for this anthology.

And last (but certainly not least), a very special thanks to our respective partners, Thomas A. Feldman and Douglas K. Freeman, who gave their support, devotion, and countless hours to completing the final anthology. We are only as great as the sum of our parts. We luckily had many parts to make this anthology a success. Thanks to everyone!

A Chance to Belong
An Anonymous Letter to the Lambda 10 Project

Dear Lambda 10 Project:

Being gay and a member of the Greek community has been a frustrating experience, to say the least. Because of the intense paranoia people have about gay individuals, I have only admitted my sexual orientation to one other person. There is no doubt whatsoever that I would have been pushed out of my chapter had my homosexuality been revealed, and my fraternity experience meant too much to risk losing it that way. Therefore, if I wanted to stay Greek and active in my fraternity, I had to "be" straight. It wasn't hard, as I've had to do that my whole life. But I feel no one really knows me as I really am.

I am the kind of guy no one would ever think was gay, other than the fact that I haven't seriously dated a woman in a very long time. I'm straight-acting, frequently hit on by lovely women, president of my fraternity chapter as a senior... but as much as I want to be straight, I know I'm not, and I suppose I never will be. It's really difficult for me to realize that the contributions I made to one of our national fraternity's top chapters would be completely discounted had my sexuality been made public. I wasn't president of some lame chapter; we're one of the best they've got! And we're consistently selected as the top fraternity on campus. Yet for me to have admitted being gay would have instantly discredited me from any values I brought to the chapter.

One of our chapter brothers was coming to terms with his homosexuality but found himself ostracized because of it. We were notified a couple of years later that he had committed suicide, feeling alone and pushed aside from both family and friends. Yes, he was dealing with issues other than his sexuality that led to such a tragedy, but his inability to find acceptance from those he wanted it from was undeniably a significant factor. Yet I'm not sure things changed much in the minds of our active members and alumni.

I know of at least one other brother from our chapter who is gay yet held significant leadership roles within the chapter while active. I wonder how many more? If our brothers could see what goes on in the minds of closeted gay members when homophobic slurs fly around the house, would they care? If I was truly a brother when I was seen as straight, why can't I be as a homosexual as well? My deep friendship and unquestioning loyalty to my brothers and fraternity were never suspect before: why would my being gay change anything?

I am still closeted and might possibly be so the rest of my life. I care too much about some relationships between relatives and friends to admit my sexuality right now. My parents are just not ready to handle that reality, and my fraternal friendships still mean too much to throw them away. Yet I know that I will never be able to "act" my way to being straight.

I think this book will show that I'm not alone in my experience. There are many men in fraternities who are gay but live a straight life for fear of being shunned. Some would really be surprised to learn of certain chapter members' being gay. Indeed, I know of homosexual men in every fraternity on campus. But until the larger Greek community is ready to be a brother to another person regardless of his sexual orientation, these Greek members will continue to live a lie among their chapters, trading their true identity for a chance to belong.

We received this anonymous letter less than two months after initiating the Lambda 10 Project. The letter poignantly describes the struggles of being gay in a college fraternity and the necessity of this book in breaking the "cycle of invisibility" that perpetuates homophobia in the Greek system.

Out on Fraternity Row will be the first published anthology on being gay in a college fraternity. The stories recall different experiences, ask many questions, and, most important, acknowledge that indeed there are gay men in every college fraternity. While a few writers chose to use pseudonyms, such stories bring light to the fear that still exists for brothers in coming out to their fraternity chapter, family, and friends.

The writers selected for publication represent many different fraternal organizations, eras of fraternity membership, levels of the coming-out process, and attendance at colleges and universities across the United States. We also intentionally kept the original writing style of the authors in an attempt to reflect their true voices.

The stories were collected through an initiative titled the Lambda 10 Project. The project solicited stories from gay fraternity men nationally through an official "call for writers" and utilized professional college-affiliated newsletters, computerized distribution lists, publications that targeted gay audiences, and other readily available forms of publicity. The Lambda 10 Project was not created on the basis of a value-laden hypothesis, identifying fraternities as positive or negative in terms of the experiences of gay members. Rather, it was focused on the gay members' experiences within the context of how fraternities describe themselves. Contributors were asked to describe their pledging experiences, the nature of brotherhood in their chapters, their roles within the chapters, and their continued fraternity involvement after leaving college. Writers also were asked to identify when they first realized that they were gay, if and when they came out to fraternity brothers and others, and who was most influential in shaping the nature of their experiences.

Douglas N. Case provides a context for readers in the introduction by drawing on his research on fraternities and sororities, his experiences as a gay member of the fraternity system, and his current role as a professional student-affairs administrator and adviser of a college Greek system. His introduction includes a discussion of major themes identified from his research and from the stories. The book is then divided into four sections characterized by the different experiences of the gay brothers, similar to a coming-out process: Silence; Struggle, Fear, and Isolation; Truth and Honesty; and Camaraderie and Brotherhood. The conclusion and educational interventions section translates the stories into action-oriented ideas for the Greek community to move forward educating on issues surrounding sexual orientation.

While we believe the stories share a diversity of fraternal experiences, we also recognize the limits of the Lambda 10 Project. We realize that gay men who have written for the book may be personally invested or more positive about their fraternal experience in college. Such a perspective may have biased the book with more positive experiences.

With this in mind, we recognize that fraternity men who were impact-ed more negatively by their fraternal experience (for example, kicked out as pledges) may not have taken the same time or interest in writing their stories.

In addition, this anthology was intentionally limited to the male ex-perience in the college fraternity and includes stories about both gay and bisexual men. The fraternities described in the stories are all-male fraternities, mainly local and national social fraternities. As such, we be-lieve the stories bring attention to homophobia among men and its im-pact on male friendship, alcohol abuse, and sexual objectification of women. The Lambda 10 Project hopes to collect and publish stories at a later time accounting for the female experience in the college sorority.

Before you begin reading the anthology, we also must explain that both of us have a personal interest in this topic. One of us is a gay fra-ternity man who considers coming out to his fraternity chapter his most rewarding undergraduate experience. The other is a woman whose daily work in student ethics and antiharassment programs makes her readily aware of the acts of harassment and violence toward gay, les-bian, and bisexual students that occur on a college campus. Despite this, the Lambda 10 Project still has been an eye-opening experience for both of us.

Out on Fraternity Row reminds us of the complexity of how homo-phobia hurts everyone and gives visibility to an invisible minority in the college fraternity. We have received and continue to receive numerous congratulatory remarks praising the book and the need for such an an-thology to bring gay fraternity men out of the Greek closet. While re-sources continue to grow on this topic, we believe *Out on Fraternity* Row provides a much-needed qualitative account of the stories from gay brothers (both closeted and out) on being gay in a college fraternity. We hope the book will not only serve as a resource to gay fraternity brothers but also provide an educational tool for the Greek communi-ty and for institutions of higher education.

The anonymous letter shared above remarks that there are gay fra-ternity men in every chapter on campus. Indeed, we believe such is the case on many college campuses. Gay brothers remain invisible—feeling alone, isolated, and fearful of coming out to their chapters, friends, and families. We hope this book will let gay brothers know that they are not alone in their experience. We invite you to share this book with others, straight and gay alike. Read the stories to help understand what it is like being gay in a college fraternity. Give the book to someone who has recently come out to you. Let us together break the "cycle of invisibility"!

About the Lambda 10 Project

Developed in the fall of 1995, the Lambda 10 Project works to heighten the visibility of gay, lesbian, and bisexual members of the college fraternity by serving as a clearinghouse for resources and educational materials related to sexual orientation and the fraternity/sorority experience. The Lambda 10 Project pledges to provide educational resources on issues of sexual orientation within the Greek system as well as to maintain a Web site that lists updates, provides educational materials, and encourages dialogue on being gay in a college fraternity.

Lambda 10 Project
Office of Student Ethics & Anti-Harassment Programs
Indiana University Bloomington
705 East Seventh Street
Bloomington, IN 47405-3809
(812) 855-4463
fax: (812) 855-4465
E-mail: lambda10@indiana.edu
http://www.indiana.edu/~lambda10

Inter/National Fraternity Chapter Listing

Acacia
Alpha Chi Rho
Alpha Delta Gamma
Alpha Delta Phi
Alpha Epsilon Pi
Alpha Gamma Rho
Alpha Gamma Sigma
Alpha Kappa Lambda
Alpha Phi Alpha
Alpha Phi Delta
Alpha Sigma Phi
Alpha Tau Omega
Beta Sigma Psi
Beta Theta Pi
Chi Phi
Chi Psi
Delta Chi
Delta Phi
Delta Psi
Delta Lambda Phi
Delta Sigma Phi
Delta Tau Delta
Delta Upsilon

Farm House
Iota Phi Theta
Kappa Alpha Order
Kappa Alpha Psi
Kappa Alpha Society
Kappa Delta Phi
Kappa Delta Rho
Kappa Sigma
Lambda Chi Alpha
Lambda Phi Epsilon
Lambda Theta Phi
Omega Psi Phi
Phi Beta Sigma
Phi Delta Theta
Phi Gamma Delta
Phi Kappa Psi
Phi Kappa Sigma
Phi Kappa Tau
Phi Kappa Theta
Phi Lambda Chi
Phi Mu Delta
Phi Sigma Kappa
Pi Kappa Alpha

Pi Kappa Phi
Pi Lambda Phi
Psi Upsilon
Sigma Alpha Epsilon
Sigma Alpha Mu
Sigma Chi
Sigma Lambda Beta
Sigma Nu
Sigma Phi Epsilon
Sigma Phi Society
Sigma Pi
Sigma Tau Gamma
Tau Delta Phi
Tau Epsilon Phi
Tau Kappa Epsilon
Theta Chi
Theta Delta Chi
Theta Xi
Triangle
Zeta Beta Tau
Zeta Psi

Uppercase Greek Alphabet

Alpha	A
Beta	B
Gamma	Γ
Delta	Δ
Epsilon	E
Zeta	Z
Eta	H
Theta	Θ
Iota	I
Kappa	K
Lambda	Λ
Mu	M
Nu	N
Xi	Ξ
Omicron	O
Pi	Π
Rho	P
Sigma	Σ
Tau	T
Upsilon	Y
Phi	Φ
Chi	X
Psi	Ψ
Omega	Ω

Breaking the Cycle of Invisibility
by Douglas N. Case

In April 1994, Fox aired an episode of its then popular television series *Beverly Hills, 90210* featuring a situation in which the members of Kappa Epsilon Gamma (KEG) fraternity suddenly discover that their chapter president is gay.[1] As a university administrator whose primary responsibility is advising social fraternities and sororities, I was skeptical of how network television would portray a fraternity (especially a fraternity with the acronym KEG), but since I have done research on the topic of gay fraternity men, I tuned in to watch the show out of curiosity.

In the program, a KEG member, Steve, has car trouble and goes into a coffeehouse to use the pay phone, unaware that it is a place catering to gay men. In the coffeehouse he sees the KEG president, Mike Ryan. Soon, word of Mike's sexual orientation spreads through the chapter. At the next chapter meeting, a fraternity brother, Artie, calls for Mike's expulsion:

"Forget about our reputation on campus, though from now on, whenever they refer to us as the jock house, it is going to have a whole new meaning. No, I think you guys need to think about the future. What kind of pledges are we going to attract? Who's going to show up to rush a gay fraternity? And what about our alumni? We can't survive without their donations. What's going to happen when they realize what this fraternity has turned into? I think the choice before us is pretty clear."

Mike is given the chance to respond:

"When I first came here today, I thought I was going to apologize for being so dishonest with you guys. You see, I didn't think that I could trust you to see that I'm the still the same person I've always been, the man you elected president. Then I started to think about some of the

brothers and the history of this fraternity, and I realized that I was sell-
ing you guys short. I thought about the first African-American pledge
that dared to challenge this fraternity's color line, and now we take it
for granted. And what about the first Hispanic brother? And I thought
about the first Jewish brother and the first Asian-American brother.
And then I realized the problem is not really about me being gay. The
problem is about people being afraid of what they don't know."

Artie retorts:

"What I want to know is how can you compare yourself to them?
You're talking about race. I'm talking about sex—sex with another guy."

Steve, who has made peace with Mike for insensitively spreading rumors, stands up for Mike:

"You're wrong, Artie. This isn't about race, and it isn't about sex. It's
about brotherhood, about loyalty, something you guys pay a lot of lip
service to. Is that all it is, lip service, a slogan on a plaque, secret handshake? Is that what we're talking about here? Because if it is, this fraternity and everything it stands for is a joke. I move that we allow Mike
Ryan to remain a fraternity brother and that we also allow him to remain as president."

In the end, the chapter overwhelmingly votes to retain Mike as president.

Is this story just Hollywood fantasy? Is it realistic to expect that on
our college and university campuses brotherhood can prevail over homophobia? The stories in *Out on Fraternity Row* describing the experience of gay fraternity members and their brothers will help provide the
answer to that question. I wish that *Out on Fraternity Row* had been
available for reading when I was a college student 20 years ago, and I
hope that this anthology finds its way onto the shelves of college and
university libraries so that today's students can learn from the stories
told herein.

Like most gay men, I knew even as a young child that I was somehow different, and when puberty arrived I knew that I was sexually attracted to men. It was not until my 20th birthday, however, when I had
my first sexual experience with a man, that I began to accept the reality that I am gay. When I joined Kappa Sigma fraternity a few months
later, in the fall of 1975, I never considered the possibility that any of
the other members might be gay. As a pledge, I was told that a paint-

ing hanging in the chapter house was the work of a brother who had been expelled from the fraternity when it was discovered that he was gay. I never ascertained the accuracy of that story, but I learned that my sexual orientation was something I needed to keep hidden. A couple of years later, a fraternity brother at the chapter where I affiliated as a graduate student privately asked me if I had ever gone to a popular gay disco, commenting that he thought it was a good place to go dancing. Even though he was obviously trying to discreetly come out to me, while also letting me know that he had figured out my secret, I was too afraid to say anything.

When I began my career as a university administrator advising fraternities, I made a similar assumption that I was the lone gay person in my field. While attending my first annual joint national conference of the Association of Fraternity Advisors and the National Interfraternity Conference in New Orleans in 1980, I wandered into the gay section of Bourbon Street and ran into several fraternity headquarters staff members and fellow campus fraternity advisers. I discovered that I was not alone.

Like most of my colleagues, I kept my sexual orientation very private...until I came out in a very public way a decade later. The setting was the 1990 NIC/AFA annual conference, which, coincidentally, also was held in New Orleans. At the AFA business meeting where I assumed office as president of the professional association, I presented a "Resolution on Heterosexism Within the Greek Community," which called upon university administrators and national fraternities and sororities to "challenge Greek chapter or member behaviors or attitudes that are heterosexist in nature" and to "implement sexual orientation awareness, education, and sensitivity programs on all membership levels and to develop appropriate responses to heterosexist behaviors." A similar resolution had been tabled a year previously, largely because some within the association did not want to address the issue. Determined to make sure my colleagues understood the importance of the resolution, I made the presentation in a very personal manner, outing myself in the process. The resolution passed without dissent (although some of the "good ol' boys" were not pleased) and was accompanied by a standing ovation.

When a reporter from the University of California, Los Angeles, *Daily Bruin* called me a few weeks after the conference to discuss the resolution, I used the resulting story as an opportunity to come out to my students, my family, and the men with whom I had pledged Kappa Sigma 15 years earlier. My fraternity closet door was finally open.

For the first 12 years that I worked with fraternities and sororities at San Diego State University, I intentionally hid my sexual orientation from the students I advised, even though I became increasingly active within the gay and lesbian community. Shortly after I started my career in Greek affairs at SDSU, I ran across a story titled "How Gay is Gayley? Gay Men in UCLA's Fraternities: An Overview" (Gayley Avenue is part of UCLA's "fraternity row") in the 1979 premiere issue of *Ten Percent*, UCLA's gay and lesbian newspaper. The article began with this quote from a gay fraternity member: "Most of my fraternity brothers blindly assume there are no gay people in our house," then followed with this quote from a fraternity president: "I don't think we have any gays in our house, and if we did we'd kick them out." The author, Cass Johnson, interviewed some closeted fraternity men and concluded with this observation:

> "It is paradoxical that the minority group that may well be the most integrated into the Greek system is also the most feared and disliked. It is a situation, however, which perpetuates itself: fraternities voice hostility toward gay people; gay people, therefore, conceal their identity from fraternity brothers. And because gays are invisible to straight members, it supports the idea that gays are alien and threatening. Unfortunately, no one seems brave enough to break the cycle."[2]

I showed the article to the Interfraternity Council president at SDSU that year, who I had learned was gay when we ran into each other at a gay nightclub. We both agreed with the conclusions in the article, and he admonished me to keep my sexual orientation a secret if I wanted to be successful in my career.

During the years of hiding my sexual orientation, attitudes within the fraternity world toward gay members had very slowly begun to change. In 1991, four months after the *Daily Bruin* ran its profile on me and the AFA resolution, another story about gay fraternity men at UCLA was published. This time the story appeared in the *Greek Connection*, UCLA's Greek newspaper, but it was written by James R. MacCurdy, editor of *Ten Percent.* A dozen years after the 1979 *Ten Percent* article was printed, the cycle of invisibility had been broken. The *Greek Connection* story quoted Adam Ross, an openly gay pledge of a UCLA fraternity, encouraging gay and bisexual fraternity men to be more open about their sexual orientation. Also quoted was IFC vice president Dave Gatzke, who observed,

> "Though there will be a lot of resistance to brothers coming out in the current fraternity system, I think the system and its members will grow from it. An openly gay member would force a chapter to examine its purpose for being. Fraternity men should examine what their ritual says about honesty, brotherly love, acceptance, courage, contribution and strength."[3]

Fortunately, as you will read in this book, breaking the cycle of invisibility is not limited to UCLA. Yet across the country, the vast majority of gay fraternity men still feel the need to closely guard their secrets and keep their closet doors carefully locked.

A few years ago I thought it would be interesting to conduct a survey to find out more about the secret lives of gay and bisexual fraternity men. I developed a simple survey that included questions about their motivation for joining, their involvement in the fraternity, the evolution of their sexual identity and experiences, the attitudes of their fellow members regarding homosexuality, and whether their brothers ever became aware of their sexual orientation. Originally the survey was distributed primarily via word of mouth, but as the project progressed, colleagues expressed interest in my work, especially since there is virtually no published research in this area. The survey was refined and nationally publicized via gay and lesbian publications, the Internet, and referrals. Eventually over the course of 2½ years between 1992 and 1995, I received over 450 completed surveys from men.

Since the survey respondents were self-selected, the survey is not a true random sample, but the number of responses and the wide cross section of ages and geographical regions represented give validity to the results. The common themes of the surveys in my research project are reflected in many of the stories in this book.

A question I often am asked about my research is how prevalent are gay fraternity men? The percentage of fraternity men who are gay or bisexual is quite difficult to determine with reliability. In fact, despite much research, the incidence of homosexuality and bisexuality in American society is subject to much debate. Finding out what percent of the male population is gay is not as easy as finding out the percentage that is left-handed. Part of the difficulty involves methodology, and part involves definition. Most people consider sex to be one of the most private and sensitive topics and are simply too embarrassed to discuss issues such as homosexuality with a research interviewer, even when given assurances of anonymity.

The issue is further complicated by attempting to come to a consensus of what constitutes being homosexual or bisexual. When *Sex in America* was published in 1994, with the results of face-to-face interviews conducted by the respected National Opinion Research Center at the University of Chicago with a random sample of almost 3,500 Americans, newspaper and magazine headlines touted the finding that only 2.8% of men identified themselves as gay or bisexual. A more careful reading of the results, however, reveals that when measures of sexual attraction for other men and/or homosexual behavior were factored in, a total of 10.1% of the men surveyed exhibited same-gender sexuality.[4]

People cannot always be easily categorized as heterosexual or homosexual. One of the most significant findings of Alfred Kinsey's studies of human sexuality was the existence of a continuum between exclusive homosexuality and exclusive heterosexuality. Kinsey developed a seven-point scale, with "0" representing an individual who is exclusively heterosexual and "6" representing a person who is exclusively homosexual, based on measures of sexual behavior and/or sexual responsiveness. Kinsey found that only 4% of adult men and approximately 2% of adult women are exclusively homosexual (i.e., those who rate "6" on the Kinsey scale); however, if one also includes those who are predominantly homosexual (i.e., rate "4" or "5" on the Kinsey scale), 13% of adult men and 7% of adult women (an average of 10%) of the adult population could be counted as homosexual.[5,6] The title of the Lambda 10 Project refers to this commonly cited statistic, as does the name of UCLA's *Ten Percent* newspaper.

One encounters similar complexities when trying to determine how many fraternity men are gay. Many men are still developing their sexual identity while they are in college. For example, of the men who completed my survey, 93% identified themselves as exclusively or predominantly homosexual, with the remainder identifying as bisexual. At the time they were initiated into their fraternity, however, less than 40% identified themselves as exclusively or predominantly homosexual and about 20% identified themselves as bisexual. By the time they were graduated, about 60% identified themselves as predominantly or exclusively homosexual and less than 20% still identified themselves as predominantly or exclusively heterosexual. Less than half of the survey respondents had their first postpubescent homosexual experience prior to entering college.

One way of attempting to discover the percentage of fraternity men who are gay was to ask the survey respondents how many of their fraternity brothers in their undergraduate chapter they knew *with certainty* to be gay or bisexual, including those whose sexual orientation had been revealed to them after college. (Because "gaydar" is not always reliable, those members merely suspected to be gay were intentionally excluded from the question.) Using the membership size of the respondent's chapter and an estimate of the average duration of undergraduate membership, I concluded that, on average, about 5% of fraternity brothers with whom the respondents matriculated were currently known by the respondent to be gay or bisexual. It should be noted that many of those completing the survey were still undergraduates or had recently been graduated and that many of the older respondents did not learn of or confirm the sexual orientation of gay brothers until many years after college. Further, given the effort most fraternity men exert to keep their sexual orientation a secret from their brothers and the self-denial phase that many men go through, for each brother a respondent knew with certainty to be gay, there was most likely at least one, and probably more, unconfirmed gay brothers. My conclusion, therefore, is that the incidence of homosexuality within fraternities is at least as high as the incidence within the general campus population and likely even higher.

A related question is why gay men choose to join fraternities. Initially, based on the results of a multiple-choice question in my survey, I concluded that gay men join fraternities for essentially the same reasons heterosexual men join. The most common reasons given were friendship and camaraderie, social activities, and the desire to have a support group and a sense of belonging. It was very clear that very few gay or bisexual men join a fraternity to find sex partners (although about a third of those who responded to the survey did have at least one sexual experience with at least one of their fraternity brothers while in college). As Joseph Hunter Edward puts it in his story in this book, "Gay men do not join fraternities to get a date. On the contrary. Most are so terrified of even the slightest hint of their being gay that they learn to hide it pretty well. It is very much parallel with the reason gay men join the military. It certainly isn't to get a date there either. The risk of being expelled is just too great."

As I read through the stories in this book, however, I noticed another commonly mentioned reason for joining a fraternity that was not one of the choices to the question in my survey. Many of the Lambda 10 writers mentioned that they joined a fraternity as a way of hiding or denying their sexual orientation. For example, consider these statements:

"Maurice": "So when asked why I wanted to join a fraternity, I had one answer for him: to meet women and become sexually involved with them so that I would not end up gay."

Wil Forest: "Beyond the invitation to become a member, I was not sure what I sought by rushing. Maybe I wanted the opportunity for companionship, leadership, and scholarship: Maybe I wanted to appear straight to an unaccepting world."

"Chaz": "Not until now have I really understood how my involvement in certain activities in college can be interpreted as a search for three things: a need for increased self-esteem, a need to be close in some way with other men, and a need to deny to myself that I was indeed gay. I think I came the closest to achieving these three things when I became involved in a college fraternity."

"Scott Smith": "I joined my fraternity primarily because I wanted to learn to be more social and to make up for what I missed in high school. I realized much later that I also subconsciously wanted to make myself straight (by having endless opportunities to meet women in a restrictive environment where gay is taboo). I wanted to have some of that 'straight energy' rub off on me. I thought I could learn to be straight and have straight relationships by crafting platonic relationships with men and perhaps even learning to love a woman."

One way that some gay men in fraternities attempt to mask their sexual orientation is by engaging in homophobic activities. A common characteristic of the male-bonding process in exclusively male young-adult groups is that members attempt to gain group acceptance by demonstrating their masculinity to the group. Young men tend to perceive masculinity to be equated with the sexual conquest of women. The group mentality, therefore, is often openly hostile to homosexuality.

Don Sabo, a sociologist who has studied gender issues in sports, discusses this concept of "homophobic masculinity" in his essay "The Politics of Homophobia and Sport." He argues that "the flowering of homophobic beliefs and emotions in young males is intricately tied to their development of gender identity." There are strong cultural messages that equate homophobia with masculinity. In exclusively male groups, such as fraternities or male athletic teams, "young men act out the role of a gay-hater as a way of constructing their manly identity and building a reputation among their male peers."[7]

Anthropologist Peggy Reeves Sanday conducted an extensive case study of the college fraternity culture and demonstrated how the sexual objectification and dominance of women that is part of the male-bonding process in fraternities manifests itself in sexually aggressive behavior such as gang rape. She also notes the relationship between sexual domination and homophobia in the fraternity culture:

> "The brothers' concern with sexual potency and social success in the male heterosexual role masks a deep fear, hatred, and fascination with homosexuality. Brothers equate virility with heterosexuality. Some brothers reported that when they were pledges there was pressure on them "to get laid" in order to establish their virility as heterosexual males. Fraternities that don't apply this pressure are seen as encouraging homosexuality."[8]

Evidence of homophobia is seen in the fraternity membership selection process. Rushees who are suspected or perceived to be homosexual are frequently summarily rejected from consideration, and if it is learned that a pledge is gay, he is likely to be "depledged" without even the opportunity to defend himself. Fearing that the other members might question their sexual orientation if they defend the prospective member, gay and gay-tolerant brothers usually remain silent when these situations arise, thereby reinforcing the homophobia of the group. As a consequence of this "groupthink" dynamic, the group mentality expressed by fraternity chapters (and other similar groups, such as male athletic teams) tends to be much more intensely homophobic than the average view of the individual members.

Shamefully, some gay fraternity men even engage in the homophobic behavior as part of their "cover." One survey respondent told the following story: "During rush one year, a rushee who had been at our house a number of times and was nearing a bid was, in essence, 'blackballed' after a brother who had gone to the same high school as the rushee said he'd observed the rushee giving a blow job in a high school rest room. What the brother neglected to mention at the time, and I have since learned, was that he was the recipient of the blow job." Another wrote, "A rushee was blackballed because of suspected homosexuality. I was one of the three who blackballed him. Five years later I met this individual again at a bar, and we have been lovers for eight years now."

Another way that gay men in fraternities "prove" themselves to the group is by immersing themselves in chapter leadership activities. One of the more interesting findings of my research is that gay men in fraternities tend to be high achievers. Over 80% of the survey respondents indicated that they had served their chapter in an executive-committee–level office (president, vice president, secretary, treasurer, rush chairman, pledge educator, or social chairman), and, of these, over 20% had been elected chapter president.

As you read through the Lambda 10 stories, notice how many writers held high leadership positions in their chapters or on their campuses. One could argue from this that gay people naturally have greater leadership abilities, but a more likely explanation is that the tendency toward overachievement is actually a coping mechanism. Subconsciously fearing rejection from the group, gay men strive to gain acceptance and respect by demonstrating their commitment and contribution to the group through leadership roles.

Many of the writers in this book share their experiences in coming out to brothers. Most of the men who responded to my survey elected to keep their sexual orientation hidden while they were in their chapter. Only about 40% came out to even a single member, and fewer than 10% came out to their entire chapters. (Note: Choosing to come out is becoming more common today than in the past. Of those in the survey who were graduated prior to 1980, fewer than one out of eight ever revealed their sexual orientation to any of their fellow undergraduate brothers.) Some survey respondents had negative experiences, such as expulsion from the fraternity or ostracism from the group, when their sexual orientation became known. Fortunately, these cases were the exception rather than the rule. Even though gay fraternity men usually have a strong fear of rejection from their peers, both my surveys and the stories in this book indicate that the majority of the heterosexual brothers have at least a generally supportive response to the revelation that a fraternity brother is gay. The response is usually the best when the gay brother has a strategy for coming out. The most common scenario is for a member to tell a few members he trusts highly (often the member's assigned "big brother" or "little brother"), then gradually come out to others individually or in small groups. Others take a bolder approach and decide to come out to the entire fraternity at once, such as during a chapter meeting or during a chapter retreat.

One of the most refreshing surveys I received came from a student at a large Midwestern university who had been president of his chapter and vice president of the Interfraternity Council. He attached a copy of an invitation for his coming-out party ("TJ's Night Out—A Celebration of the Ultimate Revelation") along with a letter he enclosed with it. He sent out 60 of the invitations, with a note that the recipients could invite others provided they shared his coming-out letter with those they invited. Over 120 people attended the party. Prior to the event only his roommate and a few friends knew he was gay.

There is a greater probability of a negative response when the revelation is involuntary, such as when Steve in *Beverly Hills, 90210* discovers his chapter president in a gay establishment. Fraternity brothers seem to respect the trust that a gay brother places in them by personally sharing information about his sexual orientation; they seem to be resentful if they feel they have been deceived by a brother who they discover has hidden his sexual orientation from the group.

It may at first glance seem contradictory that fraternities take precautions not to let a gay member join their organization, yet when they are confronted with a gay fraternity brother they tend to be fairly accepting. The contradiction is better understood, however, when one considers that fraternities are based on the concept of brotherhood. Fraternity brothers strive—with great success—to develop the close personal bonds and loyalty to one another typical of a family. When a gay person comes out to siblings, the siblings' love for the gay family member usually, over time, supersedes any prejudice they have regarding homosexuality. Coming out to fraternity brothers has a similar dynamic to coming out to blood brothers.

As I was distributing information over the Internet about the availability of my survey, a fraternity alumnus sent me a copy of a message he originally had posted to the GayNet E-mail discussion list. The scenario he described was quite similar to the *Beverly Hills, 90210* episode, except that it involved a mid-semester blackball vote on a pledge perceived to be gay. (In this case, the process was referred to as "calling a box," most likely a reference to the traditional wooden box with white balls and black cubes used for secret blackball voting.) The brother who "called the box" said the pledge "didn't fit in," would become the object of derision if he remained, and insisted that the reputation of the chapter would suffer on campus. The person who posted the message is gay and had been the "big brother" of the pledge, yet he presented only a timid defense of his "little brother" for fear of being "tarred" by association. Instead, another brother gave a passionate speech on the value of diversity within the fraternity. The chapter's response in this case was almost identical to the reaction of the members of the KEG fraternity to the self-defense delivered by Mike Ryan (the gay president), and the chapter voted to retain the pledge. The fraternity member who posted the story on GayNet noted, "I feel certain that if the option of rushing known gay men had been put before the chapter, it would have been crushed. Yet the process of getting to know [the pledge] caused these men—these privileged, mostly white, conservative men— to question their preconceptions and take positive, concrete action in favor of diversity." Even though the member in this situation was still a pledge, the bonds of brotherhood had begun to be built and proved to be stronger than the fear of homosexuality.

I witnessed a similar display of cognitive dissonance (psychological conflict arising from incongruous beliefs and attitudes held simultaneously)[9] during my own coming-out process. When I sent the *Daily Bruin* profile of me to my pledge brothers, I received a multipage letter from a brother with whom I had often engaged in spirited political and philosophical debates during our time together in the fraternity. His letter stated, "Homosexuality I believe to be wrong. It is, to my way of thinking, perverse, immoral, and serves no productive end." He went on to blame homosexuality for the decline of modern civilization. Yet as he neared the end of his lengthy diatribe, he tried to reconcile his respect for me with his perspective on homosexuality. My pledge brother concluded his letter by saying, "We have a lot of history behind us, Doug. We pledged Kappa Sigma. We slept in the cold, wet basement [a reference to our pre-initiation weekend]; we shared many a beer; and lots of good times. We grew together into what we would someday be.... Despite our philosophical differences of past, present, and certainly future, I have been and will remain your friend."

Having a brother come out can result in the chapter being compelled to redefine its norms and expectations. Will it be acceptable for the gay brother to bring a male date to a fraternity formal dance? Is it OK to have a male date sleep over with the gay brother at the chapter house? If brothers joke around with the gay brother about his sexual orientation, will it be perceived as brotherly "ribbing," or are such comments off-limits? Will the gay brother be permitted to display posters or calendars with pictures of men in his room? If so, must he take them down during rush or parents' day? Will the chapter object if the member assumes a visible role in a campus gay and lesbian organization?

Sometimes, fearing that the chapter will be branded as the "gay fraternity" and thereby have difficulty in membership recruitment, the group may attempt to place constraints on a gay brother's behavior. The gay brother may feel obligated to protect the group's reputation by remaining discreet about his sexual orientation. If the gay member feels too restrained by the group norms, he may gradually withdraw from involvement with the chapter (i.e., "go inactive").

Simply having the opportunity, however, to discuss the challenges of dealing with openly gay fraternity brothers is a positive indication that fraternities, bastions of traditionalism, are indeed gradually changing with the times. Today, more fraternity members are electing to be open about their true selves instead of living with a constant fear of discovery and ostracism.

For me, the most moving story in this collection is the story of Sean, a chapter president and Interfraternity Council president who committed suicide after his brothers discovered he was gay. I know from some of the narratives attached to my own surveys that Sean's desperation and suicide is not a unique situation. It is my fervent hope that *Out on Fraternity Row* will create a better understanding and acceptance of gay fraternity members and that gay fraternity members will feel more comfortable being open and honest about their true identities. Perhaps the day will come when all young men like Sean will be able to experience fraternity life with pride and dignity rather than feeling a need to end their lives in shame.

Douglas N. Case is the Coordinator of Fraternity and Sorority Life at San Diego State University and served as president of the Association of Fraternity Advisors in 1991. He is an initiate of Kappa Sigma (Theta-Iota Chapter, San Jose State University, 1975) and is an honorary member of Delta Lambda Phi, a national social fraternity for gay, bisexual, and progressive men (Alpha Delta Chapter, San Diego State University, 1994). Doug has been active in many gay and lesbian community organizations, including serving two terms as president of the San Diego Democratic Club and holding several leadership roles in the San Diego chapter of the Gay and Lesbian Alliance Against Defamation.

Notes

[1]Ken Stringer, Writer, *Beverly Hills, 90210* episode titled "Blind Spot" aired on the Fox Broadcasting Network, 6 April 1994. (Spelling Enterprises: Charles Rosin, Executive Producer).

[2]Cass Johnson, "How Gay is Gayley? Gay Men in UCLA's Fraternities: An Overview," *Ten Percent*, November/December 1979.

[3]James R. MacCurdy, "Gay Men in UCLA Fraternities," *Greek Connection*, 28 May 1991.

[4]Robert T. Michael et al., *Sex in America: A Definitive Survey* (Boston: Little, Brown and Company, 1994), 169-183.

[5]Alfred C. Kinsey, Wardell B. Pomeroy, and Clyde E. Martin, *Sexual Behavior in the Human Male* (Philadelphia: W. B. Saunders Co., 1948), 610-666.

[6]Alfred C. Kinsey, Wardell B. Pomeroy, and Clyde E. Martin, *Sexual Behavior in the Human Female* (Philadelphia: W. B. Saunders Co., 1953), 446-501.

[7]Donald F. Sabo, "The Politics of Homophobia in Sport," in *Sex, Violence and Power in Sports: Rethinking Masculinity*, ed. Michael A. Messner and Donald F. Sabo (Freedom, Calif.: The Crossing Press, 1994), 101-112.

[8]Peggy Reeves Sanday, *Fraternity Gang Rape: Sex, Brotherhood and Privilege on Campus* (New York: New York University Press, 1990), 122.

[9]*Webster's Ninth New Collegiate Dictionary*, © 1986, Merriam-Webster Inc., Springfield, Mass.

SILENCE

We're all of us sentenced to solitary confinement inside
our own skins, for life!

Tennessee Williams, Alpha Tau Omega

In Flux
by L.E. Wilson

Were there any other gay men in the composite photograph I glance at maybe once a year? Forty young men, lots of raging hormones. Politically correct politics says that there ought to have been three others, and the mathematical odds say at least one more—but who was it? And why did we never recognize one another, and why did we never speak?

When he was drunk, Derek used to kiss me on the cheek, just there. And Ray had eyes like silky blue opals and a smile to melt a virgin's vow. Reeve was tall, dark, deep-voiced, the descendent of deposed European royalty, and he smoked a huge meerschaum pipe like Sherlock Holmes. And Gerry and I ran together, talked together until 3 A.M. of love and loss and family and our shadowy hopes for our changeable futures.

This is true: My two years in the fraternity were among the best and happiest of my life.

This is also true: I was deeply frustrated sexually, infatuated with half of my fraternity brothers, and constantly afraid of being found out.

This is so far beyond "mixed blessing," so much more than "it was the best of times, it was the worst of times," such a tangle of mutually exclusive emotions, that I do not know if it will go into words sensibly—though it might make sense to someone else who has been there, "there" being just one more flexible term in the flux of this memory.

In the fall of 1977, when I was a junior at Illinois Wesleyan, a small Midwestern university, I joined the local chapter of Sigma Pi, a large international fraternity. I already knew many of the brothers socially, had

dined with them, partied with them, shared classes and committees and
honor societies with them. Their house had the highest grade point average on campus as well as a policy against pledge hazing of any kind—
and no one in the house smoked or used drugs. And, perhaps most importantly (but never to be spoken of aloud), my best friend in the
theater department, a blue-eyed hunk on whom I had had a crush since
freshman orientation, was a brother. When I asked him tentatively
about pledging, and after he had spoken about me to the others, the
consensus was that I would be good for the house and that the house
would be good for me. "Good for" a very young 20-year-old, a skittish
virgin, barely out to myself, much less anyone else.

My pledge class of 20 was mostly freshmen, with a handful of sopho-
mores and one other junior. We were required to learn the names,
hometowns, and girlfriends of all of the active members of the house—
but, oddly for the Greek environment of the late '70s, the actives were
required to learn the same of us. The pledge class had to train together for a relay race at homecoming, had to dress in suits and ties one day
a week, and had to memorize the fraternity's national history and that
of our local chapter. There were no paddlings, no sleepless hell nights,
no incidents with barnyard animals (about which we had heard rumors
over at the *Animal House* frat). We were not even referred to as
"pledges" but as "junior members." Civilized. Plus, there were dances
and exchanges with sororities, float building, skit practice—all during a
semester in which I had parts in three theater productions, worked a
part-time job on campus, and stayed on the dean's list. On top of that,
I was given the "most valuable junior member" award, and I was elected an officer of the fraternity a few months later.

I was valued by my brothers, very much valued—but it was for feminine things, somehow.

I was the one asked for a massage after a brutal rugby game, asked
for advice about what a girlfriend must be thinking, and then asked by
the girlfriend for advice about the boyfriend. I was expected to tell accurate fortunes with my old tarot cards, and to play medium, soothing
the house ghost when she was restless. At Halloween, my theatrical
makeup kit was raided; and I nursed brothers through concussions and
broken hearts, planned a winning homecoming skit, baked gingerbread,
took photographs, plotted elaborate practical jokes and parties. In re-

turn, I valued my fraternity brothers, very much valued them, for the glorious, casual masculinity they projected. Having grown up in a very small suburban home with three thuggish brothers who despised me, I felt privileged to be counted as an equal among smart, funny men who did not bruise, insult, or wound me on a daily basis. Guys who did not ignore me, men who did not insist that the only version of masculinity worth having was their own. And yet…I remained deeply closeted the entire time I lived at the Sigma Pi house. I declined alcohol, knowing full well what could happen if my inhibitions were to be loosened. I was beyond "virgin." This was eunuch mode, convincing and complete, comfortable, in its way, even comforting. Falling asleep in the third floor common dorm room, surrounded by the breathing and snoring of 25 of my fraternity brothers was, well, nice. Comforting. There were a half dozen or so beds into which I would gladly have crawled, but it never happened. I told myself (and I tell myself) that I wanted it to happen, and I wondered (and I wonder) if it would have been good for me, young and confused and impressionable as I was then. "That I would be good for the house and that the house would be good for me."

There were only three brothers in the house who ever knew that I was gay, one of them my ol' blue-eyed theatre buddy, who of course saw the differences in my speech and behavior between frat house and backstage. Ray knew exactly what it meant, and he never condemned me, never seemed particularly dismayed by the agonizing-to-me revelation—and never knew that I would have lied, cheated, or stolen to have slept with him just for one night! Ray agreed with Gerry—the handsome, brilliant, temperamental blond Adonis from my pledge class, the recipient of many an asexual backrub—that I probably just had not met the right woman, and they kept introducing me to pretty sorority girls on campus.

At the end of my senior year, an outraged rumor went hissing through the house that one of the freshman pledges had been caught in bed with another man from his dorm. Turmoil!

What should they do? What should they say? How would this affect the "honor" of the house?

Should they confront him, blackball him, give him another chance? It was just a week or so until graduation, and maybe I was finally feeling the constraint of four semesters among handsome, untouchable

men, but…something snapped. I stood up in the weekly chapter meeting and declared that I was ashamed of them all, that they had never
given the honor of the fraternity a moment's thought when seducing a
drunk townie in the rec room or sweet-talking a sorority girl into a blow
job in the attic. I was angry, trembling with fury and with fright. How
dare they? How could they? These men who prided themselves on their
civility and their intelligence? And it was none of their business anyway,
any more than their own sexual preferences and partners were the concerns of anyone else.

No one spoke after me. The meeting was adjourned, and not another word was said about the affair, and the pledge, Dermot, was duly initiated the next semester with the rest of his pledge class. I was valued
by my fraternity brothers. I was to be their touchstone, their conscience,
their innocent, hero-worshiping little brother who nevertheless knew
how they ought to behave.

Just before I left campus for the summer, I wrote Dermot a note,
telling him what I had said, why I had said it, and how I had felt while
saying it—I was declaring myself to someone, at last, at last! I told him
I wished that I had shared my bed in the freshman dorm, too…but then
I graduated the next Sunday, and he and I never got a chance to talk
about what it had been like to be gay in the fraternity. I have often wondered, if I had tried harder, spoken louder, or spoken sooner, might I
have had a life with one of my oh-so-idolized fraternity brothers? With
Derek, who always kissed my cheek when blitzed on beer? With Rod,
the 6-foot-5 ex-football jock, gentle and kind and searching for God or
some substitute? Dan, the golden-haired pre-med student, eager to join
the Marines after college? Dermot, surprised in his narrow bed with the
handsomest freshman on campus? All married now, I think. I sang at
most of their weddings.

Were there any other gay men in the composite photograph I glance
at maybe once a year? Forty young men, lots of raging hormones. Politically correct politics says that there ought to have been three others,
and the mathematical odds say at least one more—but who was it? And
why did we never recognize one another, and why did we never speak?

Silence is acceptable. Silence means that nobody needs to think
about the 10% minority—need not fear, need not discuss, need not
allow space, effort, or emotion. Call me grateful for my years with my

fraternity brothers—grateful for the ability to blend, to play the threatening chameleon, for the lessons on how to behave like a ma Middle America—and sick at heart, still, that those lessons were nec sary at all. So what if I can chat with preacher or politician or farmer c jock and appear at ease? It remains just appearance. It is all masks and pretense. I tell them nothing genuine, and they hear nothing honest or real from me, all good manners and hail-fellow-well-met and expected modes of behavior and scarcely a word of it from the heart. And yet…

I was valued. I was. Eunuch, virgin, other—but I was wrapped for two years in the concern of friendly (not loving), smart (not sensitive) men, and it was wonderful to learn that not all men were like my broth-ers-by-blood, that there were men in the world who were tolerant and decent and who might value what I had and what I was. "That I would be good for the house, that the house would be good for me." How had Ray known? Was I so obvious?

Derek used to kiss me on the cheek when he was drunk, just there. It was enough then. It would not be enough now…but I would not be able to speak out today if I had not endured that anxious silence 20 years ago.

Keeping the Secret
by "Scott Smith"

I have not come out yet to any of the brothers in my fraternity, however. I have debated whether I will ever tell them, since we have become distanced over the years. Part of my distancing, I am sure, is due to not being able to deal with their possible rejection. I sometimes think that keeping the secret from the brothers has limited how close my friendship with them could be.

So why did I join a fraternity? I was always very independent in high school with a small circle of friends. I was unpopular, unathletic, shy, and not the best student, but I was a good student and a loyal friend. I hated the cliques in high school that I felt estranged from, yet I envied those who were in them. So I was an independent thinker in some ways, but I was also a conformist who desired to "fit in." I joined my fraternity primarily because I wanted to learn to be more social and to make up for what I missed in high school. I realized much later that I also subconsciously wanted to make myself straight (by having endless opportunities to meet women in a restrictive environment where gay is taboo). I wanted to have some of that "straight energy" rub off on me. I thought I could learn to be straight and have straight relationships by crafting platonic relationships with men and perhaps even learning to love a woman. A fraternity seemed like the place to learn those necessary skills, so I rushed at the beginning of my freshman year at the University of Oklahoma in the fall of 1988.

I visited over 20 houses during formal rush before making a decision. Oklahoma's mutual selection process helped to ensure that both the rushee and the house were compatible. I felt fortunate to find a house where my grades and my desire to help build the fraternity could be appreciated and my lack of athletic ability did not count against me. I liked the diversity in the chapter membership in terms of personal appearance, personalities, interests, and skills. Individuality was not discouraged, and I liked that.

My first semester as a pledge, I met an attractive guy playing the piano in the cafeteria lounge. We had music in common, and I complimented him on his piano playing. Although I am shy by nature, pledges were requested to be on the lookout for other potential rushees, and Andy seemed to be a good prospect. Soon after we met in October, he suggested that we go to a movie. I was caught off-guard when he came on to me in the car just before he dropped me back off at the dorms. I told him, "I'm flattered that you find me attractive, but I really can't be that way since I'm in a fraternity." I thought I had concealed my sexuality pretty well, but apparently not to other gay people.

My excuse was lame. I found Andy attractive as well, but I used the fraternity as an excuse not to pursue a deeper friendship or relationship. I honestly believed that I could not be both—in a fraternity and gay. That was before I understood that being gay was more about feelings rather than actions. I distanced myself from Andy the remainder of my undergraduate years. When I finally came out a year ago, I visited with Andy and discovered he was in a long-term relationship with another man. I was happy for him and wondered what might have been if I had been more honest with myself.

I enjoyed my first semester as a pledge and developed close friendships within my pledge class. That first year I was very busy with pledge activities and classes. It all seems like a blur now, but it was one of the most exciting times of my life. I was soon selected as secretary after I became an active member. My analytical and organizational skills suited me well for the position.

Living in the house with the brothers my sophomore year was a great experience. My best friend David and I roomed together in the house. We got along great since we were both very independent, shared a common faith, and related closely on a personal level. My relationship with David was assuring to me as I remained closeted in the chapter.

By this time I was well-known and respected by my fraternity brothers. After the secretary position I worked as leadership coordinator—

tracking the various committees and executive members to help them achieve personal and chapter goals. I always had a positive outlook and worked to boost the others' self-esteem by recognizing individual accomplishments during chapter meetings. It was for these reasons, I believe that I was awarded the Brother of the Year award.

While my brotherhood experience was wonderful, I still had a hard time impressing and dating women in college. Sorority girls seemed to go mostly for the good-looking, athletic, humorous, social gods. A few girls I knew seemed to really get along well with me. If they only knew that they were "fag hags"! Cindy, in particular, would always ask me for advice on her relationships with other guys. I think she appreciated my sensitivity and understanding, traits she wished her boyfriend could possess. I even wished sometimes that she might be attracted to me the same way she was attracted to her boyfriend, but she was not.

I did have a girlfriend, Janet, for a month or so during my junior year. Although the physical contact was pleasurable, it just was not fulfilling for me sexually. My fantasies always involved men, but I never told her that. I also enjoyed romancing her—bringing her flowers, taking her to the movies, and having her on my arm at fraternity socials. (Society makes it extremely easy to date in the straight context!) She was a conservative Christian who would not do anything beyond "making out" which made things safe for me. I finally broke up with Janet shortly after watching an episode of *The Oprah Winfrey Show*. The topic was gay men who came out within a midlife crisis after 20 years of marriage. They caused a tremendous amount of pain and devastation to their wives and families. I was determined never to hurt a woman like that, let alone myself. At this point I realized that my gay feelings would not go away and that I might never learn to like women in the way that my straight fraternity brothers did.

I vowed never again to seriously date women, although I continued several platonic friendships. I also imposed restrictions on exploring my homosexuality and limited closeness in my male friendships. I had resigned myself to being gay, but I was not ready to share that part of myself with my brothers. I therefore began to distance myself from the brothers and to focus solely on school.

Once I graduated from OU in 1992, I applied to graduate school elsewhere. I decided to dive into schoolwork and not have any personal life. That was exactly what I did the first three years of graduate school. I did not keep in touch with my fraternity brothers, except for Christmas cards. Only in the past 18 months did I decide to finally "get a life" and come out to my family and friends. I finally told the secret at the age of 25. It has been a truly rewarding experience.

I have not come out yet to any of the brothers in my fraternity, however. I have debated whether I will ever tell them, since we have become distanced over the years. Part of my distancing, I am sure, is due to not being able to deal with their possible rejection. I sometimes think that keeping the secret from the brothers has limited how close my friendship with them could be. I have missed several fraternity reunions because I did not want to deal with the issue of my sexuality with my fraternity brothers. As I become more comfortable with myself, perhaps I will tell at least some of my brothers in the future.

Will the brothers understand when they eventually find out? Perhaps. After all, I did contribute a lot to the chapter and was well-respected by the brothers. Who knows? Until then, the secret remains kept—a silence of not knowing and an answer for tomorrow.

Silent Rituals, Raging Hearts
by R. Derrick Thomas

Success meant I would eat Greek, take my licks, and not drop! I wanted to belong. I wanted to be a man! I had to prove to myself and to others that I could do the unexpected. I could pledge and join a black fraternity.

In the tradition of all secret societies, I will undoubtedly be killed for what follows. However, honor, a sense of justice, and my desire for social progress motivates me to divulge my experiences of joining, belonging to, and reconciling my feelings about a black fraternity. If the secrets that bind us together lead to the destruction of spirit and self, then what good are they? Following others for a sense of identity is no way to become self-actualized, and fraternity life for many gay men is a long way down the path toward inner turmoil and stress.

We were lined up in a row, all grasping each other for security, support, and comfort. We were afraid of the unknown but more afraid of what we thought would follow. I had heard stories of goats, feathers, and sexual acts. I had witnessed the scars of paddling, sparring to show heart, brands, and badges of honor. Success meant I would eat Greek, take my licks, and not drop! I prayed that I would be lucky enough to say I had done it all and survived. I wanted to belong. I wanted to be a man! I had to prove to myself and to others that I could do the unexpected. I could pledge and join a black fraternity.

"The scariest part is being exposed for others to see. Your eyes are covered, but your souls are bare. You lose track of time, distance, sanity, and truth. The only things that matter are survival, thinking as one, and knowing your information. The penalties are unthinkable. The mind games are brutal, and if those do not work, there is always the paddle or the burning sands. Now, if that does not get you motivated to join this organization, save yourself the humility of dropping line and leave quietly with no questions asked!" These first words were spoken by the chapter president.

"Am I to understand that you all mean by staying in your seats that you want to be True Blue?" Our pledge master both frightened and inspired us.

"Yes, Big Brother!" We answered in unison.

"Good, let us begin…"

I grew up in a small semiconservative white community in Florida. My mother was from a modest African-American rural community, and my father was a New Yorker. All I knew about fraternity life came from the movies *Animal House* and *Revenge of the Nerds*. I really did not know about the differences between the eight historically black and the white Greek organizations until I entered college. I had turned 18 only the previous October, and by February 25, 1992, I was pledging the Iota Rho chapter of Phi Beta Sigma. "Yo, blue! You know!" I was the youngest pledge in the history of the chapter.

I entered into the bonds of fraternal life as naively as one possibly can. I followed an older friend who had wanted to pledge for a couple of semesters. In the end, he did not even make the final pledge class. I did very little research on all the organizations, but I thought I had made the right decision. Later, people who always thought I fit the mold of another fraternity were shocked when they learned of my affiliation. "You do not look like a Blankety Blank." After such comments I explained that the pledge decision is 50% about the local chapter and 50% about the national reputation. Despite the wisdom of that equation, I pledged almost 100% based on local chapter, or rather one really great and inspiring brother.

When I got on campus and got involved in student life, I met Travers Johnson; he was a major part of the reason I joined. He recognized that I had something going for myself and encouraged me to use those talents in service to others. We talked about his fraternity, and he told me about the positive things the group did. Then he invited me to come to a meeting where they talked about some of the fraternity's ideology, principles, and the contributions of some famous brothers. After that meeting, I came home and talked to my parents about the whole situation. My mom, as usual, was inquisitive and concerned; my father took a less interested role. In the end, when I decided to pledge, it was my mother who gave me the money to pay dues and fees. I had to pay her back, but she helped me out behind my father's back and told him about it later. I always thought that my mother understood me better than myself back then. I was in a new place and tried to fit in. I did not really know what was best because I had no basis of comparison. I thought pledging a fraternity would help me become a man, learn more about my heritage, and have more fun.

Pledging was hard work, and anyone who joins a black Greek-letter organization will agree. When I pledged, the chapter was relatively large, with nine brothers at various states of being active or nonactive. On my line (pledge class), there were three others. They were all taller, stronger, and more athletic than I was, but *none* were smarter. I should have known there were going to be problems when I had to start pledging later than the other guys because of a chorus field trip. I found out that the chapter was split over my being admitted, because I would have to miss some of the "intake process." They could have waited but did not do so because they felt it set a bad precedent. Some even suspected I was gay. Once I got on line, some of the brothers felt I had to prove myself because I was late and weaker than the others. There was a reform movement going on among the eight traditional black Greek-letter organizations regarding the process of taking in new members. The chapter only had a certain amount of time to complete the process of bringing in new brothers. The regional director had given certain acceptable parameters. The time limit was part of pledge reform aimed at decreasing the amount of injuries and standardizing the process. In several chapters brothers would get carried away with secret rituals and harmful stunts (a.k.a pledging "old school").

Because of the injuries and deaths resulting from pledging "old school," all the organizations changed to new pledge processes called "intake." They completely dropped the word and idea of "pledging" in order to rid themselves of the stereotype and the potential for lawsuits. All of this started back in the late 1980s and into 1990. By 1992, local chapters were still trying to figure out the exact details of the new process. However, my line was the last to really get away with any sort of "old school" pledgeship. After us, if anyone had found out students were going through many of the rituals I went through, it would have meant certain suspension for the chapter.

In the tradition of pledging, we were all referred to by our number. The number itself was a link to previous brothers who wore the same number. We should have been lined up by height, but because of my tardiness, I ended up being Number 4—the tail dog, step master, supposedly the one with the most heart, the "anchor"! The four of us were known as the "injured reserves" because all of us had some sort of athletic injury. Number 1 had a bad back, Number 2 a bad shoulder, and Number 3 a bad knee. Then there was me, Number 4, who did not play collegiate sports and did not have any sports injury. I had to fake something. It was too ridiculous to remember. This is how we began, a little off the beaten path, and we never got back on it.

The rituals of pledging are secret, so I cannot divulge any of the actual events. When someone speaks of crossing the burning sands to earn their letters, I completely understand and identify. The entire pledge process took approximately a month. After it was over, we neophytes (new members of the fraternity) were expected to act like newborns into the fraternal family. Anyone who has gone through a similar experience knows the joys of belonging to an elite and selective group. Everything was revealed to us. We were supposed to just revel in all the fraternity's ideology and persona.

In the beginning, being in a fraternity was actually fun. We held a lot of parties, hung out together, and acted very much like brothers. I remember spending almost every waking moment with these men, because in a lot of ways they knew a part of me no one else did. We bared much of our souls together. When my schedule allowed, I tried to join my brothers, but I was always the different one. Later, as they (the organization and my line brothers) started to demand more and more of my time, it became clear that I had to make a choice about the rest of my time at college. It was either a life as a "frat" boy and doing all the things that go along with that title, or pursuing my dreams of being student body president, getting involved with the debate club, and holding other leadership roles on campus. Those differences never articulated themselves more clearly than on October 16, 1992, when I decided that I was through torturing myself and would accept and explore being a gay man. I chose to be happy first and follow my own ideas about my life.

It was not an easy decision to make. I faced many trials and confrontations because of my choice. I knew the possible consequences of my fraternity brothers' learning of my homosexuality. Many brothers made many antigay remarks during the pledgeship and had even joked that I was gay, but several others stuck up for me. In some ways, I was threatened and tested during the pledgeship to make sure I was not gay. It did not do any good. With my decision and conflict of cultures, I decided to pull back from my involvement. I used the excuse of wanting to focus more on other opportunities. I was heavily involved with student activities and sat on several university committees, so it was grudgingly understood. Over time, though, it was less and less accepted.

During this early time of exploration and my first boyfriend, rumors started to surface among the girls of a particular sorority. They were known for sleeping with my brothers. When I did not follow the custom of having sex with someone the night we "went over" (were initiated by secret ritual into the fraternity), they became suspicious. They really started tearing me apart when I actually took one of the girls on a date and did not jump her bones. That sorority was not our official sister organization, but they often provided some kind of entertainment. When people saw me, I was always with another guy. I hung around my first boyfriend and another male rumored to be gay. Certain girls with revenge on the mind put one and one together to make two, then confronted my brothers about it.

The girls did this behind my back in an effort to cause me pain and either get me kicked out of the fraternity, physically beaten up, or publicly embarrassed. My line brothers at first denied everything, because they had pledged with me and knew me. I heard about the accusations after they had gone on for several months. I guess my brothers were either tired of defending me or had started to wonder themselves. The first to confront me was Number 2. One day while we were hanging out, he casually mentioned that some girls were questioning him and saying things. Then he got all macho and said, "You better handle your b'dness, man; can't have this shit going on!"

Number 1 was not so kind when he confronted me. It was January 1994 at the annual Martin Luther King gala banquet. I was serving my second of two terms as president of the African-American student union. He came up to me and decided that it was a good time to confront me on the rumors regarding my sexuality. He pulled me aside right before the banquet and started yelling at me and accusing me of lying. He demanded that I tell him the truth about these rumors. "You need to get your shit together because I ain't having any part of it! The way I see it, you are a liar. You turned your back on the fraternity, and your head is fucked up because you hang around an obvious faggot!" He even threatened to kick my ass.

At the time, I denied being gay, but I wished I had the strength to tell him a lot of things. I managed to keep my composure and tell him that it was none of his business or anyone else's. I said, "It should not matter," and walked off. Later that night I got really scared and angry at myself, at society, and at anyone I thought was remotely connected to the situation. I was scared because I knew it was probably a matter of time before all my "b'dness" came rushing out. I was mad because it was my "b'dness" and nobody else's. I did not think it fair that they cared one way or the other. Hell, I was still trying to sort it all out. Watching and scrutinizing my every move only added more pressure from them. I wanted to punish the entire fraternity for its ignorance, so I completely disassociated and pretended that I was not one of them. I stopped caring and actually wished them ill. After that, I tried to forget that I belonged to anyone other than myself.

During my isolation I also learned that some of the biggest hypocrites belonged to my own organization. Some of those same guys who were bashing me were involved in similar types of same-sex activities. I dated several people who had grown up in Orlando, Florida, with some of my brothers. Through some friends of my boyfriend I learned about all types of things (sexual play) they had done with guys in high school. After learning about their shady pasts, I really saw the situation for all its pettiness. Yet I was still angry and hurt that the people I trusted turned on me. Friends suggested I confront them and tell them I knew about their pasts. Others urged me to at least go back to being active. Very few friends agreed with my silence and isolation.

At that time you could not have talked me into the alternative for all the money in the world. In some twisted ways I did feel like I had betrayed them. I had lied when asked about my sexuality. I was not who they assumed me to be. Telling them, "Well, I am not sure, but I kind of have this affinity for guys sometimes," would never have gone over. They were not ready to hear what I was not ready to say. Running away never solved anything, but I could not go back and deal with them. I had to stay away.

Staying distant worked for the next two years and until I had tolerated enough. I realized that life is not about fear; I should control my own life. Being a man is about being true to yourself and not living by other people's standards. I decided that handling the death of my mother and the end of three meaningful relationships gave me strength. I gained even more strength from almost being outed in several other organizations. The fraternity was the last hurdle. Yet part of me did not even care if they knew. In a lot of ways, I felt abandoned by them. Whatever I had to say to them, I did it to put a sense of closure on the whole subject. That is why I confronted the brothers who said the most hurtful things.

I confronted Number 2 during my last year in school, and we resolved a lot of the issues between us. He admitted most of his outbursts two years earlier were about his anger. Our line did not stay as close-knit as when we were on line. He blamed me because I was the first to pull away. He was also angry that he did not know something about me when he thought he knew everything. He felt betrayed about a lot of things. He could not understand my wanting to cut the fraternity out of my life. He said, though, that whatever I did was for a reason and that he could respect that. He also said that we were brothers; gay or straight, nothing would change that. After we talked, the past and all the mistakes really did not matter that much. It had made us both stronger. Life's lessons always do.

I think part of his understanding and maturity came from the fact that he was having difficulty with the fraternity on his own. Part of his reconciliation involved reconciling things with me. We had a big fraternity meeting called by our state president to which everyone associated with the chapter was supposed to come. I planned on dealing with everyone else at this meeting. I went thinking that I and my issues were going to come up, but they did not. All the state president had to say was that he heard that some questions regarding a member's sexual preference had come up, but frankly he did not care, because it did not matter. He talked a lot about unity, putting the past behind us, and coming together as brothers. I admired him for his words, but his actions seemed to prove that he felt otherwise. I never heard from him again after that meeting. I think he had to say those words as the state president, although I have no doubt he personally did not want to have an openly gay fraternity member associated with the organization. The words he spoke about unity never meant including me, and I think that was the unspoken understanding among the heterosexual fraternity members. Very few were willing to convey a different attitude.

There were some guys who were very supportive through this whole ordeal. Travers, my original inspiration for joining, always said, "Things such as rumors about what goes on in our private lives should not matter. The fraternity should focus on what an individual can do for the chapter." Unfortunately, his wisdom fell mostly on deaf ears. The one thing I take away from him is a saying he told me immediately after making it "over" (into the fraternity). He told me, "The fraternity does not make you, you make the fraternity. Do not let anyone tell you that you need to do this or that in order to be a Sigma. It comes from within. Do not forget that."

I guess somewhere between my own fear and insecurity, I did forget Travers's words. For a long while, I did not feel like a Sigma. It is still hard sometimes. I still harbor some ill feelings toward the whole system. I do not like the control or the mind manipulation. Because of those things, I was not able to be myself. I blame the fraternity for not fostering an environment where an individual can be himself while aspiring to all the ideals and principles of being a fraternity man.

All the national black Greek-letter organizations fiercely resist pressure to openly accept their homosexual members. Amazingly, the more the world changes and gets smaller, there are continually those vestiges of culture and society that, out of ignorance, fear, or just pure hatred, refuse to accept the obvious changes. They fight a losing battle to hold on to the status quo, which does not even serve their own interests. In the end, though, they will find themselves outdated and struggling to survive. There are gay members in every organization. They serve in leadership positions, as loyal members, and are often the most respected. Sadly, they often participate without being open about their sexuality, and it is the chapter that suffers. Many who do associate with fraternities put up with the harassment and the pressure to hide their true identity. That kind of homophobia is detrimental and unacceptable.

As I look back, I credit the fraternity with making me able to confront difficult situations. It helped me to understand the nature of individuals who long to belong to a group, some of the dynamics of group interaction, and prejudices. The difficulties I faced taught me a lot about people and myself. Most important, those difficulties taught me that I am ultimately responsible. It was a difficult lesson. Perhaps a better lesson would have been the importance of accepting an openly gay man into a fraternity to learn about brotherhood, service, and personal growth.

No Difference At All
by Ted Plaister

In those days I was ashamed of being gay, and the crying was likely a manifestation of my self-loathing coupled with my feelings of guilt.

In 1941 I enrolled at the University of California, Davis, which then consisted solely of its college of agriculture with an enrollment of less than a thousand. Compared with today's student population, the university was tiny. The students were predominantly male, with a handful of women who were (disrespectfully) called Aggie Baggies. There were six fraternities, one of them national.

My first semester I lived in a funny little ten-room hotel. Given the small student body, I soon became acquainted with members of the different fraternities. I had not given any thought to joining a fraternity when I enrolled, but when rushed by a local fraternity, Phi Alpha Iota, I gave the matter serious thought. Both of my brothers were fraternity men during college and held positive memories of the experience. I pledged my second semester. However, before continuing with my fraternity life, let me relate some particulars of my precollege life.

I grew up in San Diego, California, with my family, consisting of my parents, two brothers, and a sister. My siblings were all older than me. My mother had expressed her desire for a redheaded girl while I was comfortably residing in utero. I fulfilled the hair color request and tried my best to accommodate her on the female aspect, but only partially succeeded.

We lived in a semirural setting, kept a horse, some chickens, and the usual cats and dogs. As I grew into my teen years and the hormones kicked in, I felt no interest whatsoever in girls but definitely had an eye for the boys. I held numerous crushes on boys in junior and senior high school but lacked the nerve to approach any of them sexually.

I hold vivid memories of a new student who enrolled at our high school and immediately captured my heart. Each gym period I would anxiously await the opportunity to watch him walk around in the buff. I awarded him a perfect "ten" in every aspect. He was quite a handsome young lad and soon had a pretty girl hanging on his arm. He was very friendly, seemed to like me, and we became friends. One memorable day in the gym, I noticed him squatting down, buck naked, removing his clothes from his locker. On impulse, I approached him, bent down, whispered in his ear that I loved him, and kissed him on the cheek. Then I panicked, realizing I had placed myself in considerable jeopardy. He reached up, patted my hand resting on his shoulder, smiled and said, "That's nice." He could have spread the story throughout school and made life hell for me, but he did not. Today, I wish I knew where he lives, because I would like to communicate to him my appreciation for his graciousness in not exposing me.

Back to my fraternity experiences at UC Davis. I was determined to become the perfect pledge in my small, 30-member fraternity and worked hard to achieve that end. I am positive I was its sole gay member, and I was completely closeted. We were a close-knit group, always attending campus functions together and helping each other with our studies. Social life was limited because of the scarcity of female students; moreover, Davis was (and remains) a tough school, so studying took priority. My closest friend in the fraternity—I shall call him Desmond—was one of the brightest people I have ever known. Desmond was handsome, well-built, for some reason quite devoted to me, and as straight as that proverbial string. We lived together at the hog barn one semester as student assistants, and living so intimately with someone I was totally in love with proved difficult. Somehow, though, I managed to remain firmly ensconced in the closet.

I rose through the ranks in the fraternity, held a number of house officer positions, and was vice president when the Japanese decided to rearrange the landscape in and around Pearl Harbor. In 1943 the campus was taken over by the Signal Corps, Uncle Sam beckoned, and off I went to make the world safe for democracy in the company of General Douglas MacArthur.

Military service proved an eye-opener in terms of learning about gay life. My Army home was the XI Corps Headquarters—a small tactical unit with many officers and relatively few enlisted men. I had not been in the corps long before I met two gay soldiers while standing in the chow line at Fort Riley, Kansas. Directly in front of me waiting to enter the mess hall were two rather swish soldiers. While I observed them, one thrust his hand inside the front of the other's fatigue jacket, triggering the remark, "Be careful—that's where I keep my grapefruit." They noticed me smiling, struck up a conversation, and in no time at all, we were out to each other. I felt no qualms about revealing my true nature to them, probably because of their openness. In a few short weeks, we boarded a transport ship bound for New Guinea and the war zone. My new friends identified the other gay officers and enlisted men, and the number of them amazed me. Moreover, and important, during the course of the war, we were never forced out of the military, even though some were blatant in their gay behavior. This speaks directly to the hypocrisy of the government and its policies toward gays in the military. During wartime it was obviously permissible to be gay, and sometimes openly so, because we were needed to further the war effort. Our corps was a highly efficient unit, and the gay soldiers contributed significantly to that efficiency. In my own case, I was awarded the Bronze Star Medal. During the war years I had only one sexual experience with one of the two soldiers mentioned previously. We have kept in touch over the years, but there was never any romance between us.

In my experience, numerous similarities exist between fraternity and army life: all male, living in close proximity, privileges of rank (upperclassmen versus pledges, sergeants versus privates), male bonding, development of close friendships, general camaraderie, and so forth. At Davis, though, I had no gay friends. I was the only gay person in my fraternity, whereas in the army, I had several close gay friends.

At the war's end, I entered business briefly on a small farm in Illinois with one of the gay soldiers from Army days, but soon realized I belonged back in college. I returned to Davis in June 1946.

Shortly after rejoining the fraternity, a significant event in terms of fraternity life occurred. There were many new faces in the fraternity along with my great love, Desmond. Most of us were veterans who had achieved a certain maturity during our military service, and as we scrutinized the fraternity's policies and practices, we concluded drastic changes were in order. Although the number of us who championed these changes was relatively small, we were determined to initiate significant improvements in our house. First, we rewrote the constitution removing all racist statements. Next, we eliminated "hell week" in its totality. Finally, we discontinued paddling, substituting instead a system of constructive punishment for rule infractions—such as washing the windows of the long-suffering widow who lived next door. Quiet hours at night were strictly enforced, with everyone required to wear slippers or socks to reduce noise. During the week, freshmen were not allowed to leave the fraternity house in the evening unless bound for the library. These rule changes proved to be positive moves because they resulted in a more harmonious house and a significant increase in the degree of camaraderie experienced among the members, to say nothing of a significantly improved GPA. I sometimes ponder what would have transpired if I had broached the matter of sexual orientation being used as a criterion for membership.

I continued being a very active member, holding a number of offices, including the presidency. I took pride in wearing my fraternity pin and worked diligently to improve the house. I resumed my close friendship with Desmond, with no diminution of my love for him. There was a great deal of affection openly displayed among the members in those postwar days, with considerable hugging and sharing of beds on Sunday mornings with quantities of silly talk and giggling. I remember one member who was forever climbing onto people's laps, begging them to scratch his back. I was up to my old ways of kissing people by sneaking up when they were seated, throwing an arm lock around their neck, and kissing them on the cheek, a practice sometimes greeted with a "Get away from me, you fucking queer," but I experienced no real hostility. In retrospect, there was one action that may have spoken to my behavior. I carried the nickname "Count" because I played the piano and was an admirer of the late, famous jazz pianist William "Count" Basie. In fact, my fraternity brothers, other students, faculty, and townspeople all addressed me as "Count," never as Ted. But one of my fraternity brothers often referred to me as "Countess."

Another example of open affection concerns one member who fit the tall, dark, and handsome cliché to a T, an evaluation shared by all the members. This handsome chap was a legacy, not overly endowed in the mentation department, although I cannot say the same for the physical area. His physical beauty drew me to him, we became quite friendly, and we soon reached the point where we engaged in considerable hugging. One day while doing chores together in one of the dormitories, we paused to talk. This led to a hug. I remember looking in his eyes and expressing my love for him. This remark led him to gently but firmly kiss me full on the lips. I thought I would faint, but I certainly did not object. Nothing further came of the incident because he was straight and would have been offended if I had propositioned him. I can only surmise that in his own way he loved me and did not think a little kiss to demonstrate this was a big deal.

I also became quite close friends with another interesting fellow who had joined the fraternity following the war. I shall call him Fred. Fred grew up in Hollywood, where his father was involved in the movie business. He was extremely bright, possessed a great sense of humor, and was quite popular. As our friendship grew, I came to feel I could trust Fred completely, which led to my decision to come out to him. My evaluation proved correct, and he accepted my coming out as if I were telling him I had just bought a new pair of shoes. Moreover, my being gay never became an issue in our friendship. In fact, I used to tease him by suggesting he really ought "to try it" just once. He would respond by telling me to keep my filthy hands off him and by calling me a God-damned queer, along with other insulting remarks, all said in jest. To my knowledge, he never betrayed the trust I had placed in him.

The question of dating arose from time to time as more and more women students enrolled at UC Davis. I offered a variety of reasons for not dating, and it happily never became an issue—with one exception. Our house enjoyed a certain fame for its annual party, the social event of the year. Although it was basically a dance, we went to great lengths to decorate the entire house, inside and out, employing various themes. All members were expected to bring dates, and this posed a problem for me. But I found the perfect answer. My solution was to volunteer as cook for the party. We always served dinner at these events, and, fortunately, I possessed reasonably good cooking skills. Clearly, I could not properly escort a date if I was slaving away in the kitchen. During the party I would table-hop, flirt with the women, and dance a little. Assuming the role of the cook proved to be good cover, and I employed it on several future occasions.

There was an incident related to dating that took place one evening following a beer bust. I was not living in the house because I had graduated and was working on campus, but I still played an active role in fraternity affairs. I was friendly with a young professor, one of our honorary faculty members, and he offered to drive me home as the party broke up. We pulled into the driveway of the cottage I was renting and sat chatting a bit about the success of the beer bust. Suddenly he mentioned that he had never seen me with a date at any fraternity social function and wondered why. I panicked momentarily, but I had not ingested too much alcohol to think straight. I fed him a cock-and-bull story about having been wounded in the war, which made it impossible for me to... and let my voice trail off. He backed off in some embarrassment and immediately changed the subject. Three years ago we met at a fraternity reunion and had a very pleasant visit talking over old times. After returning home I decided to write and tell him the truth and apologize for having lied to him so many years ago. I received an extremely cordial reply that hinted strongly that he had eventually figured out that I was gay. Now I wonder what would have happened if I had told him that evening that I was gay. What if I had told all of my brothers?

One eventful evening during a break when most of the members had returned home, Desmond dropped by. I was vice president and that office provided me with a private room, shared with the president. I invited Desmond to come to my room for a beer. After a couple of beers, something, perhaps the alcohol, emboldened me, and I literally begged him to let me have oral sex with him. I was both excited and scared to death at my boldness, but to my surprise (and delight), he said, "Sure, why not?" Afterward, he patted me on the head to console me because I began to cry and apologize for my actions. This little scenario was enacted one more time, and that was it—the sum of my sexual experiences in college. In those days I was ashamed of being gay, and the crying was likely a manifestation of my self-loathing coupled with my feelings of guilt.

Following my graduation in 1950, I accepted a one-year appointment on campus and was subsequently invited by the dean to accompany him to Thailand as part of the U.S. foreign-aid mission. It was in Bangkok where I learned what gay life was all about—in spades! I lived a total of nine years in Thailand before accepting an appointment at the University of Hawaii, where I taught until retirement.

I lost contact with my fraternity brothers, but four years ago I received an invitation to a reunion of those of us who belonged to Phi Alpha Iota. The local fraternity affiliated with Sigma Alpha Epsilon during my last year. I wrote the convener, told him I was gay and that I did not think I would attend the reunion because I was now out and would not brook any faggot jokes or gay-bashing talk. Moreover, I told him I did not wish my presence to put a damper on the occasion. Thinking back, I wonder why I made the assumption this would happen. I received a surprisingly supportive letter in which he said he did not think any problems would arise and that it mattered not at all to him about my sexual orientation. Circumstances were such that I could not go, but I did participate in one three years ago. Prior to this I had visits from two former fraternity brothers I had not seen in 40 years. I came out to both of them. They were very accepting of my disclosure, as were their wives, and urged me to attend the fraternity reunion. I went to the two-day affair and wore a lavender triangle that no one commented on, probably because they had no inkling of its significance. I renewed old friendships, and one fraternity brother in particular seemed very pleased to see me. We did a lot of reminiscing, and after returning home, I wrote to him telling him that I was gay. Once again I received a wonderful letter declaring that insofar as he was concerned, it made no difference in our relationship whatsoever. We continue to write on occasion.

These positive responses from my fraternity brothers after they learned of my sexual orientation have caused me to speculate about what might have happened if I had come out when I was an active member back in the 1940s. No definitive answer is possible, of course, but somehow I believe I would have been accepted for what I was: a well-respected fraternity brother who devoted his all to his house, who just happened to be gay. This could be wishful thinking on my part, but knowing the membership as intimately as I did, I would like to believe it would have made no difference—no difference at all.

Invisible Identities
by Gerald Libonati

Openness is always the burden of the gay person. Heteros cannot be held accountable for their ignorance if we continue to allow them to believe the absurd myths that surround gay men and lesbians. It is impossible for fraternities and sororities to reprogram their attitudes about gay people if they think they have never seen any.

Things were different in the late '60s. My first year at Broward College in Fort Lauderdale, Fla., was a time of confusion and liberation.

Confusion because my parents had raised me incorrectly, thinking that I was heterosexual. But my hormones, which knew better, had already kicked in at the speed of fright. Experience was sorely lacking, and my self-image achieved the clarity of meatloaf.

Liberation because I suddenly felt independent. I had my own car and wandered a huge, new campus, free of former restrictions. I was no longer compelled by law to attend classes but did so because my parents were paying incredible amounts of money.

As the only living homosexual in the Western Hemisphere (other than Truman Capote), I chose a field that was reputedly liberal. I became a journalism major and, as such, it seemed only logical that I pledge the communications fraternity, Sigma Theta Chi.

My friend and classmate, Bill, suggested that we pledge the fraternity together. He was a likable, easygoing guy who shared my passion for the music of Jim Morrison. It was a fraternity made up of men with an interest in print or broadcast media. Meetings were not held on campus but in the secluded broadcast building of a local radio station known as Rockin' Big Daddy. As if to mirror my sense of isolation at that time, it was located in a dense forest beyond the boundaries of civilization. Social events took place at the ranch-style houses of members and the restaurants and hotels of Fort Lauderdale Beach.

Along with Bill and a number of other pledges, I was subjected to the usual midnight kidnappings and pranks one endures like a pilgrim making a treacherous journey to a sanctuary where he knows fulfillment awaits. Jim was the jock of our pledge group. He was the popular one— handsome, trim, a little rough around the edges. Though I found him more attractive than anyone else I'd met on campus, I kept my distance. This was a habit I learned to reinforce during my college days. Attraction always equaled distance. Jason was there too. He was the diplomatic one who could talk his way out of any situation and usually did.

Our final test as pledges came in the form of a list of items and tasks to be collected or performed by us. We were dropped off in a desolate area to begin our adventure on foot. We worked frantically through the night in an effort to do all that was required of us by dawn. And when it was over we sat huddled and exhausted in Jason's kitchen. He was covered in a blanket, talking about how we'd soon be brothers. Jim was babbling about how girls were attracted to fraternity men. Bill was sitting at the table, caught up in Jim's fantasy. I was avoiding the conversation by staring blankly at the coffeepot waiting for it to perk.

Finally, we were gathered around a long swimming pool at the home of one of the members. We stood side by side, feet apart, hands in front of us. It was dark except for the eerie reflection of blue light from the illuminated water below shimmering across our faces. That was the night I was inducted into the brotherhood of Sigma Theta Chi. We were all congratulated, and I can say that each of us enjoyed a sense of accomplishment as well as solidarity.

But this was the decade of social revolution, and I was inducted not only into a fraternity but also into the ranks of the great unsatisfied— seeking meaning in a world we found unacceptable. Our real teachers were not the six men and women who spoke to us every day from a lectern but the priests of pop culture whose music pointed the way to our ever-unfolding awareness.

We were steeped in mysticism and sought to understand the nature of being as described by the Beatles, the Rolling Stones, and Janis

Joplin. (One should always question any philosophy based on the music of Janis Joplin who raised cheap thrills to the status of sacrament.) There was "the known and the unknown and in between [were] The Doors," said Jim Morrison. He was remembering William Blake, who said, "If the doors of perception were cleaned, everything would appear to man as it truly is, infinite."

The American tribal love rock musical *Hair* had taken over New York, and we were preparing for a new age. Aquarius would be the great social leveling, an informed era when men and women would understand the commonality of all humanity. We expected and acted, perhaps naively, to initiate an age of human transformation when prejudice and isolation would fall to acceptance and community. We would be a new generation, unhindered by longtime devotion to outdated ideals. A generation of people who would light the fuse to blow away the old, crystallized caste system.

But because we were to be the catalyst, there was no system in place at that time to ease the yoke of difference. This was especially true for gay and lesbian people. There were no gay youth groups on campus. There were no movies or television shows with gay characters. There was no comfort by school counselors about accepting our uniqueness. There was not even Richard Simmons.

I never wondered if my friend Bill might be gay because I assumed that everyone was heterosexual. Gay men like myself and lesbians grew up isolated, believing themselves to be alone in the world. Parents never admitted to the existence of same-sex couples, much less talked about them. Older gay men and women did not reveal themselves to the upcoming generation of gay Americans because homosexuality was equated with sinfulness and with child molestation. Certainly, the doors of perception had been smeared. It was the great social conspiracy to spoil the truth and spare the child. Even in college I believed I was the only one, alone.

Though I was one of the brothers of Sigma Theta Chi, they did not get close enough to know my sexual orientation. Or perhaps it is better said that I did not get close enough to them to disclose my sexual orientation. Openness is always the burden of the gay person. And gay people cannot be equal until we can endure the discomfort of disclosure. Heteros[1] cannot be held accountable for their ignorance if we continue to allow them to believe the absurd myths that surround gay men and lesbians. It is impossible for fraternities and sororities to reprogram their attitudes about gay people if they think they have never seen any. I believed the myths myself, simply because I *thought* I had never met a gay man or a lesbian. Their identities were invisible, and silence was all too common.

It was because of the conspiracy of silence that I remained closeted in my fraternity. The choice to do so was based on the misinformation at hand and my own youth, ignorance, and lack of experience. That would change later.

Dr. Freud had already stated 19 years earlier, in 1951 (without my knowledge), that homosexuality was not a mental illness. It was a provocative announcement that was not readily accepted because it contradicted the prevailing societal belief system. Yet all of the information and research obtained about gay people prior to 1960 was gathered from people seeking psychiatric treatment or from prison populations. Researcher Joseph Norton wrote in *The Journal of Sex Education and Therapy* that if we were to construct images of the average heterosexual based on heterosexuals who were in therapy or in prison, "we would arrive at equally skewed impressions about the psychopathology inherent in being heterosexual." It is like trying to understand heteros by interviewing Ted Bundy.

In the meantime, I played the role of the fraternity man with relative ease. Certainly, I did not fit the mythological description of what a homosexual man should be. I was not effeminate; I did not have delicate features; I was not an interior decorator. Between efforts to change the world, I smoked cigarettes but did not inhale, drank beer that I did not like, and dated beautiful women who left me empty. At the end of those awkward dates, I tried to figure out how to save face without giving it.

Of course, I also participated in secret meetings and activities designed to bond the brothers of Sigma Theta Chi fraternity. But in truth I never felt any more for these men than I did for other classmates. How could I develop intimate bonds with men from whom I hid the most basic needs and aspects of my personality? Trust demands honesty. And since I did not even trust my parents with such openness, neither did I open up to my fraternity brothers. Instead I pretended to be like them.

One sunny afternoon Bill and I were lounging poolside at a hotel on the beach with two visiting women from a northern college. They were attractive, with long hair and scanty bikinis. And though I never had any romantic interest in my date, the fact that I was with her seemed to impress the others. It was this sort of empty ritual that widened the emotional gulf between myself and my brothers.

Paradoxically, the whole idea behind fraternities was to instill a sense of belonging and camaraderie. It should not be implied that I did not benefit from my experience. I developed good friendships—but not lasting ones. I enjoyed the laughter and the fellowship—but they were not deep-felt emotions.

But in 1969 my education was really just beginning. I took a job with *The Miami Herald* and also began to write a weekly column for the University of Miami newspaper, *The Hurricane*. In July of that year, I saw a magazine article that radically changed my outlook on life. They printed a picture of a man the reporter had interviewed a month earlier in June. He was standing on a street in Greenwich Village, talking about the riot that had taken place the night before. The police had raided the gay bar shown behind him called the Stonewall. That was not unusual since the police (who apparently also did not hear Dr. Freud's amazing announcement) often raided gay bars and printed the names and addresses of those they arrested in the next morning's newspaper. But on this particular night, the patrons inside the bar resisted arrest for the first time and forced the police to barricade themselves in the bar. The man said he was there at the time angry homosexuals, tired of police harassment, fought for the right to be left alone.

What struck me most about this article was not that the event had set a precedent or that social change was in the making. What astounded me was that the man in the picture was gay! He looked perfectly normal. My parents never told me that there were "normal homosexuals." My teachers never included them in discussion, so they apparently had not invented anything or contributed to society. And I had never seen one until that day. Could the view of gay consciousness through my own doors of perception have been any more opaque? Social revolution apparently takes place first within the individual. Though it was a shattering revelation for me, my fraternity brothers did not seem to be aware of the event.

The Beatles were moving into a new level of expression. They had sought the counsel of the Maharishi Mahesh Yogi, and, like myself, they were transcending. The brothers of Sigma Theta Chi were not transcending but neither were they so rowdy that they did not bow to the dictates of our spiritual leaders who spoke to us through music like "Hey Jude" and "Revolution #9."

Fraternity meetings were held on Sunday nights, the same night as *The Ed Sullivan Show,* which had earlier introduced the Beatles to American audiences. It was the only thing that could interrupt the important sessions conducted in the forest of Rockin' Big Daddy. Our pledges were not permitted in the official meetings of the brotherhood but were kept in another room. It was their duty to maintain a vigil over the television and advise us as to the imminent appearance of the instigators of social reform.

The men of Sigma Theta Chi were not heroes or trailblazers. For the most part, they just wanted to enjoy life and, more than that, to fit in. Our rituals and initiations were nothing less than guides in the struggle for identity, not unlike the oral-sex rituals of those primitive tribes in the Hebrides (which the American Anthropological Association forbade researchers to divulge), only far less enjoyable.

My own efforts to fit in were still pinned on maintaining my secret identity. Bill and I attended the now-famous Miami concert by the Doors. It was held in an old seaplane hangar in Coconut Grove. And once again I struggled to conform by setting us up with dates for the concert. My cousin agreed to go as Bill's date, and I asked a younger student whom I knew would not ask for romance after the event. The concert never got under way. Morrison was drunk, the audience was angry, Bill was in the backseat with my cousin, and I was in denial.

As a group, the members of my fraternity continued to broadcast and to write and to photograph through the waves of change overtaking the country. We identified with that change and, indeed, we were part of the body that participated in it, even if only to establish our difference from the World War II generation—our parents' generation. The civil rights movement was sticking its foot in the door and would not let staunch opponents close it. Martin Luther King Jr. was assassinated after the nation reeled from the violent deaths of President Kennedy and his brother Robert. We were protesting violence at home and the atrocity of war abroad. Some of us refused to go to Vietnam, choosing exile over combat. Our critics were saying that the ubiquitous peace sign was actually the footprint of a chicken. We were shocked by the slaughter of our peers at Kent State University and repulsed by graphic photographs from the battlefields of Asia. It was reason enough to stay in college.

We found comfort in mass gatherings like the one just outside of Woodstock, where the lords of the counterculture came together to sing its praises. Not only did they sing of love, sex, and drugs but they also voiced our condemnation of violence, war, and prejudice.

I knew that other minority groups would have to be successful in their efforts to change prejudicial attitudes before gay men and lesbians could even consider it. Equality was a radical idea taken up against the wishes of our parents and the Supreme Court. But I was only beginning to learn that the greatest battle for the equality of gay and lesbian people would be fought within ourselves. We would wage personal wars against low self-esteem, learned self-condemnation, and the need to hide our vision from the world. We would have to clean those doors of perception regarding the way we saw ourselves. And once done, we would have to recognize that neither equality nor acceptance was free. We had to give up our invisible identities and reveal ourselves to others in order to show them how good and talented and noble a people we were. But revelation was expensive, and we risked the loss of friends and family along the way.

My parents turned out to be supportive, but I never found out what would have happened if I had told my fraternity brothers. At that time they may not have understood my orientation, since they were as ignorant as I was about gay men and women. But promoting a positive image of gay consciousness does not always mean a formal announcement. I could have corrected negative comments made in my presence and demonstrated positive feelings toward gay people. Or I could have simply stopped ending all of my sentences with the word "man." If I met those brothers today, I suspect their opinions might be more flexible.

Notes

[1] I never call heterosexuals "straight" because the word implies correctness and is an indirect insult to people who are not straight. Straight is thought to be proper, good, honest, drug-free, holy, and right. People who are not straight are thought to be addicted, dishonest, crooked, mentally unbalanced, and, apparently, gay.

Don't Ask, Don't Tell
by "Chaz"

...my sexual prowess was yet another piece of the denial dynamic. If I did not appear to hook up or have sex with a lot of women, the other guys might think that I was gay. In this sense, women were almost seen as trophies to prove that you were a real man.

I have distinct memories from my grade-school days of being called "fag!" While these vivid memories may be a part of the inescapable scars that every person has from growing up, I really believe that this type of name-calling contributed to a low self-esteem and a denial of my real self that I have not been able to sort through until two years ago. Not until that point could I really understand how my involvement in certain activities in college could be interpreted as a search for three things: a need for increased self-esteem, a need to be close in some way with other men, and a need to deny to myself that I was indeed gay. I think I came the closest to achieving these three things when I became involved in a college fraternity in the spring of 1992. However, my initiation into and participation in this brotherhood was not sufficient to fill these lifelong needs.

When I went away to college in the fall of 1989, I saw this new experience as a way to improve myself beyond the concept of becoming an educated person. I saw it as my chance to become, for lack of a better term, "cool." Coolness was certainly not something I enjoyed in grade school or in my extended awkward years in junior high school and high school.

Perhaps it was no accident that I was often called "fag" in grade school and beyond, because in my opinion, unenlightened ten-year-olds may only understand that being a "fag" is synonymous with being "uncool." So, in reality, one might be called "fag" simply because his brown corduroys were a little too short (in the suburban Detroit city where I grew up, these pants were called "flood pants") or if he was not very athletic or was a little thinner than the others. In grade school, I met all three of these criteria. Were some of my taunters exercising a childhood version of "gaydar" (the supposed ability of gay people to spot other homosexuals just by looking at them or catching "vibes" from them)? However, knowing that "fag" was a term for me became especially painful when I began to experience same-sex attractions around puberty time. These scenarios contributed to a vicious cycle of low self-esteem and difficulty making close male friends. These items were among the baggage that I took with me to college my first year.

My decision to join a fraternity was an attempt to satisfy many needs, not the least of which was denial. However, before I became involved in Greek life, I was a part of something that was even more risky for a gay man—ROTC. For the first two years of my under-graduate experience, my life revolved around my involvement in the Reserve Officer Training Corps, a military officer training program for college students who pursue their program of study while learn-ing about military leadership. Upon successful completion of the four-year program, each ROTC member receives an officer's com-mission in one of the armed services along with his or her bache-lor's degree. I had a wonderful experience with ROTC. Although ROTC is coeducational, I really felt that I was beginning to establish friendships with other men that were real, and I was respected as a man (in a male gender-role stereotype sense) because I could do "rough" things like rappel off a 30-foot tower, shoot an M16, wear combat boots, and eat snake. My involvement in ROTC, for the short term, really increased my confidence. At the same time, I was really in love with some of my fellow male cadets. I recall one incident in particular when I spent the night at another cadet's apartment after a night of consuming a little too much alcohol. We slept in two sep-arate beds, but I remember wanting to join him in his bed for a lit-tle "loving." At the time, I thought these feelings were part of a phase, but they were the content of fantasies for weeks to come. Simply having these feelings could have resulted in my dismissal from ROTC and the loss of a life that I had known since I stepped foot on campus.

One of the most difficult things I had to do in ROTC was answer some standard questions regarding my sexuality on a form that had to be completed prior to committing myself to the ROTC program. The questions on this exam were similar to these:

"Have you ever been attracted to a person of the same gender?"

"Have you ever had sex with a person of the same gender?"

"Have you ever wanted to have sex with a person of the same gender?"

These types of questions were standard in the era prior to the "don't ask, don't tell, don't pursue" policy currently in force. For the record, I answered "no" to all of these questions. It is true that at this time, like many 19-year-olds, I was in the process of questioning my sexuality. I questioned my attractions for a short time but was pretty sure that I was straight, because I was not like the gay people I had seen on television or in the movies. With no other frame of reference, I assumed that I had to be straight. I reasoned that my attraction to other guys was a part of growing up.

My ROTC career ended after my sophomore year when I was not recommended to continue in the ROTC program and be commissioned as an officer in the United States Air Force. My flight training officer who evaluated me at an intense four-week field training camp at Lackland Air Force Base failed to see my leadership potential. I disagreed, and after my appeal to the Air Training Command regarding my FTO's recommendation was denied, I concluded that my dismissal was their loss. I was bitter for a long time after this happened, and my self-confidence plummeted. My academic and social worlds had been defined by my life as an ROTC cadet for two years. My involvement in ROTC had served to boost my self-esteem, bring close friendships with other men, and deny my gayness. Since I had largely identified myself with my ROTC involvement, I was left searching to fill the void that was left by the abrupt end to my short military career. I thought I had found a way to fill this void one night when a friend from ROTC invited me to a frat party.

Up until this time, I had thought very little about becoming involved in a fraternity. I never really had time with ROTC, and I honestly did not think that I was the fraternity type. I was, therefore, pleased to find that my friend's fraternity was possibly my type of fraternity. I felt that the guys

were friendly, down to earth, and pretty much like me. This was a pleasant surprise, and I decided to rush and subsequently pledge my friend's
fraternity the next term. When I was initiated, in the spring of 1992, I recall feeling an increased level of confidence with the onset of my new identity. For the next year, I frequently and prominently displayed my fraternity's letters. With this new identity, I once again felt that I had close male
friends and a high level of self-esteem. I was deep in denial.

Greek life revolves around heterosexist traditions like date parties,
tuck-in nights with sorority women, and serenades on sorority row. By
nature of the manifestation of heterosexism in our society, the assumption in most organizations, including my fraternity, is that everyone is
straight. Perhaps the Department of Defense does not assume all of its
members are straight, because they have actively and explicitly made an
effort to exclude homosexuals. Of course, the official questions regarding sexual orientation were not the norm in my fraternity, except for the
occasional, half-joking accusations such as, "Chaz, are you some kind of
faggot?" or "Why are you wearing that yellow Polo, you queer?" or "You
look like such a liberal fag with that goatee."

However, when we were selecting new members just prior to handing out bids, homophobia often reared its ugly head. On many occasions during these "hashing" periods, statements were uttered such as
"That guy is such a fucking faggot, I don't want him in my house. If he
gets in, I'll fucking quit." These statements were painful for me to hear
from my brothers. Such statements were common, and each time I
heard them, I was hurt in ways that I am only now beginning to realize. At the same time I heard these statements, the same person might
make comments about the appearance of the rushees. There is no denying that many of the guys in my fraternity were interested in bringing
the more-attractive looking men into the fraternity. Most of them admitted that this was true, reasoning that the best-looking brothers attracted the best-looking women. Other members would become angry
about this type of recruiting of "chick-magnets" because, unlike others,
ours was not a "face house" that wanted only good-looking guys for its
membership. Part of me believes that this type of recruiting is a form of
latent homosexual desire that most men would strongly deny.

I did not feel a real sense of true brotherhood in my fraternity because of homophobia and heterosexism, but also because of a lack of

common purpose, such as I had experienced in ROTC. As an ROTC cadet, I shared a common purpose with the other cadets: the pursuit of an officer's commission. Teamwork was encouraged in tandem with a healthy competitive spirit. In pursuit of these goals, I felt challenged and supported in a positive way by my fellow cadets. In my fraternity, I felt that brotherhood was valued as a concept most often when it was convenient to get something from a brother. I saw this most vividly during my senior year when I became a resident assistant in my residence hall. Some of my brothers saw my membership in their house and my job as an RA as incompatible. I was told by a few brothers in no uncertain terms that busting people while wearing letters made the entire house look bad. The expectation that I be a good brother and become a little more lenient was a one-way street because they were not willing to support me in my tough position of holding them accountable for their actions. I soon began to feel that the best way to experience brotherhood was through the use of large amounts of alcohol. Toward the end of my senior year, I decided that this behavior was not compatible with my new role as RA.

Alcohol and intoxication often are used in the fraternity as a way to foster brotherhood—a way for men to get close to other men both emotionally and physically. I have noticed many times that men of any orientation are more willing to touch each other and talk more openly when they have been drinking.

Many of the guys in my house were very concerned about others' perceptions of their sexual prowess as well. I too have been guilty of this, trying to convince others that I frequently "hooked up" with women. In my case, my sexual prowess was yet another piece of the denial dynamic. If I did not appear to hook up or have sex with a lot of women, the other guys might think that I was gay. In this sense, women were almost seen as trophies to prove that you were a real man.

I never dated women during my active membership in the fraternity. In fact, I have never dated a woman in my life. However, I must admit that it was important to me to be seen with women at parties, even exchanging a few kisses. I feel a sense of guilt now for leading these women on. I was a confused person confusing others.

That was all several years ago. I do not see much benefit coming out to my fraternity brothers at this point. I have since moved away from

Michigan and surrounded myself with people who I believe are more accepting of who I am. Many of these people are gay, but some are not. I feel that I have nothing to gain from brothers or other people who do not mean that much to me anymore. The few friends that I would tell will be told when the time is right.

I believe that the intense homophobia I saw displayed by my fraternity brothers was most certainly a sign of denial. I believe there were more than a few brothers just as closeted as myself. There were men in my fraternity who fulfilled the gay stereotype much more than I, who set off my own "gaydar." Few would suggest that these guys were gay. This type of denial is what one gay studies writer has referred to as the "big lie." The big lie allows people in our society to assume that there are very few gay people in the world. For me, finally meeting someone who had the courage to be out was a step in a positive direction toward a life of self-acceptance instead of denial.

So what's the bottom line? I was looking for some pretty substantial things: self-esteem, fulfillment of a need to be close to other men, and a way to deny that I was different. Changing my identity through my involvement in ROTC and Greek life worked in the short run, but accepting my gayness was more important. I feel better about myself, and I feel as if I am living a more full life. It took me ten years to discover what was missing. It saddens me that I cannot share these feelings with those who should be closest to me. Some may say that coming out would eliminate this homophobia, but it also could lead to more hurt and rejection. I feel that it is for me to decide. That's a decision I still have to make.

Deaf First, Gay Second
by Dan Brubaker

We were perfect zombies—unable to talk or even laugh or smile. For those out-siders, we were shrouded in mystery and suspense because they had no inkling of what was happening inside. If they happened to know, they kept the silence.

As a Deaf[1] person, I grew up in a world heavily immersed in Amer-ican Sign Language and Deaf culture. I am a third-generation Deaf fam-ily member. I grew up in both mainstream and residential schools for the Deaf. I was surrounded with Deaf adult role models (some of whom were members of the Kappa Gamma fraternity at my deaf school), Deaf clubs, and Deaf conventions; my father was Kappa Gamma. (For disci-pline, my father even used the Kappa Gamma paddle.) I was bred to be one, well-prepared for the "blue" brotherhood ever since I was only a few years old.

Kappa Gamma, a local fraternity at Gallaudet University in Washington, D.C., has had an illustrious (as well as notorious) history since its incep-tion in 1901, a third phoenix after the demise of earlier fraternities. It has approximately 1,500 members, which is why it is called the Chosen Few.

It was a natural choice for me to attend Gallaudet, the only liberal arts university for the deaf in the whole world. It was also a natural choice for me to want Kappa Gamma—the one and only fraternity I wanted to be a part of. *Woof!* However, being gay is also natural! It was not even a choice to begin with.

I did not have a great freshman year, mainly because of my struggle with my overall self-identity as a Deaf and gay person. I did not come out as gay until about the end of the academic year, and this did not happen without a great deal of agony. One of the reasons that I had such difficulty coming out was that I wanted desperately (just like many other boys) to be admitted to this particular fraternity; and in order to be one of the Chosen Few, I needed to be straight.

In 1984 Kappa Gamma had orchestrated standing-room-only protests at several student congress meetings where the representatives were in the process of recognizing a student gay, lesbian, and bisexual organization called Lambda Society. Those circuslike debates were the only things students were talking about in the cafeteria for weeks, and most of the student newspaper was filled with opinionated pros and cons. Even the Kappa Gamma representative, who happened to be gay, voted against the establishment of Lambda Society, much against his personal wishes. (The student congress denied Lambda Society formal recognition twice in two years before the administration forced the student body government to honor its request).

At one of those weekend parties in a freshman dorm, a few boys decided to roughhouse Shelby, a well-known gay boy who was obnoxiously drunk. Their roughhousing went overboard, and they bloodied his nose. Shelby was tripped as he ran in the hallway; and before he knew it, he was sprawled all over the floor. The party boys got a fire extinguisher to clean up Shelby's face so it would not look as bad as it did. The horror of all horrors—I laughed when they told me this story the following day. I did not want them to know that I was like him in any way. So much for my internalized homophobia! In two or three years, after their university probation (instead of expulsion), the party boys would be my blue brothers.

In January of 1986 I was ultimately honored to be bidded in the middle of the night by the Chosen Few (which had its probation, now known as pledge period, once a year). At the same time, I was scared to the bones with all those vivid images of how they would taunt and mock me for being such a "fag." But I knew there were also gay members of Kappa Gamma fraternity, which relieved my worries somewhat. If they could make it, then I could too.

When the fraternity announced its pledges as we ascended Telegraph Hill down toward Hanson Plaza (where all the high-rise residence halls and cafeteria were), many people were stunned that I was one of them and yet not so surprised. They knew I had worked hard and deserved it through fellowship, leadership, and scholarship.

During the monthlong probation, I had been continually and mercilessly taunted and mocked, not only because I was a lowly pledge but also because they suspected I was a queer who would not make it. They thought I would be the first to quit—and two pledges did resign after three days—but not me!

We were perfect zombies—unable to talk, or even laugh or smile. We would walk in lines and make sharp L turns when going different directions. To outsiders, we were shrouded in mystery and suspense because they had no inkling of what was happening inside. If they happened to know, they kept the silence.

I made it through four weeks of sequestered silence. The Kappa Gamma pledges were not allowed to sign or speak with anybody at all, except when necessary for classes or work, nor were we allowed to sleep in our own rooms; we slept at the pledges' headquarters or brethren's rooms instead. (The aforementioned in-house rules have since been "outlawed" by the university.)

The brethren had difficulty accepting me for who I was. I even found out that my name was actually blackballed before they admitted me. When they debated into the wee hours as to who would make up their 86th congregation, one of the gay members stood up and nominated my name, to their dismay, even though they knew well enough that I had exceeded their qualifications. And since it had to be a 90% vote of approval before an applicant would become a candidate for pledgehood, I was an easy candidate for being blackballed. (This occurred when one or two brothers dissented to a popular applicant, suggesting a package deal that another applicant be admitted before this popular applicant could be likewise.)

What I did not realize was that most of the gay brethren were in the closet during their pledgehood (and came out afterward) and that I was one of very few out pledges. This outness did not last for too long, because I fell in love with a girl soon after pledgehood, and we became an item. The whole student body was floored! They believed that the almighty Kappa Gamma fraternity had converted me! What they failed to know was that we were dating for some time before my initiation, and I was so much in love with her that I thought I would be straight. *Knock, knock on my head.* It was genuine love; I had no thought of trying to be straight just for the sake of family, friends and society.

However, during the ensuing months, my sexual orientation became
more of a reality than an illusion. I had to face issues of my identity—as
a gay male as well as a member of a heterosexist fraternity. Most of my
gay friends could not understand why I would choose to be with my
blue brothers over them, on outings to bars, dance clubs, parties, and
sporting events as well as camping out on weekends or even doing community service. One of the main reasons was that most of my gay friends
identified themselves as gay first, Deaf second.

I would stand up for Deaf rights more than I would for gay equal
rights. I consider myself a deaf advocate (just like my fellow brothers)
who also happens to be gay. It was like a tug-of-war deep down inside
me. I cringed when my so-called gay friends would stab me in the back,
calling me a hypocrite for my preference in hanging out with my
straight brothers. As far as I know, I have always identified myself as a
Deaf person first, and as a gay person second. And Kappa Gamma is one
of the bastions of Deaf culture and heritage.

I also cringed when my brothers made faces when they learned I was
going out with my gay friends.

"You gotta be kidding, that fag is your friend?"

"You're going out with this lesbo?"

When I would point out that I was also one of them, they would always
say, "Oh, you're unique, you're different, you're so much unlike them because you're so fun, and you'd not flaunt it, but him or her, bloody hell!"

Those who were too effeminate, too flamboyant, too butch, too mili-
tant, too this or that would be persecuted verbally and physically. A few
skirmishes off-campus occurred as well. And my protests would go in
one ear and out the other, if one deaf man can say that of another.

They would say, "Why can't they be just like you?" I would say I am
me, they are them. But we are the same family. They would flinch. Deep
down inside me, I would be hurt. We are not any different, yet they did
not see this the way I did. No words could comfort my gay friends as
to why they were insulted or harassed by my own brothers. On the
other hand, I could not explain why I still bonded to the fraternity with
Paul Bunyan-size double standards. Before I became a pledge, I fully
knew what I was getting into, and that was my choice.

Even though I graduated in 1989, I stayed with the university for my graduate degree as well as professional employment until 1996, maintaining close ties with the Kappa Gamma fraternity.

One of my achievements during my fraternity years was that I did manage to change some of my brothers' attitudes toward gay people, and that included Joely. He and I grew up together in Kansas, went to the same school as well as college together, bicycled across America (4,220 miles in 70 days) together, and came from Deaf families who celebrated an occasional Thanksgiving together. He thought that gayness was an unacceptable choice (and I am not going to go into detail, for you all know the same story over and over again as to how morally wrong homosexuality is with the church and all that jazz). But Joely still remained my close friend all through the years. He remained very supportive, and over time he finally came to accept me for who I was. He even went to two gay bars, fussed over my flaws, and stood up for me in several situations. Joely is still my best friend and will always be.

On the other hand, Raven (also from a Deaf family) hated me for who I was. He could not stand what I believed in. He even admitted to having taken part in several gay bashings. Then one summer we ended up being roommates. He started to realize that I was not as bad as he had imagined, that I was about the same as everybody else, and that there were different kinds of gay men (those who would physically "bother" straight men, and those who would "respect" straight men). We would end up doing things—going on various outings or working on projects together. Raven was one of very few extremists whom I "converted" from hating me to enjoying my company. I just wish I could say the same about several brothers who did not want to change or would superficially change because it was politically correct to respect gay men and lesbians.

It was brothers like Joely and Raven (as well as several others) who were influential toward my sense of belonging to the Kappa Gamma fraternity. Their evolutionary acceptance of who I am also influenced me to accept those brothers who did not accept me.

Regardless of the Chosen Few's traditionalist (and homophobic) overtones, it had evolved slowly within a short time frame—ten years. The Chosen Few had subtly and subconsciously elevated my self-esteem and self-awareness in dimensions far and wide (and I believe the same went for all other out gay brethren). They had strengthened my deaf identity, and the end result was an even more strengthened gay identity. Regardless of most brothers' beliefs, the fraternity as a whole never ostracized me for who I was, even though my relationship with the brothers was jagged at times. I thank them for who they were—and for accepting me and trying their best to understand.

Notes

¹As mentioned in *Deaf in America* by Carol Padden and Thomas Humphries (1988), as well as many other publications that followed a proposal by James Woodward (1972), I am using lowercase *deaf* to define an audiological condition of not hearing and uppercase *Deaf* to define a particular group of people who share American Sign Language as well as a culture. A person may be audiologically "deaf" without being culturally "Deaf." To be considered culturally "Deaf," one has to come from a residential school, from a "Deaf" family, or from a total immersion of an all-Deaf environment using ASL.

Good Ol' Boys
by Allen Ward

Homophobia within fraternities is a tragedy that perpetuates ignorance and plays on irrational fears. The dominant heterosexist attitudes prevalent in most fraternities shut out minority voices and create an intolerant atmosphere where gay bashing is actually applauded. Fraternity professionals who are silent on this issue advance the notion that gay bashing is part of the "good ol'" fraternity experience.

In 1985 I was beginning my sophomore year at Tennessee Tech. My friends were mainly fellow students who were members of the Church of the Nazarene or members of Inter-Varsity Christian Fellowship. That year I had gotten the politics bug and had begun what was to be a three-year stint in student government. The last thing my friends or family expected to hear from me was that I was considering joining a fraternity. To my friends, fraternities were perceived to be secular, alcohol-centered social clubs. To many of them, the only respectable reason one might venture into the realm of Greekdom would be missionary work.

I did not see it quite that black-and-white. I knew and liked several Greeks, and I was beginning to question some of the fundamentalist teachings that are popular in the rural South. Joining a fraternity was, in part, an initial rejection of those rigid moralities. I also recognized that if I wanted to play in the student-government arena, it would not hurt to have Greek votes. My campus Christian coalition could only attract so many voters, even on a Southern campus.

I would not have admitted it to myself at the time, but joining a fraternity was also a kind of personal search. The internal conflict I had experienced since early adolescence over being homosexual was becoming more of a nightmare. As I moved through college, it became clearer that these feelings of attraction toward other men were not going away. The church's handy recipe that gays should simply pray and faithfully wait to become straight was a horrible failure. I had tried that self-oppressing road for years. Looking back, I think I was naively hoping to find more acceptance in a less rigid crowd. It did not happen.

It was on a Friday evening in January that a group of brothers from Phi Gamma Delta fraternity, often referred to as Fiji, knocked at my apartment door. Earlier that week I had attended several nights of rush. I had gone to one other house (there were about 15 or so on Tech's campus), but I felt more comfortable with Fiji. That evening I had attended the final rush event. It was a great spectacle. The brothers sang heartrending fraternity songs followed by a number of moving testimonials given by seniors and a few alumni about how Phi Gamma Delta had changed their lives. The whole experience was right out of an evangelical guidebook for revivals. It made me want to belong.

The group of brothers at my door was led by Steve. Wearing a suit coat and with serious demeanor, Steve told me that the brothers wanted me to become a pledge and then handed me a bid. He told me that the brothers found in me the qualities they look for in new members. I was very proud and honored.

One of the first things my fellow pledges and I learned about fraternity life is that the brothers would know everything about our business—much like a family. If I had had any inclination about sharing the fact that I was gay, fraternity culture quickly put an end to it.

My first job as a brother was the position of rush chair—a challenge I feared was too much, too soon. Steve, who had been elected chapter president shortly after I pledged, believed that I was up to the task. I respected Steve and did not want to disappoint him, so I agreed. Serving as rush chair placed me in an eye-opening position to see how hostile fraternities can be to gay or presumably gay rushees.

Selecting new members can be a painful process even in the best of circumstances. Each prospective candidate is reviewed thoroughly for what he might contribute to the brotherhood. This review can (and frequently does) drag into areas that are irrelevant or divisive issues. Votes are conducted secretly in the dark. A single member could prevent a prospective candidate from receiving a bid without offering a word of explanation.

Not surprisingly, our chapter had its share of "good ol' boys" who could spark a xenophobic debate at any moment. During one rush my chapter went through rancorous discussions when the first African-American student accepted our invitation to attend. One brother, who was initially opposed to allowing African-Americans into membership, passionately argued that allowing a black man into the bond would forever change what it meant to be a Fiji. Ironically, he was right. Learning to accept racial diversity and our new black brother made us better.

Dealing with race was one thing, but dealing with homosexuality was quite another. Just prior to my joining the fraternity, one of the brothers nearing graduation told another brother that he was gay. As fraternities work, this news soon spread among the membership, causing an uproar. Many of the brothers felt the best way to handle this "crisis" was to be more careful about "who we let in." They argued that we needed additional athletes (falsely assuming that that meant heterosexuality). Even suggesting that a rushee might be a queer or a fag would kill his chances of receiving a bid.

I often have wondered how these guardians of our fraternity honor would have felt if they had known how many of their brothers were gay. I remember feeling isolated listening to my brothers tell fag jokes and hearing gay-bashing comments. At that time I thought I was the only gay Greek on campus. As it turns out, there were more than a few of us.

Several gay Greek brothers and friends have had to make difficult decisions about how to live out their lives in a conservative, intolerant region of the country. In a recent conversation with one of these brothers who remains in Tennessee, I was told that after several years of marriage, his wife still had no idea that he was gay. A few other brothers are so self-oppressed that they have not verbally acknowledged their own sexual orientation, even though the manifestations of their denial are too obvious and numerous to ignore.

Since graduating, I have had the opportunity to revisit my chapter and to discuss homophobia with several of my brothers. Reactions have been mixed. After I came out several brothers ended all communications. Two of them were particularly disappointing because I had helped to recruit both of them into the fraternity. Both of them, like me, had come from rural, religious backgrounds.

Relations with other fraternity brothers have not been affected by my coming out. In fact, some relationships have become more meaningful. One of the most empowering experiences I have enjoyed since being open about my sexual orientation was attending the 1993 March on Washington for Gay, Lesbian, and Bisexual Rights. Standing among hundreds of thousands of gay Americans joined with thousands of straight supporters and family members to speak out for equality was an overwhelming feeling. The occasion was made even more significant by having a fraternity brother to share in the occasion. Steve, the fraternity brother who had delivered my bid and had given me my first chapter position, was living in the Washington area at the time. He came into the city to see me, to meet my partner, and to demonstrate his support as a straight ally for gay-straight equality.

I am encouraged that fraternities are making some progress in their struggle to overcome homophobia. In Greek leadership programs on diversity, I hear undergraduate fraternity leaders argue more frequently that sexual orientation should make no difference in the membership selection process. Last fall, on the campus where I now work as a Greek adviser, the president of the gay and lesbian student association received a bid from one of our strongest fraternities. I hear colleagues talk of similar progress at professional association meetings.

This advancement, however, is too slow and too isolated. Professional leaders of America's fraternities are guilty of promoting intolerance and sanctioning gay bashing by their silence. National fraternity conferences and conclaves include little or no education about issues of sexual orientation.

There is an amazing irony to the widespread existence of homophobia within fraternities. Having worked with fraternities for nearly ten years, I am convinced that gay Greeks make up a significant number of fraternity members. The contributions of these individuals are unknown to most but, to a disproportionate extent, sustain the fraternity world as we know it. Despite the significant number of gay fraternity men and the prominence of gay issues in our national dialogue, fraternity leaders exclude any references to homosexuality or bisexuality in their Greek vernacular.

A blatant example of this obvious shutting out is fraternity literature, which has, with very few exceptions, nothing to say about homophobia. In the past few years, several widely circulated fraternity publications featured major articles on diversity in the '90s without a single reference to sexual orientation. Is it any wonder that undergraduate fraternity men interpret this ostracism of homosexuals as permission from their headquarters to bash gays?

Institutionalized homophobia absorbs Greek life and causes fraternities to ostracize gay students as the least desired and most harassed segment on campus. Homophobia within fraternities is a tragedy that perpetuates ignorance and plays on irrational fears. The dominant heterosexist attitudes prevalent in most fraternities shut out minority voices and create an intolerant atmosphere where gay bashing is actually applauded. Fraternity professionals who are silent on this issue advance the notion that gay bashing is part of the "good ol' " fraternity experience.

Stories of gay Greek men are just beginning to be told, and the cost of silence has not yet been fully measured. This issue reminds everyone that fraternities have not yet learned fundamental history lessons about the price of exclusion and discrimination. Professionals who work with fraternities have a moral imperative to live up to the values they say they believe in.

College campuses should be places for students to expand their intellect and to learn about how to live and work in an increasingly global, diverse community. If American fraternities are to have a place in the future, they cannot operate on obsolete fears that promote bigotry and ignorance. Fraternity leaders must move aggressively to combat all forms of discrimination and prejudice, including those based on sexual orientation. To do any less is inconsistent with basic fraternal values.

The Ultimate Road Trip
by Joseph Hunter Edward

I was sitting there talking to the intramural king of the chapter—well-respected and the guy-that-every-member-wanted-to-be. And here was this 6-foot-4, 195-pound rugby player telling me that he might be gay. Still, I thought, "This guy is just trying to feel me out and when I say, 'Don't worry. I'm gay too,' he is going to kick the shit out of me, and they will be dragging the everglades for my body."

My fraternity experience, like that of most members, is something that profoundly affects me today. From the beginning, I knew that the friends I was making would be with me for the rest of my life. Six years since graduation, my fraternity brothers are still the people I call when I have good news to share or when I have had a particularly bad day. Phi Delta Theta's motto, "A Fraternity for Life," is not just some phrase at the bottom of a rush brochure. Rather, it is a belief that is proved daily by men of high character, the likes of which I have yet to find in any other circle.

It was this group of leaders that first inspired me to further my fraternity experience after college. While serving as chapter president at the New Mexico Alpha chapter at the University of New Mexico, I hosted many visits by the general headquarters staff. These fraternity missionaries were the people who encouraged me to apply for a position as a chapter consultant. As a chapter consultant, I would travel around North America and visit chapters, offering guidance and leadership on everything from chapter organization to finances to answers about social planning. In the nearly 150 years of Phi Delta Theta, fewer than 100 men had been chosen to act as ambassadors for this great brotherhood. That is why when I was offered the opportunity to serve my fraternity, I forgot about my acceptance letter to law school at Notre Dame and moved to Oxford, Ohio.

Along with the other five chapter consultants, I reported to Oxford in early July 1991. Our tours were scheduled to begin in late August, and the interim weeks would be filled with training, role playing, bonding, and, yes, lots of happy hours. On one of the first days, one of my fellow fledgling consultant brothers, Marc, commented, "I feel like I've just met my new best friends." The feeling was unanimous. We all bonded instantly. After work ended at 5 p.m., we would take in a workout or a run, reconvene for dinner, and then later head to High Street to some of our favorite bars. (I do not think the guys will ever forget the sight of my being "removed" from Attractions and tossed onto the sidewalk by a very large bouncer who did not like the fact that I refused to pay the cover charge.)

It was the best summer of my life. But even with my new family and as close as we had become in a very short time, I knew that I had to keep a part of me quiet. This was "good ol' boy" country, Middle America, where homosexual people are believed to exist only on the coasts.

At the beginning of my tour, I still did not consider myself to be gay. All I knew at that point was that I enjoyed having sex with men (my "straight" fraternity brother, Jeff, still disagrees with my philosophy that a man can have sex with another man without being gay). It was something that I hid very well. In fact, I had become so adept in planning my clandestine adventures that I could slip away without raising any suspicions. So I guess that is how I thought it would be. I would continue to go on reconnaissance missions and still live up to my new professional responsibilities.

It was a good plan, at least on paper. However, somewhere between Vancouver, Canada and Springfield, Mo. (or was it Shreveport, Louisiana? Maybe it was New Orleans... Yes, definitely New Orleans!), something changed. This was the first time I was living my life for myself. My mom was not watching. I did not have a chapter full of fraternity brothers watching me. My girlfriend was safely ensconced in graduate school a few states away. I was free! I was free to live any way I wanted, at least while between chapter visits. The countless hours spent behind the wheel listening to Garth Brooks's *No Fences* and *Ropin' The Wind* gave me time to think. It was becoming clear that I could no longer hide from myself who I was. I was gay. I remember the first time I wrote that on paper. It was in a letter to a guy that I had met just before I moved to Ohio. I wrote to him and said, "I am gay." After writing that sentence, I fell back in my chair in one of the dozens of forgettable hotel rooms that consultants tolerate and went numb.

Now what? This was only two months into my two-year tour. I knew that I had to continue hiding myself from my peers. Not only was I not ready to tell another soul about Mr. Hyde, I feared that I would be excommunicated from the inner circle. The chapter-consultant position is held in very high regard, both by the undergraduate brothers and the well-respected alumni volunteers within the fraternity. This was a very visible position that required the utmost in professionalism and demeanor. If the year had been 1997, I might have decided to tell my boss or at least one of the other consultants, but even though this was 1991, the "gay '90s Revolution" had not commenced. I knew that I would be treated differently—or worse.

And so it was. Every six weeks the chapter consultants would travel back to Oxford and debrief for a week, sharing horror stories from the road (like the time I was awakened in the middle of the night in Wichita, Kan., to the sound of a hazing lineup in the next bedroom, or being put up in an empty bedroom in Eugene, Ore., where the chapter's mascot Labrador used to live or making that emergency crash landing in San Francisco!). It was a great time, the camaraderie unmatched. We would head back to our favorite haunts in Oxford ("Attractions," "Hole in the Wall," "Top Deck") and drink like sailors on leave.

I thought I was pulling the whole thing off pretty well. The guys would share stories of meeting women on the road, and I would tell them about the great Polo outlet I found in Lake of the Ozarks. Since I had never been one to boast of female conquests, I was never called out to talk about the sorority consultant that I had met on the road. My moniker had become Customer Service Champion since I always expected a certain level of service while traveling (but if you ask me, I'll swear I am not high-maintenance!). So while stories were being traded about picking up those two female hitchhikers somewhere in Arizona, I was talking about my stay at the Sheraton Grande Hotel in Vancouver or being upgraded to first class on United! We all had a good laugh and had another beer.

After a few nights of this, though, something would happen. I would begin to feel very alone. These guys were free to talk about their girl-friends back home and the other women they had met. I could not tell them about the NFL player that I slept with in Los Angeles or the guy I spent the weekend with in Chicago. By the end of our week in Ox-ford, I could not wait to escape to the road and return to myself. I looked forward to finding out where my travels would take me and mapping out my route. Since we had the weekends off while traveling, I would seek out bars in whichever town I happened to be. Most of the time while in these bars, I would look around and think, *I do not belong here*. I would walk in, and, especially in the small towns, everybody knew that I was "not from round here."

I do not know if I gave off some scent or maybe I had a sign taped to my back that read "In town for one night only," but men would ap-proach me and want to meet me. Sometimes I appreciated the attention, and sometimes it resulted in sex, but most of the time the sex was just sex. I never offered my real story to any of these men and certainly did not want to get close to them. I would say that I lived in Cincinnati and that I was a business consultant. I was deathly afraid of any connection being made between my extracurricular activities and my fraternity. Somewhere in the back of my mind I still felt shame in being gay and was terrified that someone—*anyone*—associated with Phi Delta Theta would find out. I took extra precaution not to be wearing any fraterni-ty letters if I went to a bar. Since I have my fraternity letters tattooed on my ankle, I would have sex with my socks on if it meant not letting the guy see my tattoo. It was pretty bad. Now I look back and realize how silly all of that was (I actually put a Band-Aid on my tattoo once so someone would not see it!)

All of this was because the fraternity world is not a place where gays are welcomed. This is a strange paradox considering the high percent-age of gay men in every fraternity today. Almost all of these men live in silence, fearing expulsion if their secret is told. It should not be a great surprise to learn that there are large numbers of gay fraternity men. After all, is not one of the stereotypes about gay men that we are overachievers? Certainly, the very concept of fraternity was started by men of high caliber who sought to make themselves better than the average man. It just seems logical that somewhere amidst the brotherhood is a gay college football quarterback, student body president, and IFC rush chairman.

Knowing that he is walking into a pit of pythons, why would any man choose to join a group that would probably not want him if they thought he might be gay? Although at the time I became a Phi Delt I did not consider myself gay, I knew that I was attracted to men. I joined for the same reasons that any man joins a fraternity: friendship, scholarship, leadership, and a feeling of belonging. Gay men do not join fraternities to get a date. On the contrary, most are so terrified of even the slightest hint of their being gay that they learn to hide it pretty well. It is very much parallel with the reason gay men join the military. It certainly is not to get a date there either. The risk of being expelled is just too great.

And I certainly did meet more than the hypothesized 10% of undergraduate wolves in sheep's' clothing. (For the record, I believe that the percentage of gay men in fraternities is much higher than 10%!) While visiting a school in Florida, I was finishing up a routine meeting with one of the officers when he said he had something else that he wanted to talk to me about. At the beginning of our meeting, I had found it strange that he came to talk to me wearing only a tight pair of Umbro shorts. I dismissed his appearance and counted him as just a dumb jock. Then he asked me what the fraternity's policy was on homosexuality.

I was stunned. This was the first time this topic had come up. As I felt my face turn bright red, I asked, "Why are you worried about that?" He said, "Well, in any group of 60 guys, there is bound to be someone who is, right?" I said, "Yeah, probably." "In all of the guys that you have met while traveling around, have you met any?" Now I was really terrified. Where was he going with this? I did not know if he thought that I was gay and he had a problem with that or if he was trying to tell me that he was gay. I told him that this topic had not come up, neither in my training as a consultant nor in my meetings with any of the undergraduates. He then took a deep breath and said, "Sometimes I think that I might be gay."

Whoa! Where did that come from? I had not been coached by the general fraternity with a proper response, so I asked whether or not he thought that his chapter brothers would support him if he was. It was surreal. I was sitting there talking to the intramural king of the chapter—well-respected and the guy-that-every-member-wanted-to-be. And here was this 6-foot-4, 195-pound rugby player telling *me* that *he* might be gay. Still, I thought, *This guy is just trying to feel me out and when I say, "Don't worry. I'm gay too," he is going to kick the shit out of me, and they'll be dragging the everglades for my body.* We talked a little more about it, but I think he got nervous about the whole thing and abruptly ended our meeting. He made himself very scarce during the rest of my stay, so I did not get a chance to talk with him again.

I was very uncomfortable when Mr. Rugby brought up the subject of sexual orientation. I should have asked him more about his feelings and talked him through it. I really could have put him at ease and maybe changed the balance of his undergraduate experience for the better—I could have been a role model. And is that not what consultants are supposed to do anyway? Instead I blew the opportunity to help him, mostly because I was paralyzed and could not discuss my own feelings but also because the fraternity had not prepared us for this, and there certainly was not a manual to refer to for information on the subject. I doubt that consultants are coached on dealing with homosexuality even today, but they should be. Even providing basic training on counseling services that every university has would help in these situations. At a minimum, the next Mr. Rugby would not be met with silence or a feeling of being judgmentally dismissed.

If the Mr. Rugby scene were not weird enough, there was a school in the South that I was visiting for a second time. There was not enough room for me to stay in the house, so I stayed with one of the members who had an apartment off campus. This was fine with me, since I had stayed with him during my previous visit and we really hit it off. Trevor was a great guy with a classic Southern upbringing that taught him to be the perfect host. And he was. He always made sure that my meetings went OK and usually ate most meals with me.

Trevor had a one-bedroom apartment, and in his bedroom he had built two bunk beds with the top bed crossing the lower bunk to form an L. He gave me the top bunk, and he took the lower one. On the day before I was scheduled to leave, Trevor had a water-polo meet. He was the goalie on his school's team. As with every other event during my stay, he made sure I was invited. And it was an event. I was sitting with the other guys from the chapter along with about 300 other people. I had already seen him wearing nothing other than a towel when he walked around his apartment after a shower, but this time the sight of Trevor in a tight Speedo required that I follow his every move.

Every time the ball would get thrown out of the pool, Trevor would jump out and get it. I was transfixed but still pretended not to notice. As he bent down to pick up the ball, in the same motion he would pick me out of the crowd and make eye contact with me. The first two times I played it off and looked away. The third time, there was no hiding it. I sat there and smiled at him, and he returned it. After the meet he asked if I wanted to go have dinner and go out for some drinks. We headed to one of the college bars near the campus and proceeded to get drunk on pitchers of kamikazes.

Drunk and barely standing, we headed back to his place. We both got undressed down to our boxers and got in our respective beds.

As the room was spinning from all the shots we had, Trevor said, "I am so drunk!"

I said, "Yeah, that last pitcher probably wasn't a good idea."

He said, "I feel all tingly all over."

I thought that that was a weird thing for him to say, but I blew it off and charged it to his drunkenness. Then I almost fell out of my bed when he said, "I get really horny when I'm drunk."

We were on very dangerous ground here. When I did not respond, he asked, "Do you get horny when you drink?" I said, "Shut up, Trevor, and go to sleep."

Of course, with my heart pounding, I could not fall asleep. This was the golden opportunity of a lifetime. What was I thinking turning it down? An Adonis goalie from a collegiate water-polo team was asking me if I wanted to have sex. This does not happen to mere mortals. But I would not and could not have my professional world and my personal world meet. To have sex under these conditions would have been unprofessional and just plain wrong. So in the morning we both pretended like the whole thing never happened.

As the year ended, I knew that something had to change. I loved the consultant work that I was doing, and I certainly loved the travel, but the charade was taking its toll on my sanity. My girlfriend had just realized that we were headed in two separate directions, so she gave me back my lavaliere. She just could not understand why I was not ready to settle down with her. Getting back to Oxford meant retreating to my former self, and I really did become "myself" during that year on the road. I honestly believe that individuals become the people that they will be for the rest of their lives once they reach their mid-20s. The college years leading up to the "mid-20s revelation" are just practice.

A month after we were back in Oxford, my two worlds collided. After a night of drunken buffoonery, a fraternity brother of mine claimed that I had made a sexual advance toward him. This accusation came while I was on a two-week vacation in Los Angeles (my favorite city on the planet). That was it. The game was over. The clandestine life I had kept hidden so well for so long had just blown up in my face. So while still on vacation in Los Angeles, I drove to the beach, where I sat in a daze for hours. I woke up from that daze, drove to LAX, flew to Oxford, packed my belongings, and drove back to L.A., afraid and confused. (I still cannot account for those catatonic 24 hours of driving time between Oxford and my first stop in New Mexico!) No job. No plan. No life. Devastated.

My membership in my fraternity, the foundation that has made me the person that I am today, was in question. I did not know what would happen. After I had spent a few weeks in L.A., the drama died down and one of my fellow consultant brothers, Marc, called me and said, "No matter what, I love you, Joe." That meant more to me than Marc will ever know. I waited for the other consultants to contact me. I figured that if they wanted our friendship to continue, I would let them make the first move.

Three of the other five did contact me, and I am still friends with two of them, Marc and Conrad. Patrick and I did continue a friendship after I left staff—we even visited each other. But after I told Patrick that I was gay, he never talked to me again. This really surprised and devastated me, since we had been very close. Patrick still remains the only person who discontinued our friendship after finding out. It hurt. It hurt a lot. The "Patrick" incident is the reason today I tell people that I am gay only if they have the audacity to ask. All the important people in my life know: my mom, ex-girlfriend, and best friends. I should say to Patrick that it is his loss if he does not want to continue our friendship. But what I really say to myself is, "I miss you, brother."

My feelings about homosexuality in fraternities are mixed. While I do not believe that any man should be denied an invitation to join a fraternity nor be expelled for being gay, I also do not feel that the fraternity world is a place to espouse a radical homosexual agenda. There are other forums for this movement. Being in a fraternity has always been about men bonding together in the spirit of friendship and scholarship. Homosexuality deserves no more special attention in this definition than being left-handed or asthmatic. Fraternities are still run by men who are generally not comfortable with gay men. If all we do as gay fraternity men is to make being gay a nonissue, then we have won. I want my brothers to refer to me as "Joe, the guy who gives 110% for Phi Delt and who is a great friend and is always there when anybody needs him—oh, and he happens to be gay, but it's no big deal."

As I think back to my tour as a chapter consultant, I think about the men I may have influenced had I been out. I now know that one of the consultants who visited me when I was an undergraduate and who consequently became one of my good friends is gay. Had I known that he was gay at the time, I would have had a role model—someone to look up to, because gay men do not have enough positive role models! It would have helped in my own coming-out process. I now wish that I could have been that role model for some of the undergraduates that I met. There would have been chapters where my being gay would have been a nonissue, and there would have been places where I would have been met with hostility. I think the success of being an out chapter consultant would depend on the way it is presented. If I encountered a situation where a member came to me and wanted to discuss it (like Mr. Rugby or Trevor), I could say, "Well, you know, I'm gay, but that has nothing to do with the fact that I'm still a good Phi." It could take a lot of pressure off a troubled brother.

On the contrary, if I had begun my visits with the entire brotherhood in some random place like Oxford, Miss., with, "Hi, I'm Joe and I'm gay!" I would not have been seen as someone who was there to help with their problems and listen to their needs. In our quest to be more accepted, we cannot force change down people's throats. The soft sell is a better approach!

I am a strong believer in fate. Fate stepped in that dark morning in 1992 and forced me to leave the chapter-consultant staff and get on with my life, and I am stronger because of it. Though at the time, I felt like my world had just ended, my life now is very healthy because of that learning. I am dating a great guy, have a challenging career, just bought a home in Los Angeles, travel whenever and wherever I want, and basically live a relatively decadent life surrounded by great friends. I am happier than I have ever been. My friends now for the most part know that I am gay. The best part is that they still think of me as Joe-meet-me-in-Chicago-for-a-Cubs-game-Edward (box seats, first-base line, of course). No more dual role. No more lies.

STRUGGLE, FEAR, AND ISOLATION

Fear is not an unknown emotion to us.

Neil Armstrong, Phi Delta Theta

All-Male Cast
by "Maurice"

When asked why I wanted to join a fraternity, I had one answer for him: To meet women and become sexually involved with them so that I would not end up gay.

As a young boy growing up in the Midwest, I was very unaware of life beyond the corn, wheat, and soybean fields that surrounded my small hometown. I was too young to know that Stonewall was a bar in New York City and television had Dick and Laura Petrie sleeping in twin beds. There were very few clues in my world to inform me of other ways of living, and it was not until I was a teenager that I discovered one of those clues. In the *Chicago Tribune*, the Sunday edition, I would read the entertainment section, giving more attention to the movie advertisements, finding it hard to believe so many movie theaters could exist in one city. Within the movie advertisements, in extremely small blocks, were two movie cinemas that promised triple-X features with all-male casts. I had no idea why a movie would have an all-male cast and be pornographic, but I knew someday I would have to find out.

I did not get very far from my hometown when I finally left for college. The university I attended was only 30 minutes from my home, just across the state line. It was a small state-supported institution, which was extremely overshadowed by the flagship institution an hour down the road. Although I had not given much thought to where I might attend school, I was content with what I had found. It was 1977; Carter was president, and life was unexciting for an 18-year-old without a car, who did not drink, and who went home every weekend. When I attended summer orientation, each student completed a survey of student organizations that the university sponsored and supported. I could hear some students snickering as I was completing my survey, and I wondered what was so interesting as to provoke such a reaction. I found my answer very soon: the Gay Student Association. Although I had only a slight idea of what *gay* was, I knew that it was something that I would not want someone else to know that I might be interested in, so I checked the "no" box and continued.

I did not give much thought to the gay thing until I moved into my residence hall a month later, to discover that I had been assigned to an all-male floor. Not only was it an all-male floor, but it was the only all-male floor that was not allowed visitation by members of the opposite sex. Our floor immediately was labeled the virgin vault by the others in the hall, and those of us who lived on the floor were somewhat paranoid. However, we managed to develop a good relationship among the men on the floor, and the lack of women did not bother us too much. Some of my good friends—female friends—from my high school lived in a hall that had visitation, so I practically lived on their floor that first month. I was soon dragging my floor mates to that floor, so we seemed to be surviving our artificially contrived environment by leaving it as much as possible.

For someone who knew very little about gays before he came to college, I was learning much that first year. The event which truly wreaked havoc on my floor was the newspaper advertisement which announced gay blue jeans day: wear blue jeans if you are gay or support gay rights. We were truly in a dilemma, as most of us had nothing but blue jeans to wear (this was the pre-khaki and pre-Dockers era). I had a pair of white painter's pants to wear that day, and my friend across the hall chose to wear sweatpants, a practice that was not the norm at the time. I remember that my English instructor brought up the topic and tried to get some discussion out of the class, but I do not remember much about what was said. I do remember the shock I had when I saw that most people were wearing their blue jeans; had they not seen the notice? I began to feel a little stupid about how I had acted, but it was several years before I could wear blue jeans during a gay blue jeans day.

I was not very much interested in fraternity life my first year at school. Very few of the men on the floor pledged a fraternity, and the floor and the residence hall provided us with all the friends and activities we needed. During my sophomore year, many of us returned to the same floor (we discovered that our floor could change our visitation option, we chose to have visitation, and the virgin vault curse was eventually lifted), so there was little need to look for friendship beyond the hall. However, a number of men from some of the lower floors in the hall were joining a new fraternity on our campus. The men who were joining this fraternity seemed to be decent fellows—several of them were either resident assistants or front desk staff in our hall. We gave a couple of people a very hard time about joining this group, but I became more interested as I watched from a distance. Near the end of my sophomore year, I decided it was time for me to investigate what it was that was attracting all my friends to this fraternity, so I invited myself to a rush function. The function was nothing that I thought it would be, a group of men meeting in the old faculty lounge of the former women's residence hall. No beers, no loud music, no wild women, just a group of men sharing their fraternity experience with me and the other rushees. By the end of the semester, I was offered an invitation to join the newest fraternity on our campus, and I said yes.

Many of my friends questioned why I wanted to join a fraternity, and I gave various answers. However, when a friend from high school asked me, I gave him a very different answer. Even though I knew little about homosexuality or gay men, the truth of the matter was simple: I had been engaging in same-sex acts since I was 14. A friend from high school was my partner in the crime. There was no passion or emotion to our relationship, just raging hormones and my fear of women, instilled in me by my mother, who made it clear that I was not to have a girlfriend lest I become a father at a tender young age. I did have a girlfriend my senior year in high school, as did my friend, and the activity between us stopped. However, the activity resumed when we went to the same college and our relationships with our girlfriends ended. So when asked why I wanted to join a fraternity, I had one answer for him: to meet women and become sexually involved with them so that I would not end up gay. Although I had not met any gay men at my school, I had formulated a theory as to why gay men existed. I believed that most gay men really wanted to be with women, but because there was something so horribly wrong with them, women would have noth-

ing to do with them, and the men would have to turn to each other for
sexual gratification. This, coupled with the fact that I thought I had a
domineering mother and an absent father, certainly explained why I
was destined to be a gay man. I did not want to be one of those poor
unfortunate souls, so I had to join a fraternity, meet a sorority girl, have
sex, and become straight.

Although I was enjoying my experiences in the fraternity with my
newfound brothers, my worst fears were coming true. The first major
social event of the season was the hayride, and I could not find a date.
The chapter president offered to fix me up, but I insisted that I would
find a date on my own. However, I did not find a date. I missed the
hayride, and the rejection reinforced my theory about myself and gay
men. The next big event was my initiation banquet, and once again I
was striking out. The chapter president promised to find a date for me.
On the afternoon before the big event, he gave me the name and phone
number of a sorority woman from his hometown. I was very apprehensive about taking a perfect stranger to my initiation banquet, but I
quickly got over my fears once we arrived at the hotel. I was in awe of
the scene, since I had never been to such an extravagant affair before.
The night really hit a high note when it was announced that I was chosen outstanding associate by my fellow class brothers. I still maintained
my virginity at the end of the evening, but I knew fraternity life was for
me, and my problem became less of a concern.

As I became more involved with the fraternity and other activities on
campus, I met many women, and I rarely had difficulty finding a date
for social functions. However, it was not that important for me to have
sex with a woman. No, I had not come to terms with my homosexuality, since I was still in a state of denial about it. I was so caught up in my
chapter life, with my friends in the residence hall, and with my academic work and music that it was easy to forget about the sex part—or so
I thought. I soon discovered two dark sides about life, one on campus
and one in the college town. On campus, I found out through some
friends in my hall that the bathroom in the basement of the library was
the site of questionable activity. It did not take me long to venture out
and discover for myself what was taking place. I was a mess. I thrived
on the thrill of it all, the sense of adventure, and the anonymous, quick
gratification. Yet I was in dreaded fear of being caught by someone I

knew. In fact, I saw a man who once had lived on my floor but left to move into his fraternity house. If he recognized me, he gave no indication, and nothing happened between us. Although some of the faces became familiar to me, anonymity reigned.

I learned about the dark side of life that existed in the college town from some of my fraternity brothers. There was an off-campus telephone number that, when dialed, connected one to a constant busy signal. However, one could talk between the signal, and one could hear myriad voices straining to be heard between the pulses of the tone. This was the "hot line," and there were actually three lines which existed. Men and women—teenagers, for the most part—would yell "call me" or would chant a phone number between the pulses. Every once in a while, especially in the late-night hours, I would hear a mature male voice ask for "any men," and if there was a positive response, a phone number would be exchanged. Again, driven by the excitement of the thrill and the danger, I managed to become an active participant in the nightly exchange of phone numbers. I worked the night desk, so I had all the time in the world to work the line, and I had a pay phone to use as a number to protect my identity. I began to meet men off campus and actually became connected to a couple of different men I met over the years. However, I never used my own name, and I always had to lie about myself. I could not take the risk of letting someone know who I really was or what I was about. So by day, I was Mr. College, fraternity man, student about campus. At night, I was off in search of sexual conquests, only to return to a state of denial when morning came and the cycle started again.

I gave three years of my life to my fraternity. I was chapter secretary for one year, a position that enabled me to become better connected with other facets of the university. I participated in intramural sports, assisted with building the homecoming float, attended sporting events, played my instrument in the all-Greek theater productions, and attended most of the social events. I also did the occasional class assignment. I was giving so much of myself to my fraternity and other endeavors that it did not bother me that my college career was lasting longer than the average four years.

It was rare that the topic of homosexuality came up in my chapter. I can remember only one time when it was alluded to in a chapter meeting, when someone was expressing concern about a new member who was somewhat effeminate. A chapter officer challenged this brother, stating that there were times when the accuser manifested feminine characteristics, so he had better watch what he said. I remember it being very tense in the room, but we somehow moved past the issue and continued with business. That is the only incident I can remember when homophobia manifested itself in a formal setting in the chapter. There were times when a brother would make some joke about sleeping with another brother, but such statements were usually made under the influence of alcohol and were quickly dismissed. In many ways homosexuality did not exist on our campus, and it certainly did not exist in my chapter.

My fraternity chapter was rather large, but we did not have a chapter house, and we often found ourselves being isolated into geographical regions on campus. Each hall had a group of brothers in residence, some groups of brothers lived in suites, and we had a contingent of brothers off campus. Chapter gatherings, meetings, and events were very important to us because it was the only time we were all together as a unit. There were several people in the chapter extremely important to me, one being my little brother. He came to my aid many times when I found myself in a state of rejection. I never understood how we became such close friends, because we are different in many ways. The chapter adviser was a very influential member of our organization, and I took advantage of every opportunity I had to spend time with him. There were always groups of brothers who moved in and out of my life, like the tides, and I highly valued their companionship. However, I never felt that I was in a position where I could confide in one of my brothers about my dilemma, about the internal struggle I was fighting alone. I cannot remember a single positive portrayal of gay life that occurred during my undergraduate experience. The few people that I suspected were gay were entrenched in the closet. There were no gay role models in the media, AIDS was not a news story, and the mental health services did not provide positive support services for students struggling with their identity. Two gay students were driven out of their residence hall, and the university did not respond publicly to support them. To make my identity as a gay man public would have been the end of my fraternity experience as well as my undergraduate experi-

ence, and I was not in a place to take that risk or to seek help in re-
solving my dilemma.

I was a member of the residence life staff my last two years in school,
and my association with my fraternity gradually changed as I became
more focused on doing my job and on graduating. I managed to maintain close ties with the older brothers in the chapter, but I found myself
struggling with the names of the newer members. It was as an RA that
I became more aware of a gay student population on the campus. My
residence hall had an openly gay male, and he was dating a fraternity
member from a nearby private campus. I was hesitant at first to befriend
this person for fear of being suspected of also being gay. However, since
an RA was supposed to be a friend to all residents in the hall, I think I
managed to escape guilt by association. Through this friendship I discovered that there were many other gay students on campus, including
several people who worked for the residence life office. And to make
matters more interesting, we had our suspicions about several fraternity members who were also staff members. The possibilities excited me,
but fear prevented me from acting on any of my desires to reach out to
these people and reveal my true identity as a gay man.

During my next-to-last summer in college, I finally ventured out and
visited my first gay bar, which was located at a Big Ten college town
over two hours away from my school. I decided I was less likely to meet
someone I knew at this bar, so I thought I would be safe as I explored
this new world of music, lights, and mirrors. I was blown away the first
time I went to this nightclub because there were so many good-looking
men there—men who could have any woman they wanted, so I thought.
Even though I had had a few positive encounters with gay men, my initial theories about homosexuality had not been seriously challenged
until I discovered this oasis of gods. I made the pilgrimage to this spot
three Friday nights in a row, telling my roommates that I had met a
woman who was worth the trip. Finally, I had found a place where I
could be me for at least a few hours of the night. The trips continued
through my last year in school, and then it happened: I caught one of
my fraternity brothers with a member of another fraternity on the dance
floor. I saw him first, but I did not know what to do. I eventually gathered up my courage and walked up to him and said a very nervous "hi."
He returned the greeting and asked if I wanted to dance. We danced for

a while and then went our separate ways. Although it was wonderful to find someone, a brother, who was like me, there was also the fear that I would be exposed to others who might not be as tolerant. When we returned to campus, we never talked about our encounter at the bar. The closet door remained closed.

I had very little involvement with my fraternity my last semester of school, although I lived in the same residence hall with a number of brothers. The quest among the residence life staff to discover the gay members became more intense, and I hated myself for being a part of it. On the day that I finally graduated, my two hall directors took me out to celebrate my 25th birthday. They took me to the only gay establishment in our town, and I was excited and perplexed at the same time. Upon entering the bar and walking up to the second floor, I was greeted by the screams of fellow staff members, all friends and all members of fraternities. One happened to be a chapter brother to whom I was very close, and the group of us spent much time together that summer, exploring the life that freedom had to offer us. That was the start of my gay adolescent period, and I had much catching up to do. Although I was still fearful of being caught by someone not so understanding of my situation, I discovered that I was not alone, neither in my fraternity nor in my circle of friends.

Much has happened to me in the 12 years that have passed since leaving my undergraduate institution. I worked after graduation for three years as a fraternity adviser and a residence hall director at a small private college. I met a man at a gay support group, and we have been together for over eight years. During the second year of my graduate program, I found much support coming out to the rest of my fellow students and faculty. When I searched for a job, it was important for me to find a place where I could be gay, and it was an issue that I brought up at every site where I interviewed.

I am not officially out to my parents, my family, or too many of my friends from my undergraduate days, although most of them have met my partner and know of our living arrangement. I am waiting for them to bring up the issue when they are ready. My family situation was rarely very stable, and I was not ready to share with them this information about me. One of my cousins knows, though, and I know it is just a matter of time before I will be open with the rest of my family. After working four years in a residential life program (as an out person) at a major East Coast campus, I took an adviser position in a Greek affairs office. I came out during the interview process, assuming that word of mouth would take care of the rest. In my four years of working here, the issue of my sexuality has not been brought up by the students, but I also do not bring it up. Most of my colleagues know that I am gay, and I am told that most of the student leadership within the Greek system knows. For the students, the most important thing is that I do my job, not what I do in my off hours. I will admit that I was and am still somewhat cautious around the students, but many of them have my home number, and several of them have spoken with my partner on the phone. Since the institution does much education around issues of diversity, homosexuality is a very public topic in various facets of university life, including the Greek system. I know I will eventually be more public about my life, but for now I prefer the privacy, since I rarely get it in this profession. I have met other fraternity and sorority members who are gay, and each of them has had very different experiences within their organizations. Some chapters have been accepting, others indifferent, and some intolerant. The one thing we all have in common is that we each had to fight the battle alone, until we found someone else with whom to share the struggle.

And as for those triple-X features with an all-male cast—I finally visited one of them several years ago, on New Year's Eve when I was in Chicago. It was not all that great, but it did not matter. What a difference a few years and a new perspective can make.

I Love You, Man
by Carl Einhaus

Getting drunk seemed the only way for many of my fraternity brothers to ex-press their emotions and feelings toward each other. This was hardly a healthy or effective way for them to come to terms with their emotions, or to find out what it is to be a real man. Maybe that's why these bottled-up emotions some-times turned to depression or anger toward women. As I look back, those guys who I thought had it the most together were probably the most lost.

I was closeted when I was an undergraduate member of Delta Chi. Not only did I keep my gay identity a secret from my fraternity broth-ers; I denied it to myself as well. Deep down, a part of me did realize I was gay. However, I thought that if I consciously accepted being at-tracted to men, someone would be able to pick up on those vibes or subtleties and suspect or label me as being gay. Being discovered was not an acceptable reality to me. Labeling myself as gay was way too frightening and something for which I was not yet ready. My struggle to be accepted by my fraternity brothers was already a difficult internal challenge. The irony is that I felt like I was not being accepted because I believed I could not be my true self with many of the guys in the chap-ter. Of course, part of being my true self would mean being open about my sexual orientation, and from what I concluded from my fraternity experience, it was neither an accepting nor safe environment in which to be out of the closet.

It is important for me to note that I did not have a miserable exis-tence as a fraternity man. In fact, I have rich memories that will last a lifetime. I made a few strong connections and friendships that are still very important to me. The leadership and growth opportunities I took advantage of in the fraternity system provided me with invaluable skills and knowledge that I continue to use. If I had to live my college days over, I would join Delta Chi again with no question in my mind.

Indeed, much of my fraternal experience made a positive impact on my life. Being in a fraternity assisted me in getting the most out of college life—it was one of the main reasons I joined. But it also significantly hindered the development of my identity—not just my gay identity but my self-confidence and self-worth. It seemed as if whenever I revealed my true self and individuality, members in my fraternity were certain to knock me back down in disapproval of my differentness. After all, a fraternity is usually made up of like-minded individuals who limit variance in personalities (much like society). If a member consistently exhibited a personality or character trait that crossed over an understood and unspoken boundary, he was in some way pushed out of the fraternity. This was usually done by giving an individual the cold shoulder or making fun of him when he was not there to defend himself. I admit that I took part in this form of exiling. Perhaps I figured as long as there was someone else who was more different than me, I would be safe from being informally squeezed out myself.

Honestly, I do not know how different my fraternity brothers perceived me as being. I do believe that many of them liked me because I was genuine, personable, and had a good sense of humor. I was not usually effeminate to the point that people could outright label me as being gay (although I suppose a few could have suspected it). To be stereotypical, my music collection certainly did not out me. I never owned (and still do not own) Broadway show tunes; just supposedly heterosexual alternative rock and roll (like Midnight Oil and Elvis Costello). I did, however, reveal many qualities that traditional males in this society are influenced not to display; for example, I was very open with my feelings and emotions. It took me a while to realize that expressing feelings and emotions is not reserved for the female population but for the secure and the aware. A few of my fellow Delta Chis, in all fairness, did exhibit these qualities, but they were by no means the norm.

The leaders, just as in most organizations, set the norm in Delta Chi. The chapter's executive board was especially strong and influential in my first years as a member. Many of us respected these leaders for many reasons; they worked hard for our chapter, were effective in giving us common direction, and served as good role models. These leaders influenced me the most because of the immense respect they held in our chapter. They sent many positive messages; for instance, they emphasized the importance of taking initiative and getting involved and our responsibility as Delta Chis to volunteer in philanthropies. However, they also reinforced many negative notions, including that to be a man you must party like a rock star, have sex with women to gain status, and never show signs of weaknesses or feelings. Because of these factors and who I was, it was difficult for me to feel I could gain respect very easily.

My way of trying to be accepted and fit in was through taking on leadership positions, playing a few sports (which I did and still do enjoy), and drinking like hell. I did not drink just to be accepted, but it was another common interest I could share with my brothers, and it also served as "liquid confidence." Luckily, drinking never became a serious problem for me, but it did for a few of my fraternity brothers. It was scary to see how some of their personalities drastically changed when they drank; they could become violent, taking advantage of women sexually, and I heard rumors of some brothers physically abusing women as well.

We always made fun of the "touchy feely" drunk who got all teary eyed and emotional when he drank. These were the guys who got uncharacteristically sentimental when they were wasted. They would put their arms around another fraternity brother and say something like "I love you, man." It was fun to laugh at but sad at the same time. Getting drunk seemed the only way for many of my fraternity brothers to express their emotions and feelings toward each other. This was hardly a healthy or effective way for them to come to terms with their emotions or to find out what it is to be a real man. Maybe that's why these bottled up emotions sometimes turned to depression or anger toward women. As I look back, some of the guys who I thought had it the most together were probably the most lost.

I was very rarely sexually attracted to women. Often the only way I could become sexually interested in women was to get drunk. This was important because a way to gain respect in the fraternity (besides periodically grabbing your package) was to get laid. The frequency with which you had sex with women had a direct correlation with the level of your manhood. If you did not get laid a lot, you were low on the "becoming a man" graph. I remember the morning after every party, many of us would end up in someone's room in the fraternity house, wearing just boxers and T-shirts, laughing about people's sexual accomplishments and other assorted drunken escapades from the night before. Upon hearing that a brother got lucky, the members of the house were able to update their mental chart of who was closer to being a respected real man.

Needless to say, my contributions to these party stories were usually kept to hysterically stupid tales about myself or others who got butt-wasted. I sometimes felt left out when I had no sex stories to share. Also, I became depressed because I was missing out on the intimacy that I thought my brothers were experiencing. A few times, however, the moon aligned with Venus and I managed to hook up with a woman. Of course, I was able to do this only because I was drunk, with my inhibitions down and hormones soaring. (These drunken flings with women, by the way, never came close to the incredible and fulfilling experiences I have had since with men.)

When I was sober I could not gather enough desire or motivation to approach a woman with intimate intentions in mind. I recall fraternity brothers giving me advice claiming I was not "direct" or "forward" enough. I just was not interested enough. I had become close with many women but strictly on a platonic level. So, besides the few occasions when I did hook up with a woman, you could see me late at night at a party doing one of the following: drinking around the keg and raiding the kitchen with a few other surviving partiers or passed out in the hallway or my bed (sometimes with ceremonial markings drawn all over me by my fraternity brothers, a branding reserved for those who could not handle their alcohol). I think I am proud to say that I was usually the former and not the latter.

It is sad to think that I was always drunk during the few occasions I had intimate experiences. Further, my relationships (if they could even be called that) never lasted longer than two weeks. This is something I battled daily. I wanted so desperately to be in a relationship like some of my fraternity brothers were in or to at least have enjoyable sex without the assistance of desensitizing alcohol. As a result, my desperation led me into fits of depression. I felt I was cursed with a karma that pre-

vented me from experiencing rewarding relationships. This was a re-
curring issue that I had struggled with since junior high. It would hit
me hardest at parties, when alcohol played war games on my emotions,
bombing me into a self-absorbed depression and loneliness. It became
worse when I saw friends hooking up with women. I thought, *If they're
doing it, how come I can't? It has to be because I am not desirable enough.*

Deep down I realized that I *was* desirable and felt I had so much to
offer a partner. So what was my deal? I was decent-looking (even
though I had a roommate who jokingly called me "clownface"), possessed a good personality, and got along with most everyone. Still, it
seemed I was doomed forever to be the faithful escort for girlfriends of
my fraternity brothers (who probably did not see me as a threat) when
they could not go to date parties.

The truth was sometimes unavoidable. I could not stop fantasizing
about men. I tried to dismiss it when it happened, thinking that all I really needed to do was "find the right woman." As a result, I developed
a habit of trying to replace the men in my fantasies with women. My determination to condition myself into lusting after women was very
strong. I believed if I wanted to pass as a heterosexual, I had to think
as a heterosexual. Even though I fantasized about men, I still would not
allow myself to accept that I was gay. Again, that would have been too
horrifying a realization for me to handle. At the time, I did not feel that
my chapter was a supportive enough atmosphere for me to take such a
great personal risk as coming out. Moreover, I relied too much on others' opinions of me to build my self-esteem. I could not withstand rejection from a group of people whose acceptance meant so much to me.

Fear of rejection and the need for acceptance seemed to be a driving
force in motivating behavior for many of my fraternity brothers, not just
myself. It would have helped to realize that I was not the only one in
my chapter who was not "self-actualized." I recall many of my brothers
speaking and acting out of character, probably in the hope of being
more popular with the other D-Chis. For example, a normally respectable brother was once caught trying to have sex with a sleeping
woman; another brother threw a log through a neighboring fraternity's
picture window over some minor overdramatized dispute, and yet another decided to defecate on a brother's car from the second floor
porch (just to get laughs out of people).

Those are just a few of the innumerable offensive stories I could relay that would make most people turn away in disgust. However, my intention in describing these stories is not to criticize the fraternity system. My bet is that most nonfraternity college students were witness to or a part of more ignorant situations than the ones I have revealed. (It is fascinating how quickly some people judge fraternities' actions when they have been guilty of equally repugnant acts themselves; they just have the luxury of being out of the media spotlight). My intention, however, is to convey steps some fraternity brothers took in trying to be accepted.

I was never blatantly homophobic. I suppose that at some level I knew that if I bashed gays, I would be bashing myself. Also, would I be seen as protesting too much? I could not risk that. Sometimes when I teased my friends, I would jokingly call them "gay" or a "fag," but that was the extent to which I expressed any homophobic sentiments. The homophobia held by others in my fraternity, however, was much more blatant and descriptive. Frequently, vivid and violent comments about gay men's sexual acts were spoken for guaranteed laughs and to ensure that homosexual hatred was shared. It was made quite clear to me that queers were seen as weak, lesser, and feared individuals. Also, it seemed sometimes that my brothers acted homophobic to prove that they were heterosexual. Displaying dislike toward gays was a way to authenticate their manhood.

I remember a few fraternity members who were suspected of being gay, but there were never any real confirmations. Much of this suspicion came simply from the fact that they did not seem to fit the definition of "Delta Chi material." We somehow let those slip in from time to time. In attempts at "loser infiltration prevention," one fraternity brother announced at a bidding night (a member-selection event), "If you cannot imagine going to a bar with him, then he is not Delta Chi material." Fortunately, this member was not very well-respected in the house, and his suggestion was laughed off. Besides, there were only a few Delta Chis who desired going to a bar with *him* (to remain objective, he had problems relating to most people).

One occasion comes to mind when we seriously thought that one of our fraternity brothers, Ed, was gay. It was quite the gossip. Gay jokes involving Ed were flying. It was rumored that he hit on a guy in another fraternity and tried to get him in bed. Ed was already looked at as a little too "flamboyant" for the Delta Chi mold, so I guess it made it easier for us to chastise him. He must have caught wind of the rumors, because I do not remember seeing him around much after the news broke. I believe it was a loss for the fraternity, because he was a good guy. I never got to know Ed very well, because he did not live in the fraternity house or come by very much. However, through our pledging together I came to know him as funny, very dependable, easygoing, and a person who would assist anyone in a time of need. I cannot imagine the mental anguish he must have gone through at this time. He did not even have a chance to defend himself. It was probably that time of year to "squeeze" someone out of the fraternity. Also, it sent a clear message to every closeted brother in our fraternity: stay closeted or be pushed out of the chapter. Kinsey's studies are often interpreted as suggesting that 10% of our population is gay; applying this theory to Delta Chi, there were at least nine closeted gay men in the chapter at the time.

It was very challenging at times to keep my sexual orientation a secret, especially when I developed crushes on my fraternity brothers. I learned to live in a contradiction; I pursued a heterosexual identity while having strong same-sex attractions. This issue, I imagine, may be a subject of concern for my brothers who now know that I am gay. "Did Carl have a thing for me? Did he stare at me when I came out of the shower? Shit! He saw me naked!"

Actually, I had very few crushes on my fraternity brothers. I did develop one that was intense. We were roommates for a semester, which made getting over it very difficult. He was sensitive, handsome, funny, intelligent, personable—basically, almost all that anyone looks for in a partner. However, I knew that he was very heterosexual, and therefore I kept my attractions to my denying self. It was extremely difficult to be attracted to someone who I knew could not reciprocate. But the alternative—revealing my feelings to him and possibly being thrust out of the chapter as a result—was not an option even to be considered.

Quite possibly, I might have remained closeted during my undergraduate years even if I had not been in a fraternity. But the fraternity was very significant in teaching me that being gay is wrong, somehow subhuman. As a result, my self-esteem was butchered, and I remained in the role of the closet king.

Considering my fraternity's nonsupportive environment, staying closeted when I was an undergraduate was the right choice for me. I was not ready emotionally and developmentally to be out quite yet. I came out a year after I graduated, when I was in graduate school at the same Michigan institution. Coming out was the best choice I have ever made, personally and politically. I can now live life to its fullest. However, what made it such a great decision was the timing. I want every gay, lesbian, and bisexual person to come out at some period in their lives, but it has to be at the right time for them. Identifying trusting friends or mentors who can support you in the coming-out process is a big part of that decision making. Coming out can be very challenging (the best word to describe that period in my life is still *funky*), but it is also extremely rewarding.

My advice to closeted fraternity members is to examine your situation. Are you ready emotionally to come out? Do you have people whom you can trust for support in revealing your identity? Can you afford to stay closeted? My suggestion for heterosexual fraternity members is to attempt to be understanding if a brother comes out to you. He is still the same person. You have just found out another piece to his puzzle. Besides, you should feel honored that your brother trusted you enough to reveal something so personal. He will be extremely vulnerable and will need someone to listen and to be a friend or ally.

I still have bittersweet feelings about my fraternity experience to this day. One day I will think about how invaluable a life experience it was, and the next day I will tear it apart for its inconsistencies and the way it destroyed the self-esteem of so many brothers. Like most life experiences, being in a fraternity had its negative and positive aspects, but I have decided that it is counterproductive to obsess on the negative aspects. Searching for someone to blame will not help me to regain the time I lost not being out or the missed opportunities to experience rewarding relationships. Instead I tend to look back on being a Delta Chi very proudly: We were the number one fraternity on that campus for my years of stay, I made some strong friendships, I gained some great skills that I will continue to use in the future, I have some great memories (and pictures), and I am part of a "brotherhood of a lifetime." I am still very proud to say that I am a Delta Chi. I am even more proud, however, to be a gay man.

Hidden Agendas
by Jim McAleer

Drink more, fit in more—easy. The only problem was waking up, wondering if the cover had been blown in a blackout. Did somebody find out that I was gay?

A sore head, a dry mouth, and a pledge pin—what a night! Actually, I was not really sure if it was a pledge pin. What did one look like? Given fuzzy memories of a fraternity house, massive quantities of liquid explosive called "hunch punch," and a dark room with strange men and candles, chances were good that it was a pledge pin. Shit.

It was 1989 and my first two weeks at a state university. Even if it meant being lonely and scared to death, it was about damned time I was on my own. No matter how often I had dreamed of going off to college, it was really strange to actually experience being alone. Year after year of recoiling into a shell of others' expectations had finally given way. The volcanic pressure of staying home had overcome the fear of leaving small-town Georgia. Now was the time to explore it all. No more of the old games; it was time for a new playing field.

There was not much question about the sex thing—even early on. Furtive struggles with neighborhood boys at 12 had given way to late-night sex on the beach with strangers. By the time I was 16, most of what could be done had been, and what had not been done had been dreamed about. No one was supposed to know I was gay, of course. After all, a strict family, a strong religion, and a small town added up to one hell of a roadblock to being out.

College was going to be different. Finally, here was a chance to be free—whatever the hell that meant. For the first time, it was possible to explore being gay and not worry that the preacher—or worse yet, my mother—would drive by. It was time to come out singing "I Am What I Am" in surround-sound stereo. After 22 years in a small town where *gay* meant *pervert, pedophile* and worse, I just wanted to belong—to be wanted and accepted for who I was.

I had no idea what being lonely was until those first two months at school. My best and only friends were a bottle of Jack Daniels and the video store. The gay bar on the outskirts of town was a dump, and it was not easy to waltz in and own the place, as it had been back home. It was frightening to come and go from the gay bar at school. Even so, I ended up spending every night at the bar, leaning against a wall, sucking down booze and being alone. So much for liberation.

I did not know a soul in town, and had no idea of how to meet people. After years in a small town where everyone knew everyone, here was real anonymity and it sucked.

After a couple of months, I was desperate to find a way to meet people, so I volunteered for a local nonprofit that worked with people with mental retardation. The group was organizing a big sporting event in town, and I agreed to coordinate the recruiting of volunteers from the college. After a week or two of knocking on doors, I began to work the fraternity and sorority circuit, speaking at chapter meetings and events.

At first it was not a question of joining or being asked to join the fraternities that I visited. The goal was just to be around people and, hopefully, to make friends. Party invitations soon followed, and of course I went. There was something nice about being asked to party with the campus elite. I had never been one of the in crowd, even at home. It was a rush to go from being a geek to being a Greek.

It did not take long to figure out that gay men had to be in the back of the closet with fraternity guys. Fag jokes were part of the routine, and you could practically cut the testosterone in fraternity houses with a knife. The brothers who did not have a girlfriend made sure they constantly talked about sex with women. This still beat the hell out of being alone. Besides, it was belonging to a group of men! The whole concept was fascinating and scary. Here was the high school PE locker room all over again—being petrified of an erection but craving belonging at the same time. All of those guys were part of some great, mysterious team, and I wanted in. I was 22 years old and desperate to be one of the boys for the first time in my life.

At the beginning it seemed possible to hide the gay thing. Looking back, I probably just wanted to be a straight man, accepted by other straight men. Normal. Desperate to belong. A group of 75 men decided that they wanted me to be on their team! After years in high school of being the last one picked, this was heaven. Damned if I would blow any chance to be normal!

That dusty-mouthed morning with a pledge pin gave way to a quarter of learning the ropes and trying not to be gay—trying hard not to be gay. Fortunately, I could drink like a fish and did. The booze gave dimension and identity to the new pledge in the house. Instead of being the token "gay guy," he was the "big drunk." Everyone drank in the house. The amount you drank was a point of pride. You scored a point on this team for every shot glass emptied.

As long as it did not go too far, I could get by. As an older pledge, you could buy a lot of loyalty by buying liquor for younger brothers. Drink more, fit in more—easy. The only problem was waking up, wondering if the cover had been blown in a blackout. Did somebody find out that I was gay? This constant fear of discovery prompted more drinking, and the cycle got worse.

I slept with my first brother, an alumnus, when I was drunk as a pledge. When I freaked out, he said not to worry, it was not like we had fucked or anything. He was so sure that we had not done anything "gay." I prayed no one would find out.

Occasionally, dating women as a brother was part of the big game. After I moved into the house, it became harder and harder not to go out with the girls the guys brought around. "Scoring" took on new meaning. Living in a house with straight men and drowning true sexual nature in bourbon and beer was not everything it said on the brochure. Still, it meant fitting in. So what if that meant going out every month or so and getting laid in the car? There was still the house and the identity of belonging that came with it. A few more beers, and it was not so bad. By the end of my first six months, I could not keep the front up without the booze. I had to be drunk to play.

After initiation it was easy to throw myself into the whole business. I reorganized alumni relations, headed a crew to clean up the grounds, started a volleyball team, and drank. The best little pledge in the world was determined to be the best damned straight fraternity brother there was. There was still occasional sex with men, but it had become furtive couplings in cars or in dim apartments, giving false names. What had taken me years to accept took only six months as a brother to deny completely. This denial was the price of admission to the boys' club. At the time, admission was worth the price.

I slept with my second brother shortly after moving into the house. He literally ran from the room after it was over. We never had a conversation longer than one minute for the entire next year.

Looking back now, I wonder how any of us, straight or gay, survived. A trip to Florida for spring break tested the limits. We drank hunch punch for five days and tried to pick up any woman walking. After meeting a girl on the beach who was interested, I still spent most of the time drunkenly coming on to one of my brothers. My cover could have been exposed then, but no one said a word. I told myself they did not know. Maybe they were just playing the game too.

The more I got to know my brothers, the more desperate I was to fit in and belong. Drinking became the only way to fight the urge for men, but drinking made it hard to watch the language, gestures, and any other dangerous actions. I could not be straight sober, and I could not act straight drunk.

After the second year my time as a student and fraternity brother was winding down. Drinking gallons on weekends became drinking pints every day. Men at the house were making pretty direct hints at the truth about my sexuality, and I was close to flunking out. The joy of belonging had become the fear of discovery. After I had spent two years as a brother, fraternity life ended at midnight on a Friday, with a packed car and a trip home. No goodbyes. I quit.

For many people, the Greek experience provides a sense of self and the formation of lifelong relationships built on trust and a common experience. Much of my experience was not common with my brothers, but much of it was common. Sprinkled among the drinking sprees and fear were some laughs and companionship. Mixed with the sadness and loss is a sense of bonding and brotherhood. I miss some of the guys, even now.

After a few more years of struggle in another town, I finished school and went on for a master's degree. I now have a successful career working with people with mental retardation and have made my sexuality an integral part of my life and who I am as a person. Drinking is no longer an option. Most of the wounds have healed, and I am part of a very different team, made up of family and friends. I am beginning to realize that I might have found my place in the fraternity if I had developed a sense of self before I joined. To blame them for not accepting who I was, when I could hardly accept myself, does not seem fair.

A drive to belong at all costs is not healthy. Fraternities seem to encourage homogeneity, and most college-age men do not have a sense of self strong enough to withstand the pressure to conform. A team is made up of different talents, not the same ones. It is in our differences that we find our strengths.

Holding the Closet Door Shut
by "Anderson"

I may be a coward, but I have avoided coming out to them for this long, so why bother now?

About Me

I had no exposure to gay people when I came to Washington and Lee as a freshman.

I was quite aware, however, of my own sexual nature, since I had borne quite a few crushes on other boys during my high school days. I came close to several sexual experiences with other boys, but my own shyness, or fear of betrayal, forced me to back down and reject the others' advances. My gayness was like a nightmare to me.

In 1970 the only widely known homosexuals were extreme stereotypes: lisping fairies, transvestites, and a few notorious child abusers. Homosexuality was a subject of ridicule and cause for ostracism in high school in the '60s. This attitude carried over into college in the early '70s. I hope, by now, the stigma has been mostly eradicated.

I was 18 years old, but I looked about 15 when I entered college in 1970. I was a normal, cute teenager with an athletic build (I was on my high school track team) and a warm personality. However, back then I considered myself young, awkward, and definitely not attractive. I did not exude self-confidence.

I had passed my high school days in the company of inner-city kids who scoffed at athletics and dating. Like most of the antiwar, long-haired, drug-experimenting college students of that period, my peers were antihomecoming, antiproms, and antifraternities. I did not look forward to joining a fraternity. But almost everyone at Washington and Lee was a member, so rush was an ordeal I would get through. Besides, my dad was a fraternity alumnus from Washington and Lee. He would shame me mercilessly unless I gave rush a try.

Fraternity Rush

For me and my freshmen friends, rush was mostly an excuse to quickly down lots of free beers. Afterward we would tear around the quad raising hell. We signed up to attend three rush parties each evening for a week. The parties were blocked off into 60-minute periods, with a half hour in between to get us from one party to another. Averaging about one beer every 15 minutes, we were pretty wasted by the end of each night.

I, like many freshmen, was anxious about fraternity rushing. What if no fraternity liked me? What if I did not find a fraternity that I enjoyed being with? Was it true that there would be a place for everybody in a fraternity? Would there be a gay fraternity? If so, were the brothers looked down upon by the rest of the fraternities? Would the hazing and the initiation be as brutal as I had heard?

Phi Kappa Sigma, the "Face" House

My first rush party was weird. I am still not sure what was happening at the time, but this house was giving me some strong vibes. I was picked up in my dorm room by a Phi Kappa Sigma sophomore who was very attractive, with longish blond hair and beautiful eyes.

As he walked me down to the fraternity house, he proceeded to tell me how diverse the Phi Kapps were. Out of the blue he bragged that his fraternity was a haven for people who dared to be different. He even asserted that if I joined his house, there would be no pressure one way or another to date. He said some brothers date all the time and "some don't date girls at all"! I swear, I had not said a word about my anxiety around women, and I certainly had not betrayed my secret longing to lose my virginity in the arms of a sophomore lacrosse player. The next couple of Phi Kapps that I met were even handsomer.

Later in the year I heard that Phi Kappa Sigma was the "face" fraternity. That means it had a reputation for pledging brothers who were good-looking. I only know that after an hour of listening to the Phi Kapps sell their house, I had collected in the back of my mind vague images of platonic love-orgies with these beautiful guys, and I was ready to pledge in an instant. But during the last five minutes of the party, when everyone is supposed to make a date to return for a subsequent rush party, my chaperone disappeared.

I was never invited to return. No close friends joined Phi Kappa Sigma, and I never visited again. But their chapter was well-respected, and I heard no rumors of gays being in their fraternity. I still wonder if the Phi Kapps had a sizable gay contingent and I was being recruited for it on that first rush evening. Because I never let down my guard, I will never know.

Decisions, Decisions

My next several rush parties were unremarkable. Mostly, guys were trying to impress me with something—the quality of the women who date Sigma Chis, the athletic talent of the Delta Tau Delta house, the wealth and family connections of the Sigma Alpha Epsilons. Each house invited me back for more rush parties, and I made a date with each, some of which I canceled later.

After about 12 rush parties, I narrowed my field of interest to three fraternities. Sigma Phi Epsilon was very high on my list. There were only ten members, because the house had been through some turmoil the previous year and the brotherhood had been banned from the campus owing to a drug bust. They were still allowed to recruit freshmen, but the brothers were not allowed to live in their fraternity house for one year. I liked the Sig Eps because they were all unassuming Northerners with liberal viewpoints that contrasted nicely with the Southern social-rank values that predominated among most of the fraternities.

The second possibility was Lambda Chi Alpha. I had met some nice guys at Lambda Chi, but the house had a reputation on the whole for being wimpy and nerdy. I did not see any nerds, but there were a few really insufferable, pretentious types. But the house had strong academic credentials and a strong financial base, and I knew that my father would be happy if I joined a house like that.

The third choice was PDA. They did not boast of academic strengths, nor did they have an awesome collection of athletes. What they did have was a mixture of Northern and Southern boys, one black (the only African-American who had ever pledged a fraternity at Washington and Lee), one or two really crazy seniors who liked to play rugby and drink themselves into oblivion, some guys from poor families working their way through college, and one junior who was very sweet and effeminate. I realized that the PDAs did not have a very strong financial base, but they had diversity. Maybe they would be diverse enough to fit me in.

Of the freshmen who had become my friends before and during the rush season, two ended up joining Sigma Phi Epsilon and the rest all went to PDA. So I went to PDA too.

Dating and Fraternities

Because Washington and Lee was an all-male school, there were no women around during the week. But on weekends guys would drive over the Blue Ridge Mountains to the women's colleges and bring back carloads of females to spend the weekend in Lexington. Fraternities served as a network connected to sororities at nearby schools. They could recruit a handful of female dates on a moment's notice. Usually the matches would be arranged in advance.

So even if you had never seen the woman before, she was expected to be your date for the whole weekend, and you were expected to stay with her. Obviously, nice Southern women did not sleep with their blind dates, so there were rooming houses in Lexington, run by elderly widows offering overnight accommodations for a nominal fee. Blind dating in this context is stressful, even for straight males. There was a strong chance that you would be stuck with a date for a whole weekend that you did not enjoy. Likewise, the woman might think you were a creep.

Gays at Washington and Lee tended to stay in the closet and play the straight dating game or avoid fraternities altogether and go home on weekends. I played the straight game. This came naturally to me, since I had never been out of the closet or played the gay game.

My heterosexual dating consisted of a few big weekends in the fall and spring when there were major parties on campus. Everyone had to have a date. Outside of these weekend dates, I hung out with my freshmen buddies, drank a lot of beer, and talked a lot about deep intellectual things. My buddies did not really like the dating concept either. We were from public schools where boys and girls mixed freely and naturally during class, and this separation and sex-object casting seemed unnatural and stultifying.

On the few dates that I did experience, I learned to French kiss with a woman and to feel titties—I even went to "third base" on one occasion. Never was there any passion or physical attraction driving me, only the need to do what was expected. To be sure, the women involved got no joy either. Once as a sophomore, I had a woman spend the weekend over, and she wanted to screw. I played along like I wanted to do this too, but truly, I was fishing around for an excuse to avoid it. Luckily, when she and I went up to my bedroom to do the dirty deed, my roommate had passed out in the bottom bunk and could not be awakened. Naturally, I insisted that it was out of the question to do anything with him there. The fraternity house was a place to take your date when you were bored of entertaining her by yourself. There, other guys might charm her and, if you were lucky, steal her away from you. This was called "snaking." I always felt relieved if my date was snaked. Then I had the rest of the weekend free without the burden of a female to entertain. There were always one or two guys around to hang out with, so I never felt lonely.

Gay Fraternity Brothers

The early '70s was still a time of repression at Washington and Lee. The Stonewall rebellion had occurred just recently, but the gay liberation movement had not reached Virginia. I was one of 12 new pledges at PDA. If any of us were gay, we were in the closet—except for Cutler. Cutler must have been out of the closet in high school, because he was *way* out, from his first day of college. I remember meeting him in the freshman dorm and sitting in his room with a group of guys while Cutler put on a one-man show, talking about cute boys and oral sex and things I knew nothing about. I was intimidated by Cutler because he was so extroverted, and so "out there"—I believed his whole presentation was to be taken as sarcasm and that actually he was putting down homosexuality. Also, Cutler was beautiful. If I had really believed him to be gay and if I had had enough confidence in myself, I would have confided in him in private. Maybe then

my years in college would not have been such a struggle to hold the closet door shut. Cutler was not only a doll—he was witty and charming, a
good dancer, and popular with the ladies. He had a smoothness that only
hinted at his fine Southern upbringing and lots of old family money.

Cutler had the biggest effect on our fraternity when we were sopho-
mores. That was the year we lived in the fraternity house. That was the
year Cutler and his friends wrote GAY POWER in Wisk on the wall before
one of our PDA parties. The sign was invisible during the day, but at
the party, when the black-lights were turned on, the message was as
clear as day, right next to the band. That was the year our class first got
a say in which freshmen going through rush were singled out for recruitment. I remember the heated rush meetings when we would discuss a particular candidate and Cutler would chime in that this boy had
a very "clever" posterior or that boy "exuded animal magnetism" and
must return for another rush party, at any cost. That was the year the
new pledge class was a tiny group of six pledges, but all of them were
very cute or very gay. (It was amazing how much influence Cutler exerted in these selections.) But in fact, there were severe arguments over
whether to offer bids to certain obviously gay freshmen. I am sure this
was the first year such an issue even came up. But because of Cutler's
forceful recruitment and several other brothers' compulsion for political correctness, our fraternity was actually debating whether to bridge
the sexual-orientation barrier. I was oblivious to the actual politics involved but was careful to hold my tongue during these sessions, lest my
own gayness, God forbid, should come to light.

To actually offer membership to an obviously gay freshman? This controversy almost tore the house apart. On the one hand, discrimination is bad.
But on the other hand, if PDA got a reputation as a gay fraternity, we thought
it would destroy us the following year during rush. The compromise was
reached that two out of the three openly gay guys were given bids to join
but they would be kept out of sight during rush parties the following year.

Cutler had made an impression on me that went beyond rush. His
carefree joking and flirting with other guys allowed me to be a little bit
more flirtatious myself. Although I never crossed the line, I did feel
more free to touch other guys and to be more physical. Cutler loved to
walk around the fraternity house naked after taking a shower, and I got
a good look at what I was missing.

Frat-House Gossip

Cutler was not the only gay brother in PDA when I joined. They must have had some secret society with a gay handshake and everything. Of course, I never knew who they were until years later.

I graduated and went on a canoe trip with two ex–fraternity brothers. While one of my friends went off into the woods to answer the call of nature, the other asked me if I was gay. Taken aback by his question but determined not to retreat into the closet, I replied, "Yes." My friend never offered a confession of his own, but he did inform me that a certain Pi Kappa Alpha brother who was a year older than me had a crush on me when I was in college. That revelation really floored me. First, because I had been very attracted to the Pi Kapp in question (a beautiful soccer player) and, second, because I had no idea that this seemingly straight young man even had known I existed. Oh, the lost opportunities!

I will mention two sad stories here, because I suspect that these incidents somehow resulted from the pressures felt by young men as they struggled with their sexual identities in a culture that did not allow room for diversity. First, when I was a sophomore, a student hanged himself in his room. No explanation was ever given. It was a known fact, however, that this young man had taken dinner at the home of one of his male professors the night before his body was found.

The second case involved a fraternity brother of mine who shot himself in the early morning inside his bedroom in our fraternity house. Nothing was learned that could explain this tragedy. He had a blind date scheduled for later that evening. I know from my own experience that blind dating could create great stress—but nothing that seems worth killing yourself over. Perhaps a little more acceptance of people who are not able to fit the heterosexual norm would reduce the incidence of suicide among college students.

Being Gay in a Fraternity

When I was a sophomore, I became friends with Dante, a freshman who joined our house. Dante was creative and spiritual and dramatic and very good-looking. He practiced karate and had a body like Bruce Lee, only boyish. Dante and I were the closest of friends for a while. Our friendship was based on a religious love mixed with a craziness that only two guys can share. The two of us even started on our way to divinity school to be eternal partners in our service to God. However, ten minutes outside of Lexington, the devil caught us and made us turn down to Blacksburg to spend instead a weekend of drunken debauchery in that college town.

Dante and I loved each other, in a way. We would sometimes wrestle on the couch or the floor in the fraternity house, and if we got into a position where our lips were too close, there was always a big tension, until one of us backed away. Once, Dante brought a date to the fraternity house (hoping she would get "snaked"?), and the girl sat across the room from Dante and me while we wrestled around on the couch. At some point, I was compelled to bite Dante's neck, leaving a beautiful hickey. When the date saw this, she went off on a tirade, saying that I was a "gay queer" and should leave her date alone.

Once, when Dante and I were hiking around in the mountains together, he confided in me that he had received a love letter from another guy who was a fellow student. Dante was deeply religious, in a conservative Christian vein, and the letter left him very upset. He had told his friend never to come around again, that homosexuality was a sin, and to get himself a girlfriend. I tried to argue with Dante that his friend could not help his feelings and he should try to understand, not push him away. My arguments were to no avail, but at least I was glad that I had not sent that letter myself.

Telling My Secret

Stuart was a very attractive freshman when I was a junior. I remember the first time I saw Stuart walking by himself across campus. He was angelic. When I heard that Stuart was going through rush and that he was going to visit our fraternity house, I decided I had to use all of my influence to get this boy in our chapter. Since Stuart was really adorable, several of the other brothers also saw his positive qualities, and it was not hard to get Stuart to join. As soon as Stuart pledged, I volunteered to be his big brother. I exploited this position of power until our friendship grew into a truly deep and profound affection. Stuart and I were inseparable. Eventually I realized that I was falling in love with this young man. When he announced that he was dropping out of college after his first year, I was crushed. After he left I wrote him a letter, telling him how I felt for him. He was so moved by the letter that he called me and then visited Lexington, just to discuss my letter. He wanted me to talk about my feelings, but I was embarrassed and tongue-tied.

Anyway, Stuart clearly informed me that he was straight, and that girls were his thing. Stuart and I spent the weekend together, however, and we were very close. Up until then, I had not told anyone that I was gay. Years later Stuart visited me in Washington and met my lover and went out dancing with us. Stuart is the kind of person I would want my children to be like.

What I Got Out of Fraternity Life

When I came to college, I was trying to come to grips with my sexuality in a society that was largely intolerant. I think my desperate attempt at heterosexual dating was compelled by my fraternity membership. This was more true in my first years, when I was trying to fit in and follow the crowd, than in my later years, when I had greater confidence in my own choices. But clearly, the fraternity lifestyle perpetuated a courtly way of life that emphasized dating as a means to meet an appropriate female partner. Fraternities also put pressure on young men to perform as men, meaning to have as much sex with as many girls as possible and to brag about it as if each female conquest were further proof that women were simpleminded objects to be exploited.

The benefit I got out of my fraternity resulted from its unique diversity and its unusual efforts to include students who were outcasts from the rest of the fraternity network. Although I was not ready to come out during my undergraduate years, I learned from the views expressed by other fraternity members that conformity was not a mandate. This fraternity experience, however, was the exception, not the rule. My fraternity was very marginal in the eyes of the overall student body. The dean of students had characterized us as "a very unstable group of young men." Flattered by that description, I always took it as an indication that we reflected society itself, which was at that time in deep turmoil. My fraternity chapter disbanded within a few years after my graduation. The pressure of being on the front lines of controversy took its toll.

My Coming Out

My college was small and all-male. This insular environment was not conducive to coming out. But my exposure to Cutler and my repeated involvement with guys who were unable to respond to my attraction increased my desire to have some experience on the gay side. As soon as I graduated, I returned to the big city and explored the gay discos there but had no sexual experiences. In the fall I enrolled in a large state university and found the freedom to embark on my quest for self-knowledge, which is still unfolding. I became a graduate student at a school of 20,000 and enjoyed the anonymity. By making acquaintances at the big gay dance club, I developed a close-knit group of gay friends around my age. Fraternities were a small part of the social life at this university, and I had no contact with them. My particular fraternity was not even represented.

The friendships that I made in college lasted for about six years, then our paths drifted apart. The friendships I made in graduate school, after I came out, are still alive. If my college friends had known the complete me, there might have been more reason to maintain contact. But they knew a different person, someone with a secret. To be my friends now, they would have to get to know me as a different person. From time to time I receive a call from one of my old fraternity buddies. I return the call politely, but I do not relish the opportunity to reestablish friendships, since my lifestyle has changed so markedly. These buddies were the most outspoken homophobes back then. I may be a coward, but I have avoided coming out to them for so long, so why bother now?

Pros and Cons of Fraternity Life for Gays

A fraternity is a large group of men who socialize together and support each other.

The fraternity can shelter its members from a hostile society, or it can be a tool of society to socialize its members into conformity. Washington and Lee was a hostile environment for sexual nonconformity. Traditional values and an idealized concept of the Southern gentleman imposed a harsher climate than most college students face. Most of the fraternities at Washington and Lee in 1970 did not foster a high degree of individuality. The few that I considered joining, however, had the potential to accept a broader spectrum of the student body and could have been welcoming places had there been any degree of consciousness raising or support provided within the fraternity context. If there had been more support for gay students within the fraternities, my college experience would have been more satisfying, and I would have been more loyal to my fraternity. Because of the homophobic climate, Dante was forced to cast aside his friend who loved him. If the school or the fraternity had provided more enlightenment on the subject of male relationships, he could have kept his friend. Cutler dropped out of college altogether by his junior year. He tried his best to advocate his openness among others, but he was alone. Although there were several other gays around, including myself, who could have supported Cutler when he needed it, the overall climate of shame and ridicule kept us in the closet, unaware of each other. If Cutler had found acceptance of his lifestyle within his fraternity, he could have stayed in school and graduated. As for me, if I had found acceptance in my fraternity, I could have let down my guard and let everyone know the complete person I eventually became. Then I would not feel dread upon hearing from my fraternity buddies 20 years later, because I would know they were my friends, not just the friends of the straight person I was pretending to be.

I hope the attitude on campus has changed in the last 25 years. Most colleges have gay student groups, and kids nowadays are more aware than college students in the 1970s were. Eventually, some fraternities will adopt a policy of inclusion toward gays. In the same way that certain churches have reached out to gays in the community, some fraternities will adopt gay-positive policies. Many churches that have reached out are prospering, and I predict that the fraternities that welcome us in the future will be stronger and more popular than those that choose to exclude us. We have a long way to go, but we are much closer than we have ever been.

A Question of Rejection
by Oscar R. Jones

I knew I was gay. I feared what my brothers would think of me. Staying in the closet was safer and easier. Maybe if I tried to date women, I would "learn" to be straight; then there would be no need to tell anyone that I am gay.

I was scared. *What if the brothers find out I'm gay? What if during my pledge period I gaze inappropriately at another brother? What if the brothers can read my mind and see that when I talk about women, it's just talk, because I truly feel that I was meant to have a relationship with a man?*

Ready or not, in the spring semester of my sophomore year, I decided to seek out membership in Delta Sigma Phi fraternity. After going through rush, I was given and accepted an invitation to become a pledge of Delta Sigma Phi. For approximately eight weeks, I would learn about Greek life and life as a Delta Sig. I readily took this challenge. Throughout those eight weeks, I and my 14 other pledge brothers embarked on the journey to becoming active members of Delta Sigma Phi. Those eight weeks allowed the Delta Sig pledges to become close friends. During that time, we often hung out together and learned about each other. At a brotherhood retreat, while trying to fend off the practical jokes of active brothers and plotting ways to retaliate, we were sitting in a quiet area of the campsite where our retreat was being held. After we were sure that the actives did not know where we were, we relaxed and began to share various bits of information with each other. Where is your family from? What are you planning to major in? Why did you decide to join the fraternity? What did you do before college? Are you dating anyone? What is her name? As our conversation turned toward dating and relationships, I became very quiet. At the time I was not dating anyone. However, if I were dating someone, I would rather it be a guy. This is what I wanted to say, but I said nothing. "Peter" was talking about what kind of girl he liked to date and how beautiful this one girl he went out with was. Of course, this was followed by an onslaught of witty and all-in-good-fun taunting about his lack of ability to find any woman who would even be willing to go out with him. The conversation about girlfriends continued, and eventually I was asked what I liked in a woman. Because I was in the closet and did not want them to find out, I began to make up fictional women I had dated and what type of woman I was attracted to. After making up all these lies, I felt even worse. Here I was, wanting so badly to be myself and tell my brothers that I am gay but not being able to because I feared the possible ridicule and hatred they would have for me.

As we were walking back to the cabins, I reflected on why I did not have the courage to be honest with my brothers. Why did I not just tell them who I really am? One of the reasons I wanted to become a Delta Sig was the diversity in the brotherhood and the open-mindedness of many of the brothers; would not most of the brothers have accepted me for who I am? Yes, many probably would have. But there are those who would not have done so. And what scared me even more was that the main reason I could not be honest with them was that I could not be honest with myself. I knew I was gay. I knew that I was attracted to men, but I feared what my brothers would think of me. Yes, we were a diverse brotherhood in our cultural and economic backgrounds, but the one thing we supposedly had in common was our heterosexuality. Whenever a brother "pinned" his sweetheart or became engaged to his fiancée, there was a big celebration. Heterosexuality was celebrated through various ceremonies. Homosexuality was only joked about and made fun of. I did not want to be made fun of, and there were no indications that there would be acceptance and understanding from my brothers. Maybe I was being unfair and not giving them the opportunity to prove me wrong, but staying in the closest was safer and easier. Maybe if I tried to date women, I would "learn" to be straight; then there would be no need to tell anyone that I am gay.

As the weekend came to an end, I decided that it would be best to stay in the closet. After all, I was not only a member of the best fraternity at the university, but I was also a leader on campus, and many people knew me. I could not possibly face the ridicule and dirty looks of so many people on campus. Surely no one would accept me for who I am. As the semester continued, I learned the history of the Greek system and of Delta Sigma Phi. I grew closer to my brothers and felt confident that I would successfully pass the test of knowledge and make it through initiation. Throughout the entire semester I did not think about or fear that someone might find out that I am gay, because I realized that it was easy to pretend I was straight. I participated wholeheartedly in all the pledge and brotherhood activities. The excitement built as initiation weekend quickly approached. At the end of the week, all my pledge brothers and I sat together and took our fraternity test. The following evening we were led through our initiation ceremony. After what seemed like forever, the initiation ceremony came to an end. We were given our official member pin, pin number, and a nickname.

An active brother of Delta Sigma Phi, no longer a pledge—life was good. As I had hoped, I could now wear the letters of my fraternity proudly. I could look forward to the next group of pledges and being able to teach them about the benefits of being a Delta Sig. I no longer had to worry about any of the brothers finding out that I am gay. It was so easy to hide it so far, there would be no reason I could not continue concealing it. The remainder of the semester was exciting. At brotherhood activities and anywhere on campus I could give the secret handshake to a brother. If I met a man, anywhere in the world, I could tell if he was a brother by an exchange of a few simple yet meaningful words. The semester quickly came to an end, and I decided to live in the house for the summer. This, I thought, was a fabulous idea; but I began to have doubts. Now that I would be living in the house, it would be easier for someone to find out that I am gay. Suppose I inadvertently started coming on to a brother, or suppose I began talking in my sleep and said something about being interested in men. Suppose I could not continue pretending that I was interested in women. It was happening all over again. Something so exciting, with the potential to be one of the best experiences of my life, tainted by worrying whether my brothers would find out that I am gay. I knew that I was gay. I knew my brothers would not hate me for who I am. (or would they?) Again I was in turmoil— knowing that I wanted to be honest with myself and open about who I am while being afraid of the reactions of my brothers. I resolved my dilemma as I had before, by continuing to pretend that I was straight. I could hide it just as I had before. I had been able to "act" straight for 20 years of my life; so what were another few years?

I thought living at the house was going to be great. We had a volleyball net set up in the backyard so we could play whenever we wanted. I had my own room, and all the brothers who were not living in the house would come over to hang out. That summer I had a full-time job in the office of admissions. It did not seem like work because it was so exciting. Almost every weekend, if not every day, we would barbecue and celebrate the beautiful summer days of Michigan. One of our favorite activities was to pile a bunch of brothers into as many cars as we could find and head to the drive-in movie theater. Almost every Tuesday night we would forget about work and classes and go to the drive-in. Summer memories were made at the drive-in. Ten to 12 brothers and the same number of sisters from our sister sorority would hang out and "sorta" watch the movies. Since the voices on the speakers never were quite in sync with the movie, we spent most of our time talking about the characters in the movie or anything and everything else. After the movie was over, we would head back to the house. Most often, several of us would hang out and play cards.

One evening everyone decided to head home or to bed. Only another brother and I stayed up and hung out. After watching TV, we decided to hang out in my room and listen to some music. As we sat on my bed listening to the Doors, a silence fell between us. As I looked at Ralph, I began to remember thinking that he too might be gay. Actually, I had hoped that he was, because we were great friends and I found him attractive. We continued to listen to the music, and several times we would individually adjust our position on the bed, saying that we were just getting comfortable and relaxing. We ended up lying close to each other, and as one thing led to another, we became intimate.

I had finally found someone who shared my feelings! We shared that moment together. Afterward, there was an immediate and unbearable awkwardness between us. As Ralph was leaving, we agreed to keep this to ourselves, and Ralph suggested that it would be wise to never let it happen again or to tell anyone. As he left I felt an overwhelming sense of isolation and sadness. For a brief moment I thought I had found someone with whom I honestly could share my feelings. Instead I found myself fearing that I would be outed. Instead of having someone to talk to and share my feelings, I sat in my room, fearful of what might happen. How would I be able to talk to Ralph? A brother knows that I am gay. He can prove that I prefer men. That had to have been the most stupid thing I had ever done. Even though it seemed like a stupid thing to do, it felt so right. I shared an intimate moment with a man. I thought he would understand me and that I would have someone to relate to. It seemed right, finally connecting with another man. How could it feel so right even though it seemed so wrong? When I became a brother, I vowed to myself that I would never do anything with another brother. This was one way to make sure no one would know that I am gay. But I did, and I could not change that. What could I do now? There was nothing I could do. I was helpless. I felt like bolting my door and never coming out again.

For that entire night, I stayed awake. I cried to myself because I was so overwhelmed with the feeling of being alone. I was fearful that Ralph would never talk to me again. And what if Ralph told all the brothers that I was a "fag"? He might even go to the other brothers and tell them that I came on to him and deny the fact that he was just as much a participant in that evening's events. For the following weeks, I made it a point not to go to the drive-in movies. I made sure I was asleep before any of the brothers got back home from the movies. Ralph and I no longer hung out with each other. The only time we did hang out was when there were other brothers with us. It was painful to have lost communication with such a good friend and brother. It hurt not knowing if he felt the same way I did. Did he fear the possibility of other brothers and friends finding out that we were gay? Was he gay? How did he deal with it?

As the fall semester began, I made a conscious effort to put Ralph and that evening out of my mind. It was the last year of my undergraduate career, and I was determined to make it the best. As home-coming approached, my brothers nominated me for homecoming king. Campus was alive with excitement. Homecoming Saturday was also my 21st birthday. Needless to say, this promised to be a festive time. Wednesday night I was crowned homecoming king. That night we celebrated the victory. Saturday began with a parade of floats during which the homecoming queen and I led the parade in a horse-drawn carriage. Throughout the football game the Delta Sigs cele-brated. And that evening, after winning awards for our float and other homecoming activities, we celebrated by having a social. I had plenty to be happy about. I had just turned 21 and was crowned homecoming king. Wearing my crown proudly, I partied with my brothers. Events such as homecoming, completing my coursework, and planning for the future occupied my time and took my mind off what had happened between Ralph and me. That was in the past, and I could now look forward to my final semester of college.

As spring semester began I found myself engulfed in what would promise to be my most difficult semester. What I thought would be a semester full of parties and socializing became a semester of studying and preparing for my future. Even though I did not socialize as much, I found time to hang out with some of the brothers who became some of my closest friends. Earl was my best friend in the fraternity. We were both minorities on campus and in the fraternity. I am Latino, and Earl was a nontraditional student who, at the age of 35, decided to start col-lege and shortly after decided to join Delta Sigma Phi. Earl was not the kind of nontraditional student who goes to classes, messes up the grade curve, and goes home. He participated in college activities and became a leader on campus. He was also not a stereotypical brother. Many peo-ple who did not know him as well as I did wondered why he would want to join a fraternity at the age of 35. He joined because he knew he could do it and because, somehow, he knew that he would be an asset to the brotherhood.

On many occasions Earl would call me up and say, "Hey, let's go grab some coffee." There were several times I said I could not because I always had so many things to do and so little time to do them. But he was persistent, and I would often find myself sitting in his old con-vertible or in his big green van heading to the local greasy spoon for a cup of strong-enough-to-grow-hair-on-your-tongue coffee. During these times we would talk about almost anything. We would find ourselves talking about the brotherhood and the positive and negative qualities some of our brothers had. There were times he or I would have a problem and we would help each other by talking it through. There were many times Earl would persuade me into getting more involved with some of the brotherhood activities. Often we would talk about the difficulties we each faced as minorities. I would talk about some of the stuff that had happened to me in the past because of my skin color, or I would tell him about some of the more subtle forms of racism that really angered me. He would talk about the difficulties of raising a family and being a nontraditional student. We always promised one another that we would keep something confidential if the other did not want others to know.

As we continued to go out for coffee and discuss the issues of the world, I began to feel that if I was going to come out to anyone, Earl would be the one whom I could tell without reaching the gossip lines by evening. On many occasions I had planned to confide in Earl that I am gay, but I always chickened out. Even though I considered Earl my best friend, I realized that I still was not ready to come out. I promised myself that if I was ever at a point where I felt that I was ready, Earl would be one of the first people I would tell, because I knew that he would not judge me.

The months rolled by quickly, and I found out that on the last Saturday in April there would be a ceremony at the house to honor the graduating brothers. I realized that this would be my last official fraternity ritual as an active brother.

As our chapter president completed the last sentence of the ceremony, I came back to the present, realizing that my fraternity experience had been a successful one and that I would soon join the ranks of the alumni members of Delta Sigma Phi. I made it through the pledge process and became an active brother of Delta Sigma Phi. Just like many before me, I was a successful leader on campus. I was able to hide the fact that I am gay from all my brothers except one, and now I would soon graduate. At the end of the ceremony, each graduating brother received a money clip with ΔΣΦ inscribed on it. As I looked at this, I thought to myself, *This was one of the best decisions I have ever made. Even if I had no money to fill the money clip, it would always remind me of Delta Sigma Phi and all the memories I cherish about my brotherhood.*

After graduation I moved to Nebraska to become a hall director and to pursue my master's degree. At that point I decided that I had lived my life in the closet long enough. It was time for me to admit to myself and to those who knew me that I am gay and that I was ready to acknowledge that part of me. I began coming out to friends in Nebraska. I decided that I would no longer lie to myself or anyone else. I am who I am, and I have accepted myself. One by one, when talking to college friends or new friends, I would come out to them. For the most part, no one rejected me; many were surprised, but they were able to accept me for who I am. Then the day came when I would come out to Earl. We were talking on the phone and catching up on the latest gossip and catching up with each other. I looked over on my coffee table and saw my empty money clip. I began remembering all the fun times. I also remembered saying to myself that if I was going to come out, I would want Earl to be the first brother to know. I knew that he would not judge me. Halfway through our conversation I said, "Earl, I have something to tell you, and this might come as a shock to you."

"What?"

"This is difficult for me to say."

"What? Just tell me."

"It's about my personal life."

"What about it?"

"Well, Earl, I'm gay. And I hope you don't hate me because of it, but I wanted to tell you because you've always been a good friend, and I hoped you wouldn't judge me because of who I am." With that off my chest, I took a deep breath and waited for his response.

After a moment of silence and a little laughter, Earl said, "Well, I thought you might be. Bill [an openly gay alumnus brother] and I were talking about you, and he said he thought you were but just weren't ready to come out. Hey, but that's not a problem; you're still my brother."

I could not have been any happier. I was finally out of the closet, and one of my best friends accepted me for who I am. I was stunned that he had already guessed, but I was happy that he was so accepting. Earl knew, and we were still friends. As time went by, with my permission, Earl told several of the brothers that I am gay. For the most part, my brothers were accepting of me and said that my being gay did not change the fact that I am a brother. There were some who did not comprehend right away, bringing up the fact that I had dated women, so I could not be gay. Some said they were disgusted at the fact, but they were a small minority.

As I look back on my entire coming-out process, I consider myself very fortunate to have had such good friends and positive experiences when coming out to them. I often find myself thinking about what it would have been like if I had come out during my college years. Even though it has been only three years since I graduated, I definitely think it would have been a very different experience. I waited until June of 1994 to begin my coming out process. Prior to that I was not emotionally ready to face the world as an openly gay male. After much soul searching I realized that I had made the best choice. During my fraternity and college experience, I was fearful of what everyone else would think of me. Simply put, I was not ready. And as I have told friends when discussing the coming-out experience, I will always stand by my belief that no one should come out until he is emotionally ready.

My Fraternity Closet
by Robert L. York Jr.

Sean's story made the front page of the newspaper. The headline read COL-
*LEGE STUDENT COMMITS SUICIDE ON PLAYGROUND. Sean knew he had lost
everything. Sean did not want the fraternity to be plagued with the reputation of allowing homosexuals into the brotherhood of the chapter. Like so
many young gay people, Sean became another number and statistic. Why did
he have to die?*

By the time I graduated from high school, I knew I was gay. I was
terrified! How could a God-fearing, Assembly of God church boy from
Oklahoma possibly fall into the devil's hands? The homosexual lifestyle
was against the Bible's teachings. As Pentecostal holy rollers, we were
taught that this lifestyle was not to be accepted. How could a man possibly love another man? I was always taught as a kid that I would spend
eternity in hell for living and accepting the homosexual lifestyle. "Homosexuals choose to live this way. They are living a lie, and they will
perish in the fires of hell with all the other Sodoms and Gomorrahs,"
said the local pastor. As I struggled for acceptance of who I was, it was
an excerpt from his preaching that forever would be ingrained into my
memory.

High school was over! I walked across the stage and received my
piece of paper that said I could become an adult and a part of society.
I had been offered several scholarships to an in-state college. I had decided to get away from home, my family, and the church. I needed space
to find out who I was and what I would become without the influences
of the church and my family. I knew that I needed to get out and away

from the Bible Belt and learn who I was and what I was feeling inside, emotionally and physically. I went to the in-state college, two hours away from home. The distance was far enough to feel as if I were starting a new life. I continued to hide in the closet about my true sexual identity, however. I knew a few students on campus who were from my hometown, and I was terrified to think that they might out me back home if they knew I was gay.

I moved into the dorms, like all freshmen must do, and found out that a friend of mine from high school was living down the hall. David was a year ahead of me and had already completed his first year of college. I knew David through other friends in high school and had heard several rumors that he was gay. David became a very good friend that first month in college. He told me that he was gay and was involved in a relationship with someone in the local town where we were attending college. I was stunned and shocked at his honesty. He said that it was a very hard decision to make when he came out to his family and friends. David was the all-American athlete and star pupil of his class. I had heard the rumors in high school and told him about what I had heard. David knew that people were talking about him, and he also knew that his religious background would not make coming out an easy process.

Since high school I had been interested in being a fraternity man. Girls loved the thought of dating a fraternity man. My thought was that it would be cool. I would be able to belong to a group of men that people would envy. I had come from a broken home since I was one year old. Belonging to a fraternity would give me a chance to belong to a family that shared the same ideals, goals, and common bond. I would be able to party, meet new people, and meet women. Since early on, I had dreams of being a Greek man. Looking forward to rush week, I hoped I would be given a bid from a fraternity house. I would just have to wait and see.

The fall semester of my freshman year was a great one. David and I were contacted by the Office of Student Services and Activities about reactivating a chapter of a national fraternity. David and I were both on leadership scholarships, and the administration was looking for young men who could breathe new life into the fraternity. We had a pledge class of 12 young men who were all on leadership scholarships. After four months of pledgeship, David became president and I became vice president of the fraternity. David was very honest with me one day. He said that if anyone were to find out that he was gay, he would have to go public but that he would not step down from the presidency. Our national fraternity did not look kindly upon gay people being involved with the fraternity. It was considered to be an embarrassment to the chapter as well as a public image problem. It was the kiss of death. It was after being initiated, and also because of David's honesty, that I finally told him about who I was and the emotional struggle that I was going through. I was so terrified about being a gay man. I had so many questions about everything. The struggle that was taking place in my head and my heart was starting to tear me apart. David understood exactly what I was facing emotionally and listened to me with great compassion. His guidance, support, and care helped me to understand more about being gay. None of the other brothers knew that the two leaders of the fraternity were gay. If our national fraternity knew, we would have been barred for life. David and I never talked about things in the dorm or even on campus. It was not safe to talk, because we never knew who might be listening.

Shortly thereafter I decided to move back to Oklahoma City and continue my education closer to home. A university there was offering more scholarship money, and my fraternity was one of the largest on campus. Also, David had accepted a scholarship to another university in New York to focus more on his degree. A new door had opened as the other one had closed. I transferred all of my college hours and credits and petitioned to become affiliated with the fraternity chapter on campus. I was vice president at my home chapter before moving. It was rare to hold that office as a sophomore. It was also rare for houses to allow a brother to affiliate. My conversation with the chapter adviser was a long one. He said that the chapter did not often allow brothers from other universities to affiliate but that I was welcome to stop by and see if the chapter liked me. I met the president of the fraternity and most of the other officers on that day. Of course, I was asked all of the routine questions and basically rushed all over again. I told them I was really interested in affiliating with the chapter and asked if they would please consider me for membership in their chapter at the next business meeting. They held their first business meeting the following week, and not only was I accepted into the chapter, but I also was elected as vice president. The chapter had elected a vice president in the spring, and he had decided not to return to school. Another door had been opened, and it was also the beginning of the nightmare.

I began the fall semester of 1988 as the new vice president of the fraternity, and I made the varsity cheerleading team; I had also won three scholarships to help pay for tuition. By the end of the first month of school, I had become involved with a host of activities, one of which was the Interfraternity Council. This council was the governing body of the fraternities in the Greek system. The fall elections were to be held the second month after school started. My fraternity slated my name for nomination as Greek week chairman and as secretary-treasurer of the IFC. I won. My social life now was committed totally to the Greek system. I had no choice; I now had no personal or social life outside the fraternity system. My private life would become totally nonexistent. In just two months I had gone from just a face in the crowd as a new sophomore to big-man-on-campus-in-training. I certainly would not be able to tell anyone how I really felt inside and that I was gay. I perceived and feared that if I did, I would be barred from my fraternity, kicked out of office, and chastised by my peers in the Greek system.

There were several fraternities and sororities on campus. Everyone involved in the Greek system was very active in their houses, and we all got along really well together. The year before I arrived on campus had not been a good one for the Greek system; there had been some unfortunate circumstances. A member of a sorority house was killed in a car accident in the summer, and a fraternity house had lost its past president (who was also past IFC president) as a result of suicide in the previous spring. The Greek community was still dealing with the grief and loss. The fall I arrived became a time of healing and outreach for everyone. I think that is why we were so respectful of each other and got along so well together. The Greek community was afraid of losing more sisters and brothers and was working hard to strengthen the community. Although the bond was strong in the Greek community, I knew that if my homosexuality were made public, I would be banished. I was living in the buckle of the Bible Belt. I needed to be conservative, reserved, and play everything straight in order to survive as a big man on campus.

The fall semester was busy, with a host of activities and fall rush. Our fraternity was busy trying to build our membership. We had 20 men pledge our house for the fall, which was a high number, considering that the average pledge class was only about 13 or 14. Not only was the pledge class large in number, but it also included a lot of quality men. Ten were from the leadership council, and the rest were athletes from various sports on campus.

There was one guy named Jon who signed with us and who always made me feel uneasy. He was a freshman just starting college, and he was attractive; he was a magnet for all of the sorority women. He attended all of the rush parties and meetings and was very persistent about wanting to be a part of our fraternity. The chapter extended a bid to Jon, and he became a pledge. The time came for the pledges to choose a big brother, someone with whom they felt comfortable and to whom they could look as a role model. Seven guys picked me as their big brother, including Jon. I was very honored to know that so many of the new guys felt comfortable with me, but I could not possibly have taken them all as little brothers. I narrowed it down to four and took them under my wing. I decided not to choose Jon, since I just did not feel comfortable around him. Jon was pretty upset that I had not chosen him as a little brother. He had a very fragile ego. Jon started calling me and whining that I did not want to spend time with him and that I did not really want him to be in the fraternity. I soon realized that Jon was like me; he was gay, and he was needing to confide in someone.

This was a nightmare that I wanted no part of. I knew that if I reacted to his cry for help, we would be barred from the fraternity. I became very frightened. I had worked so hard to accomplish my goals. I felt as though my world would crumble if my peers found out that I was gay. I was living in fear. Why couldn't Jon quit our fraternity, disappear, and leave me alone? I became very agitated with the entire situation. My fear was blocking a friendship Jon desperately needed in his life, but I chose to hide from reality.

My facade worked just fine. Jon and I became distant, and he looked elsewhere for friendship. Jon became really close with one of our little sisters, Susan. He confided in Susan and told her about his true feelings and identity. Jon became extremely jealous of his roommate and the friendship we were developing. The pledge class was moving along really well until the last two months of pledgeship. Jon and Susan had decided they were going to break up the pledge class and try to ruin the reputation of some of the members of my fraternity. My name was first on the list. Jon made up this wild story that another member and I had accosted him on campus over by the student activities building while he was out jogging one night. He said that we had made sexual advances toward him. He notified all the pledges and told them the outrageous story, and they believed him. It was a story he and Susan had fabricated in hopes of outing me. The only thing I could think of was, *Why? Why me?* Susan and Jon wanted to see if I would run away scared or confess that I was gay.

The brothers of my chapter immediately called an emergency meeting. The other fraternity brother who was named in the accusation and I explained that the story was a fabrication created by Jon and Susan. We could not possibly have been where he said we were on the night when it supposedly happened. We were both in a president's club meeting with 50 other people that lasted three hours. The chapter voted, and many of the members knew that the story was a lie. A lot of the brothers had started to notice that Jon was different and thought that he might be gay. I was terrified that they would find out about me.

In the end, Jon was released as a pledge from our fraternity. I realized, as my brothers did, that Jon was looking for sympathy and also looking for a way to get back at me for rejecting him as a little brother. He had written a suicide letter because he did not like being rejected and was starving for attention. His roommate, my little brother, turned the suicide letter over to the sheriff's department, and Jon was taken into the custody of county officials for psychiatric care. We thought that the nightmare had ended until we found out that Jon and Susan tried to contact the school newspaper about the alleged story. The newspaper had no interest. The editor contacted our fraternity and found the story to be nothing but gossip. Jon and Susan had failed. Everyone knew it was a lie. I felt a complete sadness about the whole incident. I knew Jon was searching for acceptance, companionship, and friendship in other men and trying to deal with his sexuality. My perception still had not changed. There was no way I could be brought into the situation, since I knew I would be destroyed and cast out by my peers.

We survived that fall semester and initiated the entire pledge class, except Jon. The spring semester was pretty quiet, and I was moving on with my life by staying very busy with activities on campus. The spring semester is also a time of elections for the fall semester for the next year.

I was nominated for president of my fraternity and for president of the IFC. I won both elections. I was still hiding my gay identity. I felt I had to hide and that there was no other choice! I was concealing my identity so well that I even had a girlfriend in one of the sororities.

The entire spring semester was one I will never forget. That was only a start of what was to come for me in my college career. I knew in my heart that nothing would ever come of my relationship with my girlfriend. She was a good friend, and we enjoyed spending time together. We were engaged for a year and a half. I knew it was a stupid thing to do, but I had to hide my identity. She never questioned anything. She was a very religious girl and, therefore, not having sex was never a problem. Her family had raised her to save herself until marriage. I was very much relieved by all of this. I knew that I would never be able to do anything sexually with her. I didn't even really like to kiss her. My facade of our relationship was working. I knew I needed to have a cover to keep any minds from wondering if I might be gay. Michele was the perfect Christian girlfriend. We were the all-American collegiate Christian couple. Winning both elections forced me further into the closet and forced me to be more public with Michele right by my side. Why couldn't I just be me and live my life like everyone else? We ended the spring semester and prepared for the fall of 1989.

During the summer break I was struggling with my emotions. I had one gay friend (Russell) whom I could occasionally call, but even then I was fearful that someone would be listening in on the conversation. I was always watching my back, looking around the corner and being careful about every move that I made. Russell was very supportive and was never quick to judge me. He knew as well as I did that I was not ready to deal with my homosexuality. Once again, my perceptions were trapping me more and more each day. Russell had invited me to a couple of gay parties. I declined the invitations because I was afraid I would run into someone from college. Living in fear was starting to destroy me inside and out.

The 1989 fall semester began with a bang. Everyone had returned to school, and the Greek system was growing rapidly, which meant a busy schedule for me. I not only had to fulfill the duties of my fraternity, but I also had to look after the other fraternities and make sure they were meeting guidelines and regulations. I managed both duties quite well.

The other fraternities liked the fact that I did not play favorites and that everyone was treated fairly and with respect.

Each year the fraternities and sororities nominate one person from each of their houses to represent them for the Outstanding Greek Man and Woman of the Year competition. I was fortunate enough to win the nomination and the title for the fall of 1989. It was the highest honor a Greek man or woman could win in college. It meant a lot because you were picked by your peers for your commitment and service to the Greek community. My identity was still a safe secret. No one had any idea that I was gay. Michele and I were the happy couple, and many of our friends said we would be married someday.

The 1990 fall semester was finally here, and I was finally a senior! I was still president of my house and president of the Interfraternity Council. The 1990–1991 academic year was by far the best year of my college career. I was well-respected by my peers and by the faculty of the college. I was elected as homecoming king, received numerous campus and national awards, and was picked by the faculty and students as an Outstanding Campus Leader for 1990–1991. It was an awesome experience. I had truly become the classic overachiever of my fraternity and campus. I was very grateful to everyone for thinking so highly of me and of the hard work that I had contributed to the campus. However, I was still hiding. Hiding from my peers and from myself. I had a lot to be proud of, but deep inside my heart and soul, I was miserable. I knew that I was living a lie and being dishonest about who I really was. I wanted so much to let people know that I found men attractive and that I would one day find a man that I would love and care for as my partner or spouse. I continued to struggle with who I was, where I was going, and exactly what life was all about. Was I ready to face myself and accept being gay? It was becoming more of a possibility as I approached graduation, which would open doors that had been locked for such a long time.

Earlier I mentioned that a young man had committed suicide the year before I arrived on campus. His suicide was why I chose to hide within my fraternity closet. I will refer to him as Sean. Sean was an all-American kid. He was president of his fraternity and president of the IFC. He was a member of one of the largest fraternities on campus. He was also an Outstanding Greek Man his senior year and received a lot of the same honors I had received. Like me, he also dated a girl from a sorority on campus. He was idolized and well-respected by the Greek community, students, and the faculty. He had even been offered a position with the university after graduation.

As you've probably guessed, Sean was gay. At the time he was dating a sorority girl, he was also dating "Matt," one of his fraternity brothers. They had decided that Sean needed to date a woman as a cover so that they could continue their gay relationship. Sean and his lover thought they had planned everything perfectly. They were able to fool a lot of people, until one day when everything was turned upside down for Sean.

Sean and Matt had skipped class to be together. They had, however, forgotten to lock the door behind them at the fraternity house. One of the other fraternity brothers had stopped by the chapter house to see if Sean was there, and when he opened the door to Matt's room, he discovered them in bed together. He immediately became enraged, and within hours he had notified the entire fraternity chapter about what he had witnessed at the house. Sean and Matt escaped from their fraternity house and were nowhere to be found. Sean's fraternity called an emergency meeting, and his brothers met to decide his fate as a member. As the story has been told, they had decided to expel Sean from the fraternity and strip him of all honors. They did not want anything to do with a gay man being in their brotherhood. They did not even try to reach Sean for his side of the story. I tried several times to get the details of how things happened that day with Sean. Many of the people who were there that semester refused to talk about the incident. I believe many felt remorse and were saddened that they were not able to be more open and accepting of who Sean really was. It did not really matter what Sean's brothers had said or voted on that day at the fraternity house, because the state newspaper would tell Sean's story in the next day's headline.

Sean's story made the front page of the newspaper with the headline COLLEGE STUDENT COMMITS SUICIDE ON PLAYGROUND. Sean knew he had lost everything he had worked so hard to obtain. He could not bear to think about what his fraternity brothers would do to him. Sean took his life into his own hands and decided to spare his brothers and his house the embarrassment. Sean did not want them to be plagued with the reputation of allowing homosexuals into the brotherhood of their chapter. Like so many young gay people, Sean became another number and statistic, with hundreds of others who have committed suicide—because no one would listen, understand, or accept them when they needed it the most.

Sean had been living at home his senior year with his parents, trying to save money. His parents lived near an elementary school. That is where they found Sean that morning after the revelation. Sean had committed suicide by hanging himself from the monkey bars. Why did he have to die? Why could he not be the same person people admired and respected before the "horrible secret" came out? Why could they not have accepted the fact that Sean was in love with a man? Nothing had changed about who he was and what he was able to contribute to the Greek community.

I heard Sean's tragic story about a month after arriving at college during that fall semester of 1988. The story was very frightening and very real. It was also a story that a lot of people tried to avoid talking about. His brothers and other students were guilt ridden because they felt responsible for Sean's suicide. I was terrified after hearing that story. I was envious of Sean and Matt's relationship, and at the same time Sean's suicide scared me to death. I felt I had to stay hidden and not reveal that I too was gay.

Sean and I had so much in common. We had the same background as student leaders and had accomplished a lot of the same things as students at the university. I was scared to death that if someone found out that I too was gay, I would be another headline. *I* would be the one with the noose around my neck or the razor cuts across my wrists. I would be chastised, humiliated, and persecuted, just because of who I was. It would not matter what I had done for the Greek system, my peers, or the university. I would be labeled gay, a leper in the community. It was after hearing the tragic story of Sean that I chose to conceal my identity and to live in fear. I would hide my secret and carry it with me until after graduating from college.

I now look back and think about all the gay and lesbian students out there on college campuses. They need leaders, role models that they can look to for advice and courage. I wish I had been able to tell people that I was gay while attending college. At that time I simply was not ready to accept myself as a gay man. If I had been ready, I could have been a leader for the student gay community. But I chose to hide in my closet.

I chose to live by society's rules and the laws of the church. It is amazing how peer pressure affects all of us. I was very disappointed with my actions and my stand on gay rights while I was in college. I chose to go with the crowd and make ugly jokes. I conformed to their thoughts and their ideas about the gay community. I chose to accept them instead of accepting myself. I was living a lie and living in denial.

After graduation I came to accept myself. I started to experience a whole new world and the gay lifestyle. I could no longer hide, and I felt safety in numbers. I had joined the fraternity because I was looking to belong, and now I was a part of my real family, the gay community. My new gay friends and family were willing to accept me for who I was and not who I could pretend to be. I was in search of the fellowship and brotherhood of gay men and women. My fraternity experience had given me a brotherhood of men who were interested in the same ideals and goals but were prejudiced against certain aspects of society. I had been going through the motions to please everyone else. Now I could live openly as a gay man.

Searching for Brotherhood
by Brian Hawker

Delta Lambda Phi was created as a fraternity for gay, bisexual, and progressive men as an alternative to the standard Greek fraternities. The fraternity brought the bonds of brotherhood to a segment of the population that is often forgotten or rejected in Greek life.

Michael came to formal rush in the fall of 1993. He was what you might consider fresh off the farm. He had the stereotypical honest, natural approach to life. He was also rather ignorant about the way things were. It was his first year at Texas Tech after going to Abilene Christian University for the first two years of college life. That morning he had seen in the school paper that Delta Lambda Phi, the gay fraternity, was having their last rush event that evening. He went out to the mall that afternoon after his classes and bought a suit, shoes, and accessories. He came to the University Center in his gym clothes, the suit folded neatly in his bag. He slipped into the back bathroom and put on the clothes he had bought just for that event. Michael then quietly walked to the room and then slowly came in. What happened in that room would change his life forever. It was the first time Michael had ever let anyone else know that he was gay.

On July 20, 1995, it all came together for me: Everything I had given myself to for the past two years finally made sense. I laughed to myself; it was so simple, but yet it could not be expressed in words. I looked across the room as our national executive director told Michael's story to my fellow brothers. It showed that I had made a difference, that I had made an impact, and that the fraternity's ideals and purpose were alive and well back home. And now my brothers knew it as well. It was then that I finally discovered what brotherhood really was.

I came to Texas Tech in August 1992, full of hopes and dreams; to be honest, I also had my fears. I knew what I wanted to do, but I also knew that there would be constraints placed on what I would actually be able to do in college. I knew almost no one, and I also knew that this was my opportunity to break away, be myself, and do what I needed to do to be happy.

One thing I really did want to do was to go through Greek rush, but I was apprehensive. My older sister is a Tri-Delt, and through her I heard what happened to faggots in fraternities. I desperately wanted the brotherhood that a fraternity would bring, but at the same time I knew I could not subject myself to the real possibilities that came with it. The thought of my brothers turning their backs on me, hating me for who I was, was unbearable. I had already been through that.

In high school I knew I was gay, but because of my family, my church, and my school, I could not even think about talking to anyone about it. This left me feeling alone and isolated. As a result, I did not feel as if I could be myself or allow any new people in my life. A lot of people saw the distance that I created and gave it to me. I built this wall around me to protect myself so I could not be hurt or judged. I got that wall and that space, but I also got more hurt than anyone should have to go through.

I wanted to go to college someplace where I knew no one and no one knew me—a place where I could finally accept myself for who I was, where I could do what I wanted and not have it questioned. Funny as it is, I decided to go to Texas Tech located in Lubbock—Bible Belt, USA. Looking back, I guess I just liked the challenge of it. What can I say? I have always loved a good challenge.

I was jealous of all the guys on my floor who had gone through rush and were pledging fraternities. I thought about going through spring rush, but my first semester was very hard on me. I quickly found that people were not as accepting as I hoped they would be, and I had to learn to accept that. I also found out that most of my sister's stories about fags in fraternities were true. I was heartbroken; it would be something else that would be denied to me.

Toward the end of that first semester, someone told me about Alpha Phi Omega, the coed service fraternity that is based on the principles of the Boy Scouts. I thought a fraternity like that would have to be rather progressive, and so that spring I rushed. I soon found out that even there I would not be accepted, and I fell further into the closet. The ideals of brotherhood were there, and I experienced some of them, but I mostly had to sit back and watch the brotherhood happen with my other pledge brothers. The next two years crawled by, and I stayed in the same position that I had been in when I came to Tech.

By the last half of 1994, I was finally ready to make a difference. That summer I decided not to go back to my parents' house; it was finally time for me to break the mold and to publicly come out and be gay. That fall I joined the gay organization on campus. It opened more doors than I could have hoped. At the first meeting I was elected vice president and soon had several letters to the editor in the school paper published. My coming out publicly affected a lot of people. But it proved to be too much for many of my brothers in Alpha Phi Omega. While I did have a tremendous amount of support from some of my friends and a few of the brothers, most of my friends and "brothers" turned their backs on me. They felt the "lifestyle" was wrong or that it was sinful. Sadly, this also had a negative effect on my roommate and best friend. Most of the fraternity and the friends we shared assumed that since he lived with a gay man, he must be gay as well. Their reaction was to treat him as they treated me. While I do not have any regrets about coming out, I do feel bad about the effects it had on my friend.

The one thing that kept me in Alpha Phi Omega was my commitment to serve as sectional service chair. When I first came out, I was able to complete the duties of my office with cooperation from the chapters. However, as the sectional conference got closer and closer, more of the chapters in the section found out about me. The cooperation that was so vital began to slowly vanish. Regardless, by the time the conference came, I decided to run for sectional president. I thought my background and other leadership experience would outweigh the close-minded perceptions many of the individual chapters had toward me. I was wrong. After the meeting ended I offered my help to the new president; she politely told me that she would be in contact with me. I knew better and soon dropped my active status in the fraternity.

Since I was vice president of the student gay organization, I became familiar with what the group had tried to do in previous years. One thing was to start a fraternity chapter of Delta Lambda Phi at Tech, but little had been done to achieve that. Delta Lambda Phi was created as a fraternity for gay, bisexual, and progressive men as an alternative to the standard Greek fraternities. In February 1995 I was surprised to find a letter of goodwill from the Eta chapter of Delta Lambda Phi in our mailbox. At first glance it looked interesting. After I found out more about the fraternity's program and purpose, I knew I had found the organization for me. The fraternity brought the bonds of brotherhood to a segment of the population that is often forgotten or rejected in Greek life. The ideals Delta Lambda Phi promoted impressed me greatly, and I knew then that Texas Tech needed a chapter on campus. I quickly began to find out what I needed to do to bring Delta Lambda Phi to Tech. I researched how well the fraternity would be received on campus and what the attitude of the community likely would be toward the chapter.

While I was working on that tremendous undertaking, I was approached by another student who had already made initial contact with the national fraternity. The nationals wanted someone who could make it happen and make it a reality. And that is where the story of my real fraternity life begins.

We soon decided that Delta Lambda Phi had to come to Texas Tech differently than the other chapters in the fraternity because of the generally negative attitude toward gays on the campus. We decided we had to get all the paperwork out of the way before we could induct our first pledge class. We spent that first summer planning, dealing with administrators at Tech, building our program, and learning.

We soon filled the major positions in the executive committee, and we invited four advisers to join us. Something we soon discovered was that only I and one of our advisers had ever been in a fraternity. Instead of letting it be an obstacle, we used it to our advantage and made it a growing experience for everyone.

By August we felt we were ready for our first pledge class. We started advertising in the community and on campus. We saw only a few people at our first events, but as rush went on, more people began to hear about the fraternity and showed up. The day of formal rush the school paper ran a story about the "gay fraternity" on campus and our last event. Thanks to the story, we saw several new faces that night, including Michael's.

All of the officers were excited about our new brothers. We soon inducted the Alpha pledge class of the Texas Tech colony. I wish I could
say it was a moving ceremony for us, but it really was not. We were neither prepared nor ready, but there was nothing we could do. The feelings of brotherhood still eluded me.

The next week we held our first meeting and carried out all the for-
malities. One thing that was left unresolved was what to do with the officers; should we keep the ones we had, or should we elect new ones?
That was soon decided when two weeks later there was a motion to officially elect the officers. It passed, and nominations were opened for
elections to come the following week. I realized my position was in
jeopardy when the vice president was nominated to be the new president before I received a nomination.

I found out later that the secretary had been trashing my reputation
with the brothers. He had decided that I was not the person he wanted to look up to as president and that he had to rid the colony of my
leadership. At the time of the elections, I was not aware of that. I went
home confused, hurt, betrayed, and humiliated. Any feelings of brotherhood were virtually gone.

I pulled myself together by the next week and gave one of the best per-
formances of my life. My speech was great, but it helped nothing. I lost
the election and had to quickly readjust myself to being a regular member in the colony. My saving grace was one of the brothers of the Eta
chapter. He stuck with me and helped me deal with most of my hurt and
humiliation. He kept that spark of brotherhood burning within me. As the
semester drew to a close, I was asked to write the colony's petition to become a chapter. Seeing this as a source of redemption, I jumped at the
chance. While I worked on the petition, I was informed that the success—
or failure—of the chapter petition rested completely on my shoulders. If
the colony did not gain chapter status, it would be because I failed to do
my best. This stayed in my mind while I worked on it.

I looked at the colony and saw elements of true brotherhood among
my pledge brothers but also the lack of it. To cover that, I spun a great
tale of the brotherhood at Texas Tech, although I did not believe it. It
was an inspiring tale, built out of some truth but interlaced with what I
wanted the colony to be and what I knew existed in other fraternities.

The colony's executive committee approved the petition, and it was sent off to the national board of directors. We all waited in anticipation for the decision. On December 3, 1995, the board officially recognized the Texas Tech colony as the Alpha Lambda chapter. When I got the call, I had a bittersweet reaction.

The spring semester began, and we rushed our Beta class. Only two people pledged, of which one had been a member of the interest group who could not rush in the fall. Still, it was a new beginning for our chapter. The semester proved to be lacking because, since there was no real active program for the most part, the pledge program and the chapter program were one and the same. The lack of a pledge really pissed me off. The actives should have been there for the pledges, not the other way around. This was the cause for one of the pledges to drop out. The one remaining pledge did his best to make up for this loss and did end up doing a great job.

The first weekend in February was one I thought I would remember forever, but with time it has begun to fade. That was the weekend that the Alpha pledge class was initiated into the brotherhood. Our national executive director and national trustee came to represent the national fraternity and present us with the charter. Brothers from the Eta chapter came to perform the initiation ceremony. One thing that did make that weekend more memorable was that it happened to be the "Great Freeze of '96." Luckily, our trustee did make it to Lubbock for our initiation. It turned out to be a great weekend despite being cold as hell and there actually being snow on the ground in Lubbock. When I took my oath of brotherhood on Saturday, I thought I had finally reached my goal and discovered my path to brotherhood.

I found out later that night that I was only fooling myself. When the chapter was presented with its charter that evening, the officers of the chapter stood by themselves, none of them acknowledging a thing I had done. That was the biggest blow I had received yet. It seemed that now not only was brotherhood denied to me but also any credit due to me for the work I did founding our chapter.

These thoughts grew throughout the rest of the semester. I felt the chapter was failing and I was failing. There was no brotherhood in Lubbock where Delta Lambda Phi was concerned. Maybe as founder of our chapter, I had too-high expectations, maybe I was overly critical, or maybe it was because we had people who did not believe in the program or in the brotherhood. I do not know.

Our chapter is currently in the process of building a stronger brotherhood and rebuilding our membership after losing most of the Alpha class. It is long and hard work, but it is something the brothers in the chapter feel they must do. The brothers who have remained are incredibly dedicated to the program, to the fraternity, and to the brotherhood. They continually impress me with their individual devotion and work for the fraternity. It is their work and their devotion that reminds me daily that the brotherhood is here. We all guide our actions by one thought: We are Lambda men, and we must make our presence known.

When I think back on my experience, a smile comes to my face. It has not been an easy experience or even a great one, but it has been the most fulfilling of my life. We have started our newest pledge class. I can see that the flame of brotherhood that I sought so hard to find and keep so dear in my heart kindles brightly in our new brothers. I am certain that the Alpha Lambda chapter will continue to be, to grow, and to make their presence known. Fraternity life has been more than I could have ever hoped for, especially as a gay man.

Every time I hear the story of Michael, the young man from Abilene who felt he had to keep his sexuality hidden yet took the chance on coming out to our formal rush, I get teary-eyed. This is not because I am sad. Rather, it is because I know how badly Delta Lambda Phi has been needed at Texas Tech, because of the pride I feel in the Alpha Lambda chapter and in my fraternity, and because I have found home. I also finally understand what it means to have true brotherhood.

Pretending to Be

by Steve Wisener

I learned that sex was one of the things you had to do to be a man. So I had sex with a woman for the first time that summer. Once school started up again in the fall, I spent most of my time at the house, usually trying to get laid. I started to drink a lot because it made having sex easier, and I became one of the house clowns who made everyone laugh at our parties. I was having such a great time, in fact, that I did not have much time left to think about being gay.

I entered Eastern Washington University in the fall of 1988 after growing up in a small town in Montana. I chose to attend EWU for a number of reasons. It allowed me to leave Montana; I wanted to go to a different school from everyone else in my high school; and I saw that a gay student group was listed in the college catalog. Since I did a lot of reading, I knew what it meant by definition to be homosexual, so I had pretty much thought that I was gay early on in high school. I figured going to a new place where I could try things without the scrutiny of everyone I had grown up with would be a good plan. So I packed up my things and moved away from home the morning after graduating from high school.

I was so busy adjusting to my new life and freedom my first quarter at EWU that I did not even know there were fraternities or sororities on campus. I was involved in my residence hall and with my new friends. I was also busy trying to find proof that I was indeed gay. It took me a few weeks and a few hang-up phone calls before I finally talked to someone from the school's gay and lesbian alliance. The person on the other end of the phone told me where the office was and suggested I stop in. I found the office (which was no small task) and went in. Wow!

I thought I had walked into the wrong office at first because the man who greeted me definitely did not look like any queer I had ever seen on TV or heard talked about while growing up in rural Montana. Everyone else in the room looked "normal" too. I decided, once I caught my breath, that I had made a good decision.

I quickly made friends in the group and started learning what it meant to be gay. I was having a lot of fun. The first quarter of school went by quickly. I met a guy in the group who lived upstairs from me, and we became great friends. My roommate was leaving at the end of the quarter, and my new friend agreed to move in with me. It looked like the rest of the year was going to be great.

I came back from that winter break excited about the new friends I'd made and the experiences I'd had. I was really looking forward to the rest of my freshman year. One day during my first week back, I walked by a table of guys from the Delta Chi fraternity in the student union building. I had some spare time and was looking for a group to join. The guys at the table seemed friendly enough, so I gave them my name and room number and went on my way. I had almost forgotten about them by the end of the day when they came and knocked on my door.

I invited them in and introduced them to my roommate. They spent some time with us and invited us down to the house for some events. We went, and by the end of the week, my roommate and I were offered bids. My roommate decided this was not something he wanted to do and turned his bid down. I was not having that easy a time making up my mind.

This was the first time any guys I considered pretty cool and popular had paid any attention to me other than to pick on me. I really liked these guys, and I liked spending time with them. Because of a poor relationship with my father, for the first time in my life, I had an opportunity to learn what it meant to be a male in society. While I was doing all this thinking, I also was replaying all the things I had learned about being gay while growing up. I was having a major identity crisis. The conclusion of my thinking for a few days was that it would be better to be straight, and if I spent more time with guys, especially this group of guys, I could learn not to be gay. I thought that all I had been missing before this time was the right teachers, so I joined the house.

I became an associate member (pledge) of the Delta Chi fraternity at EWU in January of 1989. I was an officer in my pledge class and enjoyed spending time at the house. The more time I spent with the guys, the less time I spent with my roommate. I also stopped going to gay alliance meetings. The great relationship I had with my roommate began to deteriorate. It ended when I outed him to some people on campus in an attempt to distance myself from the gay students at the university. I was initiated in the spring and moved into the house for the summer.

It was a busy summer for me. I learned that sex was one of the things you had to do to be a "man." So I had sex with a woman for the first time that summer. Once school started up again in the fall, I spent most of my time at the house, usually trying to get laid. I started to drink a lot because it made having sex easier, and I became one of the house clowns who made everyone laugh at our parties. I moved off-campus into an apartment with a couple of guys from the house. I became a cheerleader and was starting to become a popular guy on campus. I liked the person I was becoming. I was having such a great time, in fact, that I did not have much time left to think about being gay.

My junior year I moved into the house, was elected vice president of the chapter, and served on the executive board of the Interfraternity Council. I loved being Greek! I also was dating the same woman for the second year. I had learned so much about being a straight man and was now passing these lessons on to all of the new pledges who joined the house. My life seemed to be perfect. Perfect, that is, except for this nagging idea in the back of my mind that kept surfacing about my being attracted to men. It had been so long since I had really thought about it for any length of time that it almost startled me. I was starting to get really confused. Things were working out as I had planned. Joining the house really had helped me learn how to live as a straight man. That was until the winter of 1991.

The house was getting ready to initiate a new class of pledges, so we had some local alumni staying with us to help out. One of the guys who was staying at the house had been in the house when I first joined but had since graduated. We really did not know each other very well. One night, after the pledges had gone to bed, I was studying, and he stopped by my room to talk. We talked for hours, and he eventually told me he was gay. I then admitted that I might be too, but I did not know for sure. I was very cautious because I had spent the past few years heavily investing my life in the fraternity and did not want to upset this. I had learned, over the past three years, that being gay meant being bad.

As the brother and I talked about being gay, I started to experience a high level of dissonance in my head. I was struggling with conflicting sets of facts and feelings and was desperately trying to find a "right answer." Since we were both over 21, he offered to take me to one of the gay bars in a neighboring city the following weekend. I could barely concentrate for the rest of the week. We went to the bar on a Saturday night. When I walked in and looked around, it was like walking into the gay alliance office three years earlier, only ten times more overwhelming. I liked what I saw in a big way, but it also scared the hell out of me. The brother asked me if I wanted to dance and I said "No way!" I was experiencing so much sensory overload that I asked to leave within a half hour. The sights and sounds of that night stuck with me, however. I now had a new set of data that I needed to sort through and process.

After initiation the brother left, and I went into a phase where I deeply examined my life. Over the years, I had been asked by a few fraternity brothers if I was gay, and I had always denied it. One guy told me how relieved he was when I said no. He said he would not have known what to do if I had said yes because he would not have been able to stay my friend. These kinds of experiences and the knowledge of how most of my brothers felt about queers made the rest of the year a difficult one for me personally.

I stayed in the house over the summer, since I was working on campus. I took the time when the town and campus were pretty empty to do some research. Since I am the bookish type, I brought a lot of reading material home to see what I could figure out. By the middle of the summer, I was again pretty sure that I was gay. But I had no idea how I was going to tell my house or my girlfriend. My entire life at that time revolved around my identity as a fraternity member. I did not know what I would do if things changed. And then they did.

At some point during the summer, while I was not home, one of the brothers went through my room and found some of the gay literature and magazines I had. He got drunk one night and pounded on my door around 1 o'clock in the morning. He accused me of being a faggot and of trying to destroy the house and told me I should leave for the good of the house. I was in shock. I could not sleep and sneaked out in the middle of the night to throw all of the books away in case anyone came the next day to gather evidence. I was so scared.

Things were pretty uneventful for a couple of days. I avoided the brother who had confronted me and hoped everything was just going to blow over and be forgotten. I invited my cousin over for a party one Friday night. One of the rooms in the house had a wall you could write on with dry erasable markers for announcements and phone messages. My cousin and I walked downstairs and into the room. I did not notice at first, but someone had written STEVE SUCKS COCK! on the wall and had drawn some derogatory illustrations to accompany the statement. I left the house and spent the evening under a tree on campus crying and trying to figure out what I was going to do. My life, as I knew it, was starting to fall apart.

The next week was very tense in the house. I knew I was the topic of conversation, since everyone stopped talking whenever I walked in a room. No one would talk to me, and I did not know what to say to them anyway. I was so uncomfortable and unhappy that I moved out of the house and moved home for the rest of the summer. It was nice to have some privacy and time to sort things out. While I was home, I got called for jury duty and met a guy working at the courthouse. We started dating. This was the last bit of proof that I needed to determine that I was indeed gay. Now the only thing I had to figure out was what to do when I went back to school.

One decision I made was to move out of the house. I did not have other friends who were not Greek, so I moved back into the residence halls. It was a tough beginning of the quarter, since I was a rush counselor for our house during formal rush. I did my duties but had very little contact with my house. Then classes started up. I thought getting back to the books would be a good distraction. Unfortunately, most of the guys in our house were business majors, and we took a lot of classes together. We also always sat together. I went to class on the first day and did not think I was going to be able to go in. I did not know if everyone knew about me or if it was only the few guys who were around during the summer. It did not take long to figure out.

When I walked into the classroom, I saw the group of my fraternity brothers in our usual place. I also noticed there was not a seat for me, and they did not even look at me or acknowledge my presence in the class. The guys I had spent the majority of my time with for the past three years and whom I considered my best friends pretended I did not even exist. One part of me was relieved to not have to answer any questions, but another, larger part felt hurt and alone. It was every bit as devastating as I thought it was going to be. I do not know how I made it through that first day. It did not get any easier either. I skipped that class so much that quarter that I flunked it.

So here I was, a senior in college living back in the residence halls and abandoned by all my friends. I also had to break the news to my girlfriend that I was dating someone else and it was a man. To this date, this is still the most difficult conversation I have ever had to have. She was surprised and speechless. She did not scream or cry or throw things at me. I think if she would have done any of these things, it would have been a little easier. She just took the information in and went home to think about it all. She stopped speaking to me a couple of weeks later and has never spoken to me since. Whenever she would see me on campus or in a store in town, she would turn a different direction or pretend not to see me. All I wanted to do was say hello and ask her how she was doing, but I never got the opportunity to do this.

Fortunately, since I was living in the residence halls, I was able to use the leadership skills I learned from the house to get involved. I became an RA and reconnected with the gay alliance at EWU. It took me another six months to fully come out to the entire campus. I soon became known as the queer fraternity guy on campus, even though I was inactive from my house and there was no communication between us. I heard from friends that the house did not like my being connected with them, but I was in a bitter stage and really did not give a damn. I loved being out and decided I would never again go back in the closet.

I finished my college career at EWU as an out gay male and learned that I had more negative experiences when people *thought* I was gay than I did when people *knew* I was gay. I again became an active leader on campus and filled the void left by my brothers with friends that I still keep in contact with to this day. After coming out, I learned that once I was able to accept who I was, others were more apt to do so as well.

I joined a fraternity to learn how not to be gay, but it turned out to be one of the brothers who helped me see how great it is to be gay. He helped me learn that being a man has nothing to do with who you sleep with.

Now I work on a college campus and have opportunities every year to help students learn some of these difficult lessons. One of the lessons that I try to impart to every student I work with is the one that I learned the hard way: If you pretend to be someone you really are not, you will only end up with pretend friends.

TRUTH AND HONESTY

What is essential is invisible to the eye.

James Dean, Sigma Nu

Tattooed
by Mike Pecen

At Blue House, a fraternity man hanged in effigy from the eaves. A banner pointed at the hanged man, reading FAGGOT. Some of the men at Orange House hung a banner from their balcony that read, NO FAGS IN OUR HOUSE. The truth? There were homosexuals in both of those chapters.

Max and I got tattooed by a couple of bikers in 1993. It was an idea we formulated while swilling Miller Genuine Draft on a country road back home. We watched the stars, gulped the brew, and talked about what we wanted to accomplish in rush two weeks later. The heat of the August night wrapped around us like a prickly blanket, mosquitoes in its folds. Genuinely excited about what the coming year would bring for our fraternity, we decided to get the Purple House crest blazoned on our left shoulders.

I had never considered getting a tattoo before Max suggested it. But since he suggested the crest, I was all for it. A rich visual representation of the moral heights to which Purple men aspire, it was the perfect image to slap on our shoulders. Too bad we sometimes failed to follow its principles.

In the summer of 1991, the century-old fraternity house creaked and groaned in the humid Indiana heat, struggling to get comfortable. Every window was wide open, screenless. The few men living there could always be found half-reclined where they could catch a breeze to cool down. And without the relentless schedule of the school year to isolate them, they got to know each other better. Being rush chairman, though,

I could not get too comfortable. Crisis was always ready to pounce upon me. That year it was particularly poised because many members talked of a rift in the house.

Lying in the sun one day, I understood what they meant. Several brothers were talking with me there on the deck. I had gotten to know them well that summer and suspected these men were homosexuals. I lay there with sweat rolling off me, shirtless, suntanned, and they sat in the shade the house wall offered. They were all the kind of young men who hate to perspire. As an hour grew into two, the shade grew less, and all five guys were eventually backed against the wall. With its shadow, the roofline of the house cast an artificial boundary on the deck, on either side of which sat men of outwardly different habits and likes.

Until that moment, every brother saw the division in the chapter except me—and it took me years to learn what took me so long. I saw that these men were a little different from the rest, on a superficial level. Many others saw these men as the "faggots" who would bring our chapter down. They would drive away members because no one wanted to be associated with homosexuals. We were becoming known as Queer House, the guys said.

Rush 1991 was less than brotherly at Purple House. It was more of a witch-hunt than a recruitment drive. Brothers had plenty of commentary, such as:

"Don't let Ryan and Bryan talk to prospectives—they're queer."

"I move we drop Meyers from the prospective list; he's a little faggot, and it'll make us look that much worse."

"Blue House rushed 20 football players this year. We don't even have one. We rushed a bunch of theater faggots. Man, do we look queer."

Brother after brother tried to persuade me not to allow the gay officers to address the large groups of prospectives at Round Robin, the initial college rush event. "They'll think we're a bunch of fags. Remember last year? No athletes rushed us. We've got to compete with the Blues and the Oranges on their own ground."

Numbers were the goal that year. The college was small enough, with barely 900 students, and we were the smallest fraternity. If we were not popular, we would suffer.

So I set out to please the masses. It was a tough feat, since the most prominent officers were homosexuals, but I assigned speakers careful-

ly. Our president, Merrill, was missing from the program. He was a homosexual, and my excluding him stung him to the core. One of my closest friends, he did not talk to me or make eye contact with me for days,
and he avoided pre-rush preparations altogether.

"How could you do that to me?" he demanded when I pleaded for
some sign of life. "As your brother, am I not fit to represent our chapter? Do I have to suffer all the stress of leadership *and* be someone I'm
not? To know that you're ashamed of me, that you can't publicly accept
me as your brother—that's the worst feeling, especially at the hand of a
friend." He wept. I wept. And I rewrote the program.

"I was wrong to leave Merrill out," I told the members. "If you don't
like it, then find another president to stand up there."

Later that year they almost did, but there were insufficient grounds
for impeachment. That is how virulently homophobic my chapter was.
We had a meager rush. A little paint cannot hide a big crack in a house's
foundation—but, man, did we love to paint.

Naturally, I lived in denial of my homosexuality, especially to myself.
I did not want to suffer like Merrill, Ryan, Bryan, and the others. After
longing for years to build strong bonds with other men—and having
forged those bonds with my brothers—I could not conceive of warping
them. I had rushed in order to enjoy the close fellowship with other
men that brotherhood offered. Having found that, I stuck with it for my
five college years and enjoyed what was, for the most part, a positive
growth experience.

I did not voice my feelings. Instead I joined the other guys in making fag
jokes sometimes. Drawing a good laugh from my brothers made me feel included and appreciated. In my naïveté, I saw common targets as common
bonds. At many times during my college days, I felt my sexuality clawing to
emerge from me, but I kept it at bay with a big straight act and a lot of hoping. I hoped I was wrong about my feelings. I hoped a great woman would
come around and change me. And I hoped none of the men on campus
would notice I was drooling over them in the meantime.

When my roommate came out of the closet, I learned that the Purple
men were more accepting than many of the others on campus. As man-
aging editor of the *College Crier*, Brad had written a column to educate
readers on homosexuality and the needless derision homosexuals suffered at the college. He used his own experiences as support for his dis-

cussion. He had let the chapter know ahead of time that the column would be published. Some members had even supported him.

The morning the article appeared was chilly—and not because winter was coming. At Blue House a fraternity man hanged in effigy from the eaves. A banner pointed at the hanged man, reading FAGGOT. Some of the men at Orange House hung a banner from their balcony that read, NO FAGS IN *OUR* HOUSE.

The truth? There were homosexuals in both of those chapters. Some of their homosexual alumni wrote letters to the editor of the *Crier* to voice their disgust. I did too. I did not do it to defend my brother alone. I defended the God-given right to be proud of who you are without enduring the base attacks of bigots. "It took a lot of guts for Brad to come out of the closet in a world that doesn't accept men like him," I wrote. "Don't slam the door on a brave man's toes."

I, however, kept my door firmly locked. I had had years of practice convincing myself I was not homosexual. Bryan, Brad, and Mark were often effeminate and gossipy; I was not and did not want to identify myself with people who were. Back in high school, the boys who were out were misfits—not their choice entirely but still not appealing to consider as peers. When I was a young boy, being intelligent and unathletic was fatal enough in my small Hoosier town, with all the taunting I endured from other kids. I did not even know what a faggot was, but they were calling me one because I was not like them in many cultural ways; they were just trying to get to me, and they chose name-calling as an easy way to cut me down. So I decided early on that I was *not* a faggot. As a teenager, I aspired to acceptance, popularity, and healthy social functioning—and, to some extent, I attained them. Aligning myself with homosexuals would not make that dream come true, I believed.

I lived with that myth until my 25th birthday. I was not a homosexual, even though I paid attention to nothing in ninth-grade health except my brawny teacher's body. I was not a homosexual, even though my "romances" with girls were fleeting and insubstantial. I was not a homosexual, even though some of my fraternity brothers stirred depths of feeling in me that went far beyond friendship. That made it difficult for me to ignore my sexuality, but I was sure it would be rejected by the people I valued. I was chicken. Had I been tarred and feathered for my homosexuality, the image would have been sadly perfect.

Brad did not figure his coming-out column would become a statewide news story. After fury erupted over the faggot-hanging and banner-waving bashing of homosexuals, an *Indianapolis Star* reporter called Purple House, asking to speak with Brad's brothers about the issue. I answered the phone and, being a journalist myself, was happy to answer a few questions and hook her up with our vice president, Max. "It's too bad that some of the men from other houses are acting so disrespectfully," he said. "Fraternity is about sticking with your brothers, no matter what other people may think of you for doing that."

Later the *Star* carried the story on the front page of the feature section, titling it, "Gay Man on Campus." It ran a six-inch-tall picture of Brad and discussed his association with the college and Purple House in depth. While the article spoke well of the chapter's acceptance of Brad, some members grew concerned when they read it. Max regretted that he had talked with the reporter. That newspaper goes all over the state. Prospective members are going to read it. Their parents are going to read it. They're going to say, "Purple House is awfully friendly to gays. Do I want to be associated with a fraternity like that?" "This could really hurt us in rush," Max said.

Our fraternity was always trying to please a public we did not even know. What were we doing for the ideals of Purple House? I was responsible for upholding the values tattooed on my shoulder that involved serving purity, growth and justice—and enduring sacrifice, suffering, or humiliation, if necessary, in the pursuit of those ideals.

"You're making too big a deal out of this," I told Max. "If anything, readers will be impressed by our humanity for not running homosexuals out of the house."

Randy, on the other hand, was almost run out when he came out. Tempers flared as brothers began to notice that he had a frequent overnight guest in his single room. A guy. Many brothers were concerned about the chapter's image. What would the Greeks on campus—both male and female—think of it? Gossip about sleeping arrangements traveled quickly among the 900 students. "I'm just doing what all the other guys are doing," Randy said. "I'm keeping my significant other overnight, rent-free." He was a senior and was as annoyed bumping into Suzie or Angie in the bathroom as we were running into Rick.

Most of the brothers were outraged. It was hard enough for a house full of homophobes to accept a gay brother, much less his boyfriend.

Can we blame them? The concept was alien to them. Most had never been exposed to homosexuals until college. And the exposure they did get was strange to them. How many heterosexuals cross-dress in parades and end up on national television? How many straight men dance down Fifth Avenue in leather codpieces? That is all television cameras often pick up for 30-second news stories about gay pride events. If this is what teenagers learn about homosexuality from the news, how will they react when their gay fraternity brother's boyfriend is showering inches away from them? I learned a great deal about the roots of homophobia by listening to my brothers.

From my brothers, I also learned a great deal about sports. Five crisp autumns I practiced football with them and became a regular player at "A-league" intramural flag football games. The sport was a hearty challenge, since I had to build my strength and overcome fears of being flattened. Tackling, on the other hand, was a fantasy fulfilled—running for another man's belt, clawing at it, and being praised for taking part of it away from him. I loved the game and still do.

Softball was another matter. In my childhood the ball would come straight at me and hit me in the head. I did not understand the sport, since I found it too dull to watch, and I lacked the coordination it takes to hit a ball with a bat. But in college I was expected to play intramurals for the chapter. The chapter's best players were on the college team, and Purple House needed bodies on the field. It was an embarrassing, frustrating experience for me. I struck out over and over.

But one day in my final year, I smacked the ball straight on and made it to first base. My brothers met me there, cheering like World Series champs, lifting me up on their shoulders. The umpire went red in the face trying to get our attention.

Most of what I know about sports was gained by sweating it out with my brothers. The brotherhood I shared with them grew stronger through regular workouts. The fraternity made more patient teachers of the jocks, and I learned all I could, just to feel the strength of the male bonding I had rarely felt before. And the skills I gained in the process made me a much more athletic man than I would have been otherwise.

It also made me a frustrated man. I was surrounded by images of strong, sweaty, manly flesh, barely clothed, in an atmosphere steeped in the robust camaraderie I was so thirsty for. I could not get enough. I developed crushes on brothers I worked out with and partied with: My little brother, John, a giant, a state champion nose guard back in high school; Kirk, a strong-legged metalhead; Troll, a barrel-chested mountain man.

Max, though, was the one I fell in love with. We were the closest of friends and spent much of our time together—in the gym, on the field, on the court, at the house. The black-haired, stocky, Irish-blooded jock grew up less than ten miles from me, so we saw a lot of each other on breaks too. Being close, we developed a routine of rowdy horseplay. The wrestling, the butt patting, the scrotal grab-for-shock-value—these acts were nothing more than friendship for Max. But they were a lot more for me.

Had it not been for Purple House, I think it would have taken many more years for me to realize my homosexuality. The warmth of the brotherhood—made stronger by sports—did much to make me aware of what was inside my heart and soul. It did much to make me the man I am today.

But the pervasive intolerance of homosexuals kept me from becoming *all* I could be. We homophobes alienated our brothers. And I alienated myself. I did not know who I was in my résumé-building college days. Interfraternity Council officer, newspaper editor, Greek Week chairman, award-winning reporter and poet, winner of the Big Man on Campus pageant. I was also depressed as hell.

The night I was crowned BMOC, the liquor flowed, stereos pounded, and I was happy. We had a candle pass scheduled for later that night. At candle passes we would turn out the lights, gather the brothers, and pass the candle, one to the other, to share thoughts and feelings we needed to get out. Whoever held the candle had the floor and gave it up only when he passed the flame on, ensuring that no viewpoint went unheard by all present. There was an outpouring of praise, support, and pride among the brothers that night. But then the candle came to me. Suddenly sober, I discussed the black cloud hanging over my head. "No honor's sunny enough to chase it away," I said. "So I'm going in for therapy tomorrow."

Finally, I had publicly admitted something big was wrong with my emotions. And it just got more wrong as I recognized its presence. I was depressed, suicidal. I punched walls and people. For months, hardly a day went by when I did not cry at some point. I spent the next three years in and out of psychotherapy. Doctors even put me on Prozac for a while. Some of my brothers feared me. Others grew weary of my polar moods and rash reactions.

I found myself turning to Max for help, and, being a true brother and friend, he offered open arms. Confused and depressed, I would take advantage of his friendship in little ways—stealing hugs whenever possible, planting a little kiss on his neck when embracing him, trying to monopolize his time, getting jealous when he enjoyed someone else's company too much. I did not know I was developing a homosexual love until it was obvious; anyone who knew us could tell I was infatuated, and I have heard recently that his girlfriend had sensed I was trying to compete with her.

But I never told Max how I felt. Why would I? He often spoke derisively of gays, just as most of the brothers did. Still, he queried me once, during one of my depressive fits of jealous anger. "Mike, I'm not asking you this to judge you, and I'm not going to be upset with you. I just want to know—do you have feelings for me, other than—as a friend?" I looked straight at him and lied. "No. Not at all."

It was the first time it occurred to me that my repressed homosexuality might be responsible for my emotional problems. No therapist had ever suggested it, but I guess therapists could tell that I was unprepared for that revelation. But one of my brothers knew what was going on from the start. I came out to him years later in a letter.

Jay wrote back from overseas, where he was teaching, telling me that he had recalled a candle pass in which I described the way *he* had felt when coming to grips with his sexuality. "I couldn't discuss it with you then," he wrote. "You weren't ready to accept it." I was not prepared to accept *myself.* Leaving the shackles of the fraternity behind gave me the distance to become secure with who I am. I had never been happier than after I accepted my own sexuality.

But asking heterosexuals to accept a man's homosexuality is even more complicated. As much as we want to lead brothers by example, we cannot expect that example to change everything those men believe. A wide range of influences, from religion and family to childhood peers and entertainment media, creates homophobia in a man. How can we expect him to ignore the teaching of 18 years or more just because his new fraternity brother demands it?

Rusty was a prime example of the issue. One of my roommates, he was a strong man—fisherman and hunter. He wore camouflage underwear and dog tags. The son of a Baptist minister in small-town Indiana, he grew up surrounded by people who rejected homosexuality. So did he. Sometimes it was an innocuous rejection, the kind many men make without a second thought. "Aw, Brown, you're not going to the titty bar with us? Well, we always knew you were some kind of homo." Other times it was malicious. "Fuckin' queers need to get the fuck outta my house," he was known to grumble over a beer. And Rusty was not the only one who would.

He was not comfortable with a brother's homosexuality. I can understand how he could not help that. But my empathy ends there. His unwillingness to try to be comfortable with his gay brothers was the problem. Rusty's remarks were vulgar and offensive on so many levels— to homosexuals, blacks, women and others—that the chapter's leadership eventually reprimanded him formally, asking that he reflect the virtues of Purple House, not its faults.

He ignored their request. "They're not down Anderson's throat, and *he* says things like that. And who thinks he can tell me what the fuck I can say?" Rusty had a valid point. Many others of us behaved in the same way. It was a travesty of brotherhood. In our rituals and our official programming, we paid fervent lip service to perfect brotherly love. And members who mocked others—for their face, their sexuality, their ideas about fraternity—were never held accountable for their lack of devotion. While Rusty was an extreme example, he was one of many.

Rusty's attitudes flourished because Purple House, like many other chapters, had become image-based instead of content-based. We worked for years to bring chapter programming and members' experiences to a level of quality—only to blow it all by concentrating on "image." I have never met a gay unaffiliated man who did not believe fraternities were little image factories. Whether we Greeks like it or not, they think that way for a reason.

There were unwritten codes for behavior among the men of Purple House. Many were positive—such as making certain all party guests had a way to get home safely. But others were malicious, and I saw them echoed at other houses:

Love your brother. But if he is queer, make fun of him behind his back anyway.

Respect your brother. But if he is not acting "macho," write him off as a faggot.

Make fun of your queer brothers—and later, when you cannot summon the skills to coordinate a fraternity event or get a job done, dump the work on *them*.

Rely on your hardworking brothers to do what it takes to keep this tiny chapter from closing down—even as you seek to shut the gay ones out.

The homosexuals who did not "act right" suffered under those codes. Because I "acted right," I did not suffer, even though I am as homosexual as the others. These codes were just cheap tools for controlling the chapter image. Many men quit Purple House while I was there. They all gave common reasons—finances, transfers, priorities. But it is no coincidence, I believe, that about a third of those men were homosexuals or bisexuals.

I would like to believe there is a strong position for homosexuals in Greek life—a stronger role than being workhorses. Interfraternity Council at the college was up to one-fourth gay. Of the Purple brothers who were most involved in the chapter and on campus, half were homosexuals or bisexuals. All of us were run ragged with the responsibilities we undertook, while many of the straight men took it easy. Were we trying to make up for a gap in our own self-esteem? Were we fighting for the approval of our straight brothers? I am certain of it.

I met a gay Purple House brother from a rival college who was out to his brothers. He told me about all the acceptance he and his lover had received from alumni and undergraduates alike. He may have told me the truth; his chapter may have been more harmonious. But I think he was leaving details out—or not noticing homophobia, unconsciously, because he didn't want to let it ruin his view of brotherhood. He also may be accepted because he does not fit gay stereotypes—his familiarity and commonality with straight brothers overcomes whatever derisions they would commit otherwise. Now he is a poster child for the out effort, always speaking somewhere about its importance and rewards.

His cause disturbs me. While I understand some aspects of homophobia, it bothers me that we even have to remind anyone that it is OK

to be comfortable with himself. It disgusts me that homosexual fraternity men must beg for understanding from their life-pledged brothers.
The insult is perpetual, pricking homosexual brothers time and again
while the others cannot feel it. I was supposed to be enthusiastic about
dances and date parties. I was supposed to sleep while my roommate
Greg's girlfriend moaned at his touch across the room at night. I cannot count the number of times I sat with a roomful of Greek men
watching television, listening to their crass comments about the sexual
attributes of the women on-screen, while I could not even quietly compliment the beauties of the bench during a football broadcast.

I look back on the moment when I first saw the divide in the chapter—the time I lay in the sun and the eaves cast a shadow upon my homosexual brothers. But it was superficial—a mere illusion that created
an image of division. The boundary was a trick of sight. Now that I realize my own homosexuality, I am convinced that we can choose to see
the truth, even though it may be obscured by superficial means.

So I choose to reject fraternal homophobia as it stood at Purple
House. We Greeks need to let go of our obsession with image if we are
ever going to make inroads to diversity. We give diversity a lot of room
in officer manuals but not enough practice in the chapter house. We are
the ones who can drive for that change. Few others will.

We need to change more than chapter behavior; we need to sharpen
the very focus of fraternity. To become inclusive fraternities, we need to
transform from *image*-focused organizations into *content*-focused organizations. In short, we need to hone in on the stuff that makes great men—
not the stuff that makes great men crazy. We can do that by making the
fraternal experience a comprehensive program of character development
and exploration. In the context of such a community, dedicated to growth,
true bigots will find no home. They will find themselves socially evicted
by their unwillingness to try to live alongside those who are different.

We homosexual Greeks can assume strong roles in an inclusive fraternal model, without hiding in the hall closet. I know those roles are
difficult to realize and may never get easier. But if we *act* our way
through the play, instead of living it, the show can be self-destructive. I
learned how to act so that I could stay alive and grow happy with the
world around me. Now I face a critical decision, whether to share my
true identity with my straight brothers.

I live in San Antonio now. Last Saturday I got a call on my home voice mail from A.J., one of my fraternity brothers. He was in Dallas on business and wanted to meet me in Austin to catch up. A.J. was an important part of my introduction to Greek life, and having survived a year together sharing a room with Rusty and Pat, we have a pretty strong bond between us.

I did not retrieve the message until Monday, and two days later I still have not called back. Despite the brotherly love that grew between us over the years, I do not know if I can communicate with him about my life anymore. How do I tell him I went to Corpus Christi for the weekend with my boyfriend? When I tell A.J. I am happier now than ever before, what do I say when he asks why? Do I tell him that I know I am a homosexual and that the satisfaction of just knowing who I am is enough to make me happy?

I would not expect him to be accepting. A.J. made fun of "faggots" all the time in college. And even though he has matured somewhat since, he may not be ready to know that he spent his senior year sleeping naked less than three feet away from a gay man.

My reluctance to share my orientation with other brothers is probably an instinct. I want to avoid pain, even though I am learning that hiding my sexuality from my friends and family can hurt much more. When another alumnus came out of the closet, A.J. said, "You know, you always wondered about Drew. He didn't have dates for parties, and he always was a big pussy." It is painful for me to just imagine A.J., one of my closest brothers, saying such words about *me*.

Memories such as these tear at my love for Purple House, just as the biker's needle tore at my skin to form the Purple House crest. I chose to endure a little pain to wear the emblem on my shoulder because it stands for ideals that I hold dear. And I endure a little more as I realize how much more we at Purple House could have done to uphold those ideals.

Night and Day
by John H. Lee

The door was broken open. My stereo speakers were kicked in. Someone had defecated on the bed. Records were smashed. Papers and books were shredded. What clothing remained was strewn about the room, some ripped up. And what would the scene be without epithets scrawled on the walls, doors, and mirrors with my own shaving cream? I had been left an unmistakable message by my brothers: "Faggot, go home!"

From the Beginning

All in all, I considered myself lucky. I was at the University of Kentucky, the state's flagship school, together with 27,000 other students. I was diving into rush week and feeling damn good about campus life.

Originally, my first choice of fraternities was Sigma Chi. Not unexpectedly, it was also the house nearest my freshman dorm and the first I visited. The brothers' ability to make rushees feel welcome and their obvious devotion to fun was infectious. Shortly thereafter I stretched my bounds and explored other houses who shared similar qualities, noticing how easily each fraternity earned a stereotype. Kappa Alpha, all Southern, all the time. Phi Tau, jock central. Sig Eps, too weird. Alpha Tau Omegas, what they lacked in brains was offset by brawn. Pikes, a little too businesslike.

Then came the Sigma Nu house. These guys fit my definition of a fraternity: balanced interests, cool house, the highest GPA on campus, and host to some of the most renowned parties each semester. During one of my first visits there, I met a girl named Elizabeth, with whom I would later go out. I also met a guy named Ken, on whom I would later develop a crush.

Toward the end of my last great Sigma Nu rush party ("great" being defined as "alcohol available," given that rush was not yet a dry event), I said my good-byes and began stumbling home. As luck would have it, I stumbled in the direction opposite my goal and ended up in front of the Sigma Pi house. And what a house it was! Here was a modern-looking three-story building, women milling about, a line of impatient rushees out the door and the promise of at least one free toilet. (Recall the alcohol consumed at the Sigma Nu party.)

In due course I found myself in the Sigma Pi basement, shoulder-to-shoulder among the brothers and other revelers. It was dark and humid, and the low ceiling added a definite "eau de Michelob" smell that hung in the air like an apocalyptic fart. This place was wild!

Hanging on to the bar as much to hold my place as to steady myself, I eavesdropped as the brothers spoke with rushees. These Sigma Pi boys lacked something that almost every other fraternity I had encountered found essential: pretentious mimicry. Differences within Sigma Pi, they claimed, were expected, promoted, and protected. It was not a big deal if Doug did not truly appreciate Kyle's soccer skills, or if Kyle found Doug's fascination with "Fourier transforms" inane. What made this house work was its tenet that everyone deserves respect, the right to be different, and a chance to behave like a brother when called upon. (Memorize these.)

Some days later I had forgotten about Sigma Nu and stood in the living room of that grand house, anxious to receive a bid from Sigma Pi and become a member of the Phi pledge class in the Epsilon Beta chapter.

Into the Fray

My pledge semester was unremarkable for the most part. We did experience a hell night (defying our national charter), but most of the 15 men in our pledge class made it through unscathed. My big brother (chosen with extreme care and consideration) steered me clear of any possible pledge mishap. The brothers with whom I played Dungeons and Dragons or accompanied to White Castle for midnight "sliders" after weekly sorority mixers were equally steady influences and seemed genuinely concerned that I have positive experiences during the pledge term.

Thus, it was not until the end of the semester that my first test of faith in Sigma Pi occurred. It was beyond mortal comprehension why most of the brothers in whom I had placed my trust would participate in undermining months of their own good deeds.

Apparently, some of the active brothers felt that the Phi pledge class flowed through the process too easily. We were too perfect, they thought. Too willing, too able. Where was the fun in that? Therefore, it was decided, we should undergo humiliation, mental anguish, and fear. In short, we were to experience a "pledge lineup."

Sure, a lineup is basic hazing and was against the national fraternal by-laws at the time. "But what the hell, brother, they are our pledges and we can do whatever the hell we want. Right? Pass me my bourbon, damn it."

The scene was again the familiar basement, only this time it was no party. The lights were out, and pillow cases covered our heads. I heard Hollywood—the pledge trainer assigned to shepherd us downstairs—whisper, "I'm really sorry about this," and he meant it.

The pillowcases removed, we found nearly the entire chapter seated facing us in the near darkness—including brothers seen only sporadically throughout the semester. It was ominous. A couple of brothers brandished desk lamps like swords, shoving the bright bulbs close to our eyes while yelling obscenities and insulting us. None of the pledges dared move for fear of calling attention to themselves and receiving abuse.

Soon the chapter began shouting questions at us, peppered with taunts and derision, and pledges were called upon to provide the correct answers. A wrong answer was worth time facing the back wall, an earful of vulgarism and profanity, a bucket of water, a splash of stale beer, or exile behind the bar to sit among the puke left over from our most recent party. A correct answer was just as likely to bring punishment as it was praise. No discrimination whatsoever.

It seemed unconscionable that my brothers-to-be could treat good pledges with such disdain and disregard for all decency. It seemed unthinkable that I could participate as an active brother in a future lineup. It seemed unlikely that I would ever step inside the Sigma Pi house again. The sound of the front door slamming added a sense of finality to my decision.

Perhaps a whole week passed, and I began mourning my time at Sigma Pi. How could I have been so deceived? Why did I believe all the bullshit about differences, respect, and brotherhood? How could my own big brother have joined the charade? Why did I consider severing my ties with these guys as a loss?

One evening there came a knock at my apartment front door. There stood about 20 Sigma Pi brothers in my hallway—nearly a quarter of the chapter—looking somewhat apprehensive.

Here's the gist of their message: "We repent, we shall ban lineups and make them against the chapter's bylaws. Please, come home."

Well, what was to be said at this point? I am a softy at heart, I really did miss the guys, and as long as we could agree that humiliation and even feigned intolerance are not part of Sigma Pi, then who was I to turn down an extended hand? It seemed that we had a win-win situation and that the chapter, as well as future pledge classes, would be all the better for it. I returned.

Dark Storm Rising

Fast-forward a few semesters. It was the summer term, and the Sigma Pi house served as home for me and a couple of other brothers. Plenty of the local guys dropped by every week, so it was anything but lonely. I had the same room that my big brother rented during the regular school year, and this somehow made the situation even more enjoyable for me.

That summer was mundane except for one minor item. In May I had come to the mind-boggling realization that I was a gay man. More to the point, I came out to myself, and that suggested I come out to the world. (Ever since, I have done a decent job of telling people one by one. With this story I am targeting thousands of you at once. I must be getting lazy in my old age.)

OK. I will grant you that this did not just "happen." It was not like flicking a light switch, and it did not hit me while shaving one morning. There was a definite process and months of agonizing, piled atop years of worry. During the spring semester, however, everything fell into place and I accepted the facts: John Lee is a gay man. I still had my 3.7 GPA, was still a very active member of Sigma Pi, was still beloved by the pledges for being their collective best friend and advocate, and remained more than mildly interested in Elizabeth. But there was a new facet to my life, one that added new dimension without destroying anything valuable. I was gay.

Well, it did not destroy anything valuable except the bonds of trust, the premise of truth, and life as I knew it. So then came the summer. Hot and sticky Lexington days were generally followed by hot and sticky Lexington nights. During the days I sweated it out in summer school, and during the nights I tended to haunt the Bar, the only gay nightclub in town. Late nights were spent at Leva's, a ritzy restaurant by day transformed into something much more decadent after closing.

Dancing at the Bar proved educational too. Altogether, I ran into seven Sigma Pi brothers there (all closeted, chapter officers among them) and met more than a few gays from other houses. From my perspective, it seemed like gay men were everywhere that summer—we always are, it turns out.

On the night of July 4, I found myself dancing with hundreds of other guys to music that was nearly deafening. In time one of my brothers pulled me aside for an introduction.

His name was "Ron," and he was the elder brother of our chapter's vice president, "Kent." This brought up an interesting situation. Ron's name was listed as a former pledge of Sigma Pi, and Kent maintained that Ron had died some years back. In fact, I suspect that when Ron came out to the family, Kent did not know how to accept the facts. Therefore, Kent lied to us all as well as to himself.

Ron and I enjoyed the next hour of dancing and headed out to the parking lot when the place closed. We leaned against his car, talking and saying good-night to passing friends when someone got out of a nearby car and headed wobbly toward us. It was Kent. He had come to hunt down his errant sibling, who had left the family's Fourth of July reunion to go dancing.

Kent was drunk, from all signs, and was focused so tightly on his brother that he did not notice me immediately. At that moment of recognition, however, it was as if Kent popped into sobriety just long enough to mutter a threatening, "I shoulda known."

Imagine me at that moment, the joy of meeting someone instantly overshadowed by a deep sense of foreboding. Kent's sudden appearance on the scene heralded horrible things. I feared, and I was none too sure that I was ready to face, my own personal lineup.

As soon as Kent was in his car and on his way, Ron said good-night and promised to catch up with me another time. Michael, a friend who had witnessed the whole incident, volunteered to let me crash at his

place instead of going back to the Sigma Pi house that night. Thank
God for friends, if not for brothers.

When Michael and I headed over to the house the following morning, I felt encouraged that the front door was locked as it should be, the
house was quiet, and no lynch mob was gathered to greet me on the
balcony. The front yard was free of burning effigies, and my key still fit
the lock. So far, so good. Climbing to the third floor and turning down
the dim hallway, my mood changed dramatically as it became apparent
that my room had been visited the previous night.

The door was broken open. Morning sunshine streamed though the
window into the ravaged room. My stereo speakers were kicked in.
Someone had defecated on the bed. Records were smashed. Papers and
books were shredded. What clothing remained was strewn about the
room, some ripped up. The rest was found together with my tooth-
brush, hairbrush, and other effects stuffed in the toilets, which had then
been pissed in. And what would the scene be without epithets scrawled
on the walls, doors, and mirrors with my own shaving cream? I had
been left an unmistakable message by my brothers: "Faggot, go home!"

Once again, all the big talk about diversity, acceptance, tolerance, balance, and respect was carelessly tossed out by a few vengeful brothers who
felt compelled by their own evil spirits of hate, intolerance, and conformity. That morning I left the Epsilon Beta chapter of Sigma Pi for good.

Making a New Bed

Months passed. The fall semester came, but I did not enroll. The
thought of attending school without being part of my fraternity was too
painful, so I abstained from both activities. My family did not know
what had befallen me that summer. I made up some lame excuse about
why I did not want to attend school and how I wanted a job instead,
and I basically kept communication to a minimum.

One October afternoon, some of my brothers, all pledges from the previous spring, approached me. They told me who had been involved in the
break-in, how some people wanted me to return, and how things would improve. They reassured me that the entire house was not suddenly filled with
Neanderthals or Nazis and that only by facing the chapter as a brother could
I challenge ignorance. (See? Being the pledges' best friend paid off!)

They did not know that I was not even attending school. Nonetheless, it seemed to me that I would only be a handicap for the chapter and that perhaps people would mistakenly stereotype Sigma Pi as the "queer house" on campus. I quickly imagined all the horrible possibilities and made a hasty excuse to leave.

I dreamed of escaping Lexington altogether, getting away from the mess. I felt guilty, as though I had done something appalling and had dishonored myself, my friends, my brothers, my family. I was willing to heap upon myself the guilt for a thousand uncommitted sins, and I wasn't even Catholic!

The time had come to forge a new path and create a new life. After some finagling and a very lonely Christmas spent apart from my family (I was still paying penance, of course), I accepted a job as a programmer for the Harris Corp. in Florida, near the Kennedy Space Center. Six months later, I was waving farewell to military work and on my way to Berkeley, California.

Fruits and Nuts

One of the first things I remember hearing about California is that this is the "land of fruits and nuts." Well, I joined the fruits, since there were already more than enough nuts when I got there.

In a moment of uncertain lucidity, I arranged to live with the Sigma Pi chapter at University of California, Berkeley, while attending school, and I vowed to not hide behind faux heterosexuality. I threw myself into chapter activities, going so far as to take on the dreaded responsibilities of kitchen steward. Early on I discovered that things were very different with the men of Iota chapter and that this boded very well. In fact, life was so good that some of my new brothers even arranged blind dates for me with gay guys they knew in other fraternities!

The difference was night and day. In Kentucky there was a lot of preaching about tolerance and diversity. At Berkeley there was no preaching but a lot of doing. At Kentucky there were a lot of promises made during times of crisis. The brothers at Berkeley worked to avoid a crisis in the first place.

In fact, the brotherhood at Kentucky was crafted out of handpicked brothers. The same could not be said of UC Berkeley in the early 1980s when fraternity membership was foremost based on the necessity for good housing. It raises the peculiar question, then, of why crafted brotherhood is not as strong a bond as brotherhood by happenstance.

Now, lest you think that I wax poetic about my time at UC Berkeley, history demands that I mention that the Iota chapter had its fair share of flaws and awkward moments. Some brothers were not quite as accepting as others, yet they never lashed out. That never would have been tolerated by the chapter at large. Overall, my experiences at UC Berkeley helped reestablish my faith in the power of fraternity and specifically in the fraternity I claim as my own.

Today, I have just passed my 36th birthday. I live with my "other half" of six years (whom my family not-so-secretly prefers over myself), and we recently purchased an extraordinary Victorian home near Stanford University with plenty of room for the dog to play. We both work in Silicon Valley, have been treated equitably by our employers, and were charter members of Digital Queers (a technology-oriented nonprofit group).

I have learned that this region of the country—so fruitful when it comes to technology products and services—is also rife with homosexuals. You do not necessarily see us; but we are here. *Invisible.* You cannot turn on any name-brand computer or connect to any big on-line service without using equipment or services designed by some queer. We are everywhere throughout "TechnoLand," thrusting the results of our creative energy onto an unsuspecting world. And it occurs to me, that this is as common in fraternities as in business.

Think about it. It is not a threat. It is a fact. And it has likely always been true.

Epilogue

The experiences you have just read about led me to a stronger belief in myself. That belief provided me the springboard to start businesses, become involved with nascent computer technologies and digital video, give speeches to thousands of people, and generally not accept anything as being impossible. When I was in college, the slogan QUESTION AUTHORITY was common on T-shirts. Today, I would alter it to read, "I QUESTION *YOUR* AUTHORITY. I QUESTION *MY* MOTIVATION. AND I REFUSE TO DOUBT MYSELF."

As for my involvement with Sigma Pi, sadly, it has waned. I am, though, still in contact with two of my favorite Sigma Pi brothers from Kentucky, including my big brother. In my mind these two men express the ultimate in fraternal ideals through their refusal to reject me.

No Regret
by Leif Mitchell

I wanted others to know that they were not alone. So I wrote a letter to the editor about being gay and Greek on campus. No bricks were thrown through the front window of my fraternity house, as I had feared, and only a few obscene phone calls came through my line. But I could not help wondering if my letter really did play a role in the ultimate closing of the house.

In January of 1992 I went through deferred rush during my first year at Miami University in Oxford, Ohio. I had no idea that I would find a group of guys who were completely open-minded and individualistic. Let us be honest here: fraternities usually breed a groupthink, animalistic mentality. I had no intentions of rushing until the resident assistant in the adjacent corridor challenged me to do so.

I remember his words clearly. He said, "Leif, if you truly claim to be so open-minded, then you should at least give rush a chance—and stop by Psi Upsilon."

I had to admit that he had a valid point. So I picked a couple of houses (mostly those to which other friends were going) and went off on my journey.

I went through the following thought process as I began rush: I reasoned that since high school I had always been a very active person. I was in plays and musicals, on the speech and debate team, and part of the literary magazine staff, but I never felt that I truly belonged. I knew coming to Miami University that I wanted to get involved. I was active in a couple of student groups but felt that I had made only a bunch of acquaintances. I wanted to know a close group of people on a different level than I had ever done before. The Greek system, which comprised over 40% of the student body, offered the perfect opportunity for me to develop such friendships.

As I went from house to house, I tried not to prejudge any of the fraternities; however, some expected stereotypes continually prevailed. I felt as though they wanted me to act other than myself, to be exactly like them. When I was asked a question about some football game played earlier that day and I did not know the answer, they laughed. They also expected me to have a girlfriend. I felt very uncomfortable that they assumed I was straight.

I wanted to remain open-minded and avoid generalizations, so I took my friend's advice and stopped by Psi Upsilon. As I walked over the threshold, I felt the tension of conformity lift off my shoulders. I had finally happened upon people who made me feel completely at home. As I looked at the faces of the brothers in the main room, they gave me a sense of openness and diversity that I had not received at other chapters.

I still remember the first brother I met, Matt. He talked about Psi U's individualistic attitudes and strong sense of brotherhood. I knew the minute I left the Beta Alpha chapter of Psi Upsilon that, if I were going to become Greek, this was the place for me.

A couple of days later, I was walking through a clearing in the frost-laden western campus woods with my pledge brothers for our initiation ceremony. I felt like I was about to embark on something from *Dead Poets Society*.

Still, at the time of initiation, I had not come out. Actually, at this point I still had not accepted my sexuality. Having grown up in small- town Ohio, I did not know anyone who was gay, except my uncle Jimmy, who was living with AIDS. I felt fatalistic. I was afraid that if I were gay, then I too would contract HIV. It is a gay disease, right? (I did not know any better.)

Maybe if I had had some positive role models around me who were openly gay, things would have been different. I would have accepted my being gay at a much younger age. Instead I went to a Catholic grammar and high school and was taught that homosexuality was sinful and evil. These words were seared in my memory. I felt alone, isolated, and scared. I did not want people to know that I was attracted to men, that I might be gay.

But in college I felt free. I was five hours away from my past. Things could change here.

I remember the first fraternity brother that I ever came out to was gay himself. I remember distinctly the night I told Brian that I was gay. I called

him during the day and told him that I had to talk to him about something
serious that night. We got together, and I said, "Brian, come on, you know
what I am going to say, so why don't you make it easier on me?"

Knowing perfectly well what I was about to reveal to him, he responded, "I have no idea what you have to tell me."

From the moment I revealed my secret to Brian, I realized that this
was something that I was going to have to address in all aspects of my
life in order to be truly at peace.

Psi Upsilon was a source of energy for me. Here, I felt that I could do
or say anything and still be accepted. The brothers in the house were
not the stereotypical frat guys. They were caring, sincere, individualistic, and accepting of each other's differences.

I started to go to the fraternity house more regularly the semester
after I pledged. I enjoyed just hanging out with my brothers, talking
about politics and philosophy. I recall one night when about ten of
us stayed up until 5 A.M. discussing the hypothetical question, "If a
tree dropped in the forest, does it make a sound if no one is around
to hear it?"

We liked to challenge one another. We brought our individual knowledge and experiences to the table, laid them out, and discussed our
feelings on every issue imaginable, from abortion to gay rights. Although not all of us completely agreed, we were able to have a civil debate and then leave the table with the utmost respect for each other's
opinions. Psi U gave me the strength that I was not finding in myself
but I knew existed. And through this bonding, I began to discover more
about myself. I began to realize that I was hiding an important part of
me, and what bothered me the most was that I was not being honest to
myself or to my brothers.

Brian, the first brother I came out to, became my mentor and helped
me to truly accept all of who I am as a gay male. It was only a couple
of months later that I began coming out to my closest friends, family,
and other fraternity brothers.

I became very comfortable with my sexuality, and I soon realized that
I was in a very interesting position as an out gay Greek. I had met other
gay Greeks and even heard of an "underground" group of gay Greeks
who used to meet at Miami years ago. I wanted to be a visible, out gay
leader for others and decided to do something for those gay Greeks who

remained in the closet because of homophobia and heterosexism. I wanted others to know that they were not alone, so I wrote a letter to the editor of the school newspaper about being gay and Greek on campus.

I asked my fraternity brothers at the next chapter meeting if they felt
writing a letter to the editor about being gay and Greek was appropriate. I wanted to get everyone's opinion before I went ahead with the
project. A few people said they did not understand why it was necessary, and I explained to them that I wanted to help others who were gay
and Greek to come to terms with their sexuality. No one completely opposed the idea, and many were quite supportive.

I wrote the letter and received an enormous amount of positive responses from friends and faculty on campus. No bricks were thrown
through the front window of my fraternity house, as I had feared, and
I received only a few obscene phone calls. But, the overall effect of the
letter can never truly be measured.

I continued to gain respect from my fraternity brothers as a very active leader in the house. Some of my brothers said that they understood
what it must be like for me. Others felt that there was nothing different
about someone being gay. Despite this, there still was a lot of talk
among the older members of the fraternity and the alumni about the
letter I had written to the campus newspaper. Some said that I had
"used" the fraternity to come out and felt that the repercussions resulting from the letter would not benefit the chapter whatsoever. We were
still a relatively new fraternity among Miami's Greek system, and, therefore, we wanted to present and maintain a positive image.

Such fears were most evident during a chapter meeting before fall
rush 1994. Someone came up with the idea that during rush I should
hide the wall in my room that was plastered with black-and-white ads
of men from various magazines. I understood the concept of not wanting to scare away easily impressionable first-year students, but I still felt
uncomfortable.

Would we really want someone in the fraternity who had a problem
with a brother's being gay? Of course not, I thought.

But, on the other hand, would we be able to attract rushees if they knew
our house had an openly gay brother? Would first-year students make fun
of people in their corridor who may have actually liked Psi U? Would we
be stereotyped as a gay fraternity? These are all things that went through

my mind as I covered my wall with a tapestry the night before rush.

The next semester during rush, we worked hard to establish a positive image of ourselves on campus. Unfortunately, we received little response from the men rushing, and there was some talk that my letter could have been the reason. We were not the only house that was affected by low rush numbers, but I could not help wondering if my letter really did play a role in the ultimate closing of the house.

With the closure of our house, we realized that this would be the true test of our brotherhood. Would we all live together the following year after we lost our house? Would we keep in close contact?

During my senior year, eleven of us lived together in a huge house. Late one night a few of us broke into our old house to reminisce. When I entered what had been my room, I was astonished to find FAG written on my wall. I found out later that the former president of my fraternity had written it. I could not help wondering why people were not more open if they truly had a problem with my sexuality, especially someone who was supposed to be our fraternity leader.

Since graduation I have kept in touch with some of my brothers, and I will never forget the experience I had as a member of Psi Upsilon. My fraternity, for the most part, was a safe place—a place where my beliefs were challenged and I was accepted for who I am. We had something very few other fraternities at Miami had: acceptance of individuality. I do not regret getting involved in a fraternity or writing the letter. In fact, because Psi U stressed an individualistic attitude, I believe the fraternity actually compelled me to come out of the closet.

Every Man, a Man
by Jeffrey R. Driscoll

Coming out had a snowball effect on me. The more people I came out to, the more I wanted to tell. I was tired of hiding something so basic to my very nature. And for better or worse, anyone who wanted to be my friend or even be around me had better deal with the fact that I was gay—and pretty damn quickly.

Vir Quisque Vir. Translated from the Latin, it means *Every man, a man* and is the open motto of Lambda Chi Alpha fraternity. But what did that phrase mean to me as a closeted gay brother? Not much! For me, the fear and paranoia generated in the closet and the perceived homophobia of the fraternity added a sense of bitter irony to that phrase. While I was a closeted brother, I would think a lot about that phrase and the concept of fraternity and would wonder how far my chapter would really take those ideals to heart if faced with a gay brother.

Coming out was hardly an overnight process for me. I could not even say the word "gay" to the first straight person I came out to, an undergraduate brother named Brandon. I do not even think he knew what I was trying to say. I went back to talk to him later, and he seemed fairly nonplussed about it. He figured I was gay, and it was no big deal to him.

I do not know why I picked Brandon. Partly convenience: He was at the right place at the right time, when I needed to tell someone. Partly because he was one of the few brothers who did not crack any homophobic jokes or remarks. We were fairly close before I told him; but after that and over the next year, he provided the most constant support of anyone, and our friendship grew greatly. He was always there, willing to listen to me bitch and worry.

During the next several months, I came out only to those people I felt closest to and who I believed would give me a positive reaction. Friends from within and outside the fraternity were supportive and understanding, and more than one said that they had thought I was gay but they were waiting for me to say something first. My confidence grew as I was able to open up to these people who meant so much to me.

My personal relationships with men also grew and became more fulfilling because I was not afraid of being found out. I could go on real dates, talk about the men who piqued my interest with my friends and fraternity brothers, and begin to enjoy "dishing" with them.

Coming out had a snowball effect on me. The more people I came out to, the more I wanted to tell. I was tired of hiding something so basic to my very nature. And for better or worse, anyone who wanted to be my friend, or even be around me, had better deal with the fact that I was gay—and pretty damn quickly.

I came out to people in just about every way you can imagine—in person, over the phone, by E-mail, during dinner. But one of my favorite ways of telling fraternity brothers was the Snapple Talk. The name came from the way I would ask someone if he wanted to walk over and grab a drink from the grocery store behind the fraternity house. Somewhere between buying a quart of Snapple iced tea and walking back to the chapter house, I would come out to the brother, talk about what being gay really means, and let him ask anything he wanted.

These little individual coming-out sessions became known as Snapple Talks. The brothers really appreciated my personally telling them and answering their questions. It was tremendously good for me too. It finally gave me the opportunity to talk about my feelings, what coming out was like for me, and how much better I felt being able to talk to everyone honestly about my life. Thereafter, the phrase *Snapple Talk* became a euphemism for other fraternity brothers coming out. And although I wrote the company, Snapple has yet to make this story into a commercial.

The next step for me in coming out to the chapter was to take a male date to our annual Founders Day Banquet during alumni weekend. It was an event that I was also in charge of organizing. I decided to ask my friend Fred to be my date for the event; this would be the first male date for a brother at a formal, or any event, in the chapter's 60 years of existence! It was also the very first time that I would be able to be myself at a chapter function.

When I first told my brothers of my intent to bring Fred, the response was supportive except—and this was surprising at the time—from some of the closeted gay brothers in the chapter. One even thought that I was somehow "flaunting" myself by bringing a date. And while that really angered me at the time, I realize now that they were expressing more of their own fears of coming out than anything else.

On March 27, 1993, "D-Day" had finally come. That evening Fred and I showed up early. A number of brothers, those most supportive of me, angled to get a seat at our table for the dinner. I think they wanted to keep an eye out for us and make sure Fred and I had a good experience. A crowd of about 150 people, including alumni from the 1920s to our newest freshman members, was in attendance. It seemed as if Fred and I were on center stage. Dinner began, and with the fortitude of a few drinks in me, I asked Fred to dance before the speeches that inevitably accompany a fraternity formal. While we had a lot of eyes on us, nobody threw dinner rolls! The only problem that arose was deciding who should lead.

Soon after that the speeches began. During his address, alumni adviser Joe Salo greeted the audience, pointed out prominent members, and then made a point of addressing Fred and me. He spoke of how glad he was for me that I could do this and that he realized it had been a difficult time getting to this stage. I ended up getting a round of applause from everyone for having come out. Definitely not what I had expected! I was *out*, baby, I was out.

The rest of the evening went just as swell. Fred and I danced a few more times together. Everyone around us seemed to be more concerned than we were that we were having a good time. If anyone had expressed something negative about Fred or me, he would have been pounced on by at least a dozen of the brothers. They were very protective of me as their brother. I guess that is a trait of fraternities—looking out for your own regardless.

After this experience I felt more confident than ever about making the right decision to come out and to come out to everyone. My friends were still my friends, and I was even closer to many of them. There was no longer a fear of holding something back, of leaving out details of my life. But while my relationship with my friends, fraternity brothers, and even coworkers had improved immensely, I still kept my family pushed away. I knew I had to come out to them but was not ready to do that until I had sorted out the other issues in my life.

In the spring of 1994, I decided it was time to tell my parents that I was gay. I knew I wanted to come out to them, but I kept putting it off. One of the brothers I felt closest to, Dennis, was the one who finally convinced me do it. He knew how scared I was, and we talked at length about how to tell them and what their reaction might be.

I decided that the best way to tell my parents would be in a letter. There was a lot I wanted to tell my parents, and I knew I could not say it all in person. I felt one of their biggest concerns would be my life now and in the future. I decided to have my closest friends, all fraternity brothers, write my parents and tell them how much my life and my friendships improved after I came out.

I euphemistically called this project a "mail bomb." I put it together over a period of two months. My self-imposed deadline was that it would be delivered to my parents while I was at an alumni workshop held by our national fraternity in Philadelphia. The package consisted of a letter from me to be opened first, followed by letters from three straight fraternity brothers, one gay brother, a letter from his mother (a member of Parents, Families, and Friends of Lesbians and Gays), and a copy of the book *Loving Someone Gay*.

In my letter I mentioned the role the fraternity had played in my coming out and how my brothers would be sharing their thoughts with their letters:

> I started telling friends over a year ago but it was only this May that I decided, with the help of many friends, to come completely out. Since then my life has improved immeasurably! I am so much happier not having to hide anything. I am proud to say that *all* my friends have understood and been very supportive. And that was not easy for a few of them. The fraternity was the best. They helped me through so much. Several brothers have been encouraging me for months to do what I'm doing now. Since I've come out, half a dozen other brothers have started to do the same thing. I'm glad I am here to help them. I have asked several of my closest friends to write letters to you too. I asked them to write about their observations on my life and how coming out has made it so much better for me. I have asked a

fraternity brother who is bisexual to write a letter to get a different point of view from someone who did the same thing. And a letter from his mother describing how they have come to understand, accept, and support him.

In one of the accompanying letters, Neil Kindlon described to my parents what it meant to him and the chapter as a whole when I came out:

> I met Jeff not long after coming to Rensselaer and joining Lambda Chi Alpha back in the fall of 1992, and it wasn't a moment too soon. What I didn't know then was that I would soon reach the point where I'd be sorely in need of a friend. I couldn't have asked for a better one. No problem was ever too small or too stupid to talk to him about; his ear was always open. Even when life seemed to go from bad to worse resembling a bad dream, Jeff was the one thing, and sometimes the only thing, I could count on to still be there for me. It was always him that I'd turn to when I had no place else to go. I have never been so fortunate to meet anyone else who completely listens, who truly understands, and who so honestly cares.
>
> But at the same time, there was always one disturbing problem. Jeff would let us rant and rave and go an about our problems but never really said anything about himself. As far as being a sympathetic ear, he just gave so much and took so little…it made me feel ashamed. I tried asking him about this a few times and was always met with "Me? Um…well, there's not much to tell." Or something like that. But that wasn't true. There was plenty to tell—it's just that he was scared to reveal it.
>
> Finally, he got sick of always hiding who he was, and he told us all the truth. I'll have to admit, it came as an enormous surprise. I'd never known anyone gay before, or if I had, I didn't have a clue that they were. And for lack of knowing, I didn't understand the concept at all. It was just some foreign subject to me, and members of that group were equally regarded as foreign, distant, and alien. But suddenly that ended. This was no stranger, no freak that you see on *Donahue*. This was Jeff. This was the guy who had to listen to all my bad jokes and

dumb stories. This was my shoulder to cry on and my friend to hang out with. This was my best friend and my father rolled into one. And whatever great surprises he could dump on me, whatever he really is or does, cannot ever make a difference. Jeff is still my brother, and I still love him.

As I look back, all I can really feel is gratitude. I'm grateful that Jeff finally chose to share with us what he felt that he had to keep hidden for so long. In opening up to us, he's increased the strength of our relationship enormously. In coming out, he placed an enormous amount of faith in each of us. Also, Jeff's action has allowed us to learn a great deal about being gay, to reach a new level of tolerance and understanding.

The result of these letters was better than I expected or even hoped for. While it was very emotional for all of us, my parents continued to love me and accept me. My mother felt that it was the nicest way they could be told and that they appreciated my fraternity brothers for writing and helping them to understand me better.

It may sound as if I am presenting just the good parts of my coming out. Maybe I am a little. There were a lot of emotions flying around, but I truly never encountered a negative reaction from anyone.

Where does that leave me now? I am still volunteering time to my chapter, still making new friends with members as they join, and trying to live up to being an example of a good brother, a dedicated alumnus, and a gay man. More recently I created a personal home page on the World Wide Web and on it is a collection of resources and information about gay men in fraternities. Through this I have been able to correspond with many fraternity men, both active and alumni, both in and out of the closet, who have experienced the same fears and concerns I had. Often one of these men will express relief at finding out the simple fact that he is not the only gay man wearing Greek letters on his chest! By writing this, I feel I am somehow paying back the fraternity brothers who helped me with all of their support and love.

But most important, my personal life is now completely different and immeasurably richer. I am out in all aspects of my life, confident, and completely happy with being a gay man. The mental burden and under-siege mentality that I had in the closet is now gone. I feel like I have finally been able to grow up and lead a regular, if at times "fabulous," life. I know I could not have reached this stage without the unfailing support and love of a number of fraternity brothers who helped me along the way.

As for my chapter today, I feel it is still generally accepting of gay brothers. There is a need for constant vigilance, however, when you consider the turnover in membership as brothers graduate and new ones join. Certainly, there will always be a few Neanderthals in any group, but luckily in my chapter their opinion does not reflect the majority. The gay brothers in my chapter today feel they will be accepted and have looked to me and the experiences of other gay brothers for that reassurance. The maxim "Every man, a man" still holds for my chapter and, hopefully, the concept will someday apply to chapters in all fraternities.

Role Modeling
by Joe Bertolino

I watched and listened as one of these men (the president), stood up in front of the room, welcomed the rushees, and proclaimed, "Welcome to our fraternity! We have a great house, great parties, we get the 'chicks,' and there are no fags here*!" Everyone clapped and cheered. I stood there stunned.*

Homophobic. Sexist. Racist. These are just a few of the words I associated with the Greek system. I was a product of a private Catholic undergraduate institution with no Greek system, and my vision of fraternities was shaped by the film *Animal House* and the many reports citing the negative aspects of fraternity life.

Following my stint at an undergraduate college, I moved into teaching at a small Catholic high school in southern New Jersey. Never during this time period did I question my sexual orientation. Whatever I was feeling would soon go away. It was a phase, and all I needed was a good woman to settle down with in a relationship—get married, have kids—the whole family package.

After three years as a high school teacher, I moved on to pursue my graduate studies. During this process I became a graduate hall director. My fate was sealed, since this would become my destiny—the field of student affairs. Still, my attitude toward Greeks remained predominantly negative. All I saw were the stereotypes, and I believed them. During this time period, I continued to internalize my "feelings" and put all my energies into focusing on work and school.

Upon completing my graduate studies, I was offered a position as hall director at East Stroudsburg University in northeastern Pennsylvania.

This was my opportunity to leave my home, start a new life, and leave behind those "feelings" I could not quite figure out. Yet upon my arrival at ESU, I found that my urges did not change and, in fact, grew more intense.

In August 1991 two pivotal events changed my life. The first was that at the age of 27, I finally came to terms with my sexual orientation—I was gay! This had been a long time in coming, as I had long internalized my feelings by forcing myself to date women or worse, by diving into my work. While I knew whom I was attracted to, I was in complete denial. The best way for me to deal with it was not to deal with it.

I finally confronted myself, realizing that I could not possibly help my students if I could not help myself. That summer I made a conscious decision to come out to myself. In doing so, I felt as though a great weight had been lifted from my shoulders. I felt *free*. For the first time in years, I felt like a whole being

I was afraid of being rejected by family and friends, but I was even more afraid of hiding and retreating back into my shell. It was time to start being open. Over the next six months, I would tell my family and friends that I was gay. My attitude was that people would either accept me or not. In either case I felt it was time to move on.

The second pivotal event occurred when the vice president needed an Interfraternity Council adviser. No one else wanted the job, so I was recruited. While I was excited by the new challenge, I was fearful that my newly found openness regarding my sexual orientation would hinder my ability to successfully advise these groups. My first thoughts were, *Lovely! I'm gay and I'm stuck with the most homophobic group on campus.*

My goal as IFC adviser was to assess whether ESU should continue to recognize Greeks the following year. Did fraternities have any value at our university? I expected the answer to be a resounding "No!" But something went terribly wrong. As I came to terms with my sexual orientation, I found that I wanted others to understand me for who I was and to learn to develop tolerance. I realized that the Greek system at ESU needed that same understanding, tolerance, and acceptance. To that end, I focused heavily on helping the men of IFC. To my surprise, I found that I not only learned a great deal about the Greek system but also appreciated what I saw. I had accepted the Greek system on my campus, and I had fallen in love with the challenge of advising it.

Eventually, my role as IFC adviser and my struggle for acceptance as a gay man would come to a head. This convergence occurred with two incidents in the Greek system.

A year into my IFC role, two officers from an organization approached me. They were both in a relationship together and were struggling with their sexual orientation and the concept of being both gay and Greek. I attempted to help them through this time. My role was that of counselor, adviser, and resource person.

After meeting with these men, I attended their rush function. They were heading up the function and speaking to the rushees. I watched and listened as one of these men (the president), stood up in front of the room, welcomed the rushees, and proclaimed, "Welcome to our fraternity! We have a great house, great parties, we get the chicks and *there are no fags here!*" Everyone clapped and cheered. I stood there stunned. What was happening? How could these men, gay men who had come to me for help, say such a thing? It was at this point that I realized that both my students and I had much to learn and that there was much work to do!

The second experience occurred that summer. A fraternity man by the name of Ralph had come to my office extremely upset. Evidently, a colleague of mine was with some fraternity men in a local bar. The issue of my sexual orientation came up, and my colleague proceeded to tell the men that I was a gay man. Ralph came to see me concerned and upset—not because of what he had heard regarding my sexual orientation but because a colleague had been saying things to students that should never have been said. "I'm not concerned about your sexual orientation. That is your business and your private life. You work hard for us, and we respect the work you do," said Ralph. "I'm concerned about your colleague's unprofessional behavior."

My faith in the potential understanding of my students was restored. I was empowered, if not impassioned, to educate my students on the issues of sexual orientation in fraternities and sororities. My students deserved more credit than we administrators gave them. They could handle the issue and could draw their own conclusions.

As I developed into a solid Greek adviser, it came time for me to be more open with my students. While I knew this would be controversial, I also believed it was important for my own personal growth and development as well as that of my students. I waited for the perfect opportunity, which presented itself in the homecoming celebrations of October 1993.

Traditionally, the Greek system played a significant role in the homecoming parade. Each fraternity and sorority built a float and had a float building party the night before the parade. As the adviser, I would stop by each of the float-building parties and cheer people on. During this particular homecoming, before each of these events I was told, "Joe, bring a date!"

My IFC president, "Corky," stormed into my office two days before the parade and said, "Joe, I know we've never talked about your private life, but don't bring a date. I know you'll try to be a role model or something—*don't!*" I laughed and told Corky not to worry about it.

As luck would have it, my partner, Bil, was in town during homecoming weekend. Initially we debated attending the parties together, but at his prodding we decided against it. Our thought had been, *Not a good thing to do in conservative northeast Pennsylvania.* However, as I was walking out the door, I turned to Bil and said, "Wait a minute—if you were a woman, we wouldn't even be having this conversation. In fact, you would just come along, no questions asked. Let's go!" With that, we walked out the door and headed to each of the houses. Truly a life-altering decision.

By not bringing Bil to these events, what message would I be sending to my students? By not being myself and accepting my students' invitation at face value, I was not being true to myself or them. More important, would I be sending out the message that something was wrong with my lifestyle by hesitating to bring Bil or fearing their reaction? What was the message I was sending, and what would they learn? I needed to be a role model.

Role modeling does work. In 1993 the *Chronicle of Higher Education* cited a University of California, Los Angeles, study in which freshmen were asked in 1987 about their feelings regarding homosexuality. Sixty percent responded negatively. Four years later, in 1991, those same students were asked the same questions. This time only 33% of the respondents answered negatively—a drop of 27%. What made the difference? Role modeling, experience, and education made the difference. With time, patience, knowledge, understanding of the facts, and exposure to the gays, our students will learn tolerance and acceptance.

Knowledge and experience equals change!

While that first night was unusual for me and my students, it was mostly positive. Most of the students appreciated my being "real" with them and, in fact, thought it was cool and gutsy for me to be open and introduce them to Bil. By the end of the year, my students were regularly asking about Bil and eventually invited Bil and me to their formals as a couple! We were even encouraged to dance together!

During this time period, Delta Sigma Phi had continually invited me to become a brother of their organization. My response continued to be, "No, thank you," since I felt that this was a conflict of interest with my role as Greek adviser. However, the chapter was persistent, to the point where I eventually said, "When it comes time for me to leave ESU, I'll accept a bid if you still want to offer me one." I figured this would get them off my back for a while.

Eventually, the day came when I decided to move on from ESU to New York. As soon as I made my announcement, Delta Sigma Phi was at my door with a bid in hand. I could no longer avoid the issue and seriously needed to decide if I, first, wanted to become Greek, and second, wanted to become a member of Delta Sigma Phi.

My three years of experience had taught me that becoming Greek was worthwhile. The philosophy, concepts of brotherhood, community service, natural brotherhood connections, and commitment to life learning were all strong tenets that I supported. True, there were flaws in the system, but there were also many successes. While I had heard all of the arguments against Greek organizations on campus, I understood that becoming a member of a fraternity was a commitment whose rewards and opportunity for growth would last a lifetime.

I realized that as a member, I could help chapters to more fully appreciate and move back toward following the concepts of ritual and placing ritual in their everyday lives. Delta Sigma Phi provided me with that opportunity. More important, I saw Delta Sig as an organization that would be inclusive and supportive. Time and again I had seen them welcome brothers that were diverse, not just in race but also in ability and need. They were true brothers.

In May 1994 I became a proud member of the brotherhood of Delta Sigma Phi. I was accepted for who I was. In fact, the brotherhood was excited that I was their first out brother. Their acceptance and that of other Greek organizations was both refreshing and rewarding. My students and brothers had risen to the occasion. They knew how to appreciate difference and treat others with dignity and respect.

Yet my story does not end here with this happy ending. Upon moving to New York, I became a district volunteer (governor) for my fraternity. My involvement was both local and national. The national office asked me to write the fraternities' statements on HIV/AIDS and human dignity. I was honored to have this opportunity and felt proud to have been the brother chosen to develop these statements.

After many months of research, drafting, consultation, and work, I presented two statements to the national fraternity. They were unique in that they both included educational components. More important, the statement on human dignity was fully inclusive of all men, including gay men.

To my dismay, I learned that the grand council chose to eliminate the educational component, citing that "chapters could educate themselves on these issues." Even more disappointing, the council opted to remove the term *sexual orientation* saying that the brothers were "not ready" for such inclusion. Instead the council chose to replace the words *sexual orientation* with *all groups protected by the law.*

I was stunned! The fraternity that I was committed to had honored me by asking me to write their nondiscrimination statement and then subsequently omitted me from that same statement. How painfully ironic! I was angry, humiliated, and frustrated. What was worse was that no one had the courage to tell me the council's decision. I learned of it in a discreet, quick, off-the-cuff conversation with the fraternity's executive director.

While I was disappointed by these events, I once again realized that I needed to be an educator and role model, not just for my students and undergraduate brothers but for my alumni brothers and colleagues as well. I was committed to voicing the concerns of the "silent minority" of my fraternity and to fighting for the inclusion of *all* my brothers.

Furthermore, I realized that like my experience at ESU, educating the fraternity would be a process that would take time. My immediate reaction was to respond to the council's concerns and provide them with accurate information about sexual orientation, discrimination, and protection under the law. Next I took the liberty of presenting a homophobia workshop at the national convention. I chose to be a role model and a resource to my brotherhood.

There has been and still is much to do. I began educating myself, my friends, and my campus. Through time and patience, I educated my own fraternity, and then moved on to other campuses and Greek organizations. I began publishing articles and speaking at conferences and conclaves. My message has been clear: "What does it mean to be a brother? When our ritual encourages us to accept people for who they are, how accepting are we willing to be? Do we treat our gay brothers with dignity and respect?" These are good questions that have no easy answers.

Fraternities must exemplify their ritual and the true meaning of brotherhood. As individuals, we can only begin to imagine the struggle our gay students experience daily and the struggle of our Greek organizations to be accepting. If each of us "does the something we can do," our students, our Greek systems, and our campuses will only be better. Then we truly will be brothers and sisters.

Sacred Trust
by Brian D. Buchiarelli

I came to Cal State to study athletic medicine, but I was neither a jock nor a scholar—and besides, I was gay. What could I possibly have in common with these guys? Well, I found out that what we had in common was our belief in the words of the fraternity's oath: "I believe in Sigma Pi, a fellowship of kindred minds, united in brotherhood."

I have always liked guys, but I grew up in the 1950s and '60s when there were no positive gay role models and society said only heterosexuals could be happy. Queers were sick, perverted, and doomed to hell. I was constantly surrounded by that message from straight society. In the movies the bad guys were often effeminate, introverted individuals, and gay characters were mostly the object of ridicule.

Who would want to grow up and be like that? The label "queer" was enough to destroy a kid. Being queer meant ostracism at best and often verbal and physical abuse. To survive, I hid behind a mask of lies and created a straight persona that obeyed all the rules and got all the rewards straight society had to offer.

I did well in school, was a model citizen and Boy Scout, went to church, and was a dutiful son. I joined school clubs and was elected to office. I was a good boy, Mama's little man.

But all the while, I was miserable inside. I was alone and lonely. Nothing was real to me. When praised, I felt nothing because I knew that what was praised was an act. Friends could say they liked me, but how could they? They never knew me. No one got past my guard; I let no one in. I trusted no one with my dirty little secret, until I met the brothers of Sigma Pi.

I transferred in 1978 to California State University, Long Beach. I was 27 years old—quite a bit older than most of the other students. I lived close to one of the fraternities, Sigma Pi, and decided to go to one of the rush parties. I figured, *What the hell? I'm new here and don't know anyone. I will at least get a free beer and see some cute guys and maybe even meet some nice people.* I was not prepared for my actual welcome.

I was met at the door by the president of the fraternity, Patrick, who took my coat and handed me a beer. He made me feel very welcome. As I entered the living room, I saw a large mosaic of the fraternity crest over the fireplace. I walked over to it and recognized several of the symbols, the owl of wisdom and the wreath of victory. I also saw that the letters *Sigma* and *Pi* stood for the motto *Sibaste pistis.* The next day I went to the university library, found a Greek dictionary, and looked up those words. *Sibaste* means "sacred and reverence." *Pistis* means "trust and truth."

"Sacred trust, reverence for truth." These words took on new meaning in the months and years to come.

I talked with many of the brothers that first night and, for the most part, I really liked them. After a few hours Patrick came over to me and asked me to join him and a couple of the brothers upstairs. I had no idea that they were taking me upstairs to give me a bid, an invitation to join. They told me this was the first time in their history that they gave out a bid on the first night of rush. It seems as if all the brothers had agreed I was someone they would like to have in the fraternity.

I was, of course, proud and flattered. But the idea of joining a fraternity was the furthest thing from my mind. I had spent years as a paramedic and as an activist in the Vietnam antiwar movement in Washington, D.C. I had been a hippie. I had hitchhiked around the country and lived in communes, and I practiced Zen Buddhism. I came to Cal State to study athletic medicine, but I was neither a jock nor a scholar—and besides, I was gay. What could I possibly have in common with these guys?

I soon found out that what we had in common was our belief in the words of the fraternity's oath: "I believe in Sigma Pi, a fellowship of kindred minds, united in brotherhood." Brotherhood. Boy, was I into brotherhood. I wanted brotherhood pretty badly. I wanted peace and love and brotherhood since my antiwar days. In fact, I was more of a peacenik than a gay activist back then. Once I discovered what the fraternity's oath was and realized I actually believed in the ideals of the fraternity, it was not such a big step to join after all. In a way, the fraternity was another form of commune. Here was a group of guys living together, socializing together, sharing their cultural heritages and really getting off on becoming a tightly knit group of brothers.

I looked pretty closely at the brothers during rush week.

Almost all of the members were Caucasians, although there were some Asians and some Hispanics. There was no way that I would join a group if they practiced discrimination in any form. So when I saw this fine-looking young African-American sitting there with a name tag indicating he had been given a bid, I knew the place was cool. When I first saw Craig, he was sitting alone on a couch with his eyes closed. He looked like he was meditating.

So I sat on the floor in front of him and waited for him to open his eyes. When he finally did there was an instant connection between us. I can still feel that connection. In fact, Craig told me he was aware of my entering the room and sitting before him while he was meditating. I told him right then and there that I was really glad that he was going to be in the pledge class, because if there were no blacks in the fraternity, I would not want to join. Craig became one of my best friends. He is my brother in every sense. By the end of rush week, I accepted the invitation to join and started meeting all the other guys who had also accepted invitations and were going to be my pledge brothers.

Most pledges were in their teens and early 20s. Since I was the eldest of my pledge brothers and already had some experience in student government, it was really no surprise when I was nominated to become the pledge class president. I had not planned on running but accepted the nomination with the promise that I would do my best, and I won the election!

Here I was, a guy who went out for a free beer and ended up responsible for 50-some pledge brothers. It was one of the happiest periods of my life. I was in a position to be with young men and make a difference in their lives. I was respected, and my brothers looked up to me for guidance. I was creating strong relationships based on brotherhood, on caring for and nurturing each other. I was living my ideals, which were also the ideals of the fraternity. Since I had been an outsider for so long, the feelings of being welcomed and of being one of the guys were fantastic. If only I could trust them enough to share my true inner self with them. If only they could accept the one aspect of myself that I was keeping secret.

I started to think: *Why should my sexuality even be an issue? Why should I lose the respect of my brothers just because I am gay?* As these questions started to surface, I found the one person in the fraternity with whom I could really speak freely.

When you join a fraternity you choose one of the active members to be your big brother. He is responsible for helping you through your pledge semester. I had talked for quite a while with a guy named Phil during rush week and really liked him. He was a psychology major with a music minor, and he and I hit it off instantly. He played guitar and was a bit of a hippie himself. He was interested in many of the same things that I was, from spirituality to social dynamics, and besides, he was gorgeous. So I asked him to be my big brother, which we both found funny, since I was at least six years older than him.

As time passed and I grew more comfortable talking with Phil, I wanted to be totally honest with him. I wanted to be able to tell at least one person in my life that I was gay. So I drummed up all my courage and decided to trust Phil with my secret. He did not even bat an eyelid. He said something like, "Oh, I thought you might be." And it did not matter in the least to him. I even think he started to respect me more after that because of my honesty. I was not out of the closet yet, but I was willing to let a new friend peek inside.

It is amazing to look back and see how utterly afraid I was of being myself. Forcing myself to hide in a closet had been very destructive psychologically, particularly since what I was hiding was my capacity to love and the delight in sharing intimacy. It is remarkable that I was able to grow up and cope as well as I did. By coming out to Phil, I took a giant step into the world of relationships, of learning how to live without the fear of rejection. But I still had a lot of work to do to develop a functional and healthy personality. Phil helped me a lot in this process.

Phil was always there for me. He listened to me and respected my ideas. He encouraged me to be myself and to always do what I felt was right. I had a lot of feelings about what brotherhood meant and what brothers could accomplish. As the pledge class president, I saw an opportunity to put my beliefs into practice. I saw the fraternity as a place where you could stand up and hug and kiss your brothers and no one would think that was "queer." Kissing for me is not necessarily a sexual act but an act of intimacy and love. I am half Italian and grew up kissing my mother, father, and brothers on the lips. Even today, I still kiss all my friends, straight or gay, on the cheek or on the lips if we are really close.

I thought of the fraternity as a place where love and trust could be learned and openly expressed. Remember, I was a hippie. Peace, love, and brotherhood were my battle cries. I saw the students shot by the National Guard on the campus of Kent State University in 1970, and I was standing next to my best friend when he was shot in the face by a tear-gas canister. So I taught peace, and I taught love, and I taught that it was OK to have feelings and share them.

As I communicated these values to my pledge brothers, I watched them become a loving group of friends. We started really acting like brothers. We cared about each other and helped each other both on and off campus and came through the pledge period without any major incidents.

And then came hell week.

Hell week is when we were initiated into the fraternity. It was not too bad, really, and some of it was fun. It was mostly psychological game playing, and a lot of the activities were designed to instill a sense of belonging to the group—rather like the military, I should think. But for an old hippie and budding gay activist, I thought some of the activities were demeaning and had an aura of homophobia about them. I decided that when I was an active I would change this.

As soon as I became an active, I was elected one of the fraternity's officers, and the next semester I was chosen to be the pledge trainer. Here was my opportunity to make more changes—not just changes in the members' attitudes toward each other, but also in the traditional programs of the fraternity.

The pledge trainer is responsible for the education and behavior of the pledges. He is the link between the pledges and actives. One of the first things I did was rewrite the pledge trainer's manual, stressing the fact that all the pledge activities should be organized to instill the moral principles of the fraternity. I saw that the pledges were treated with respect. I also tried to make all the activities of hell week educational and inspirational.

I based the pledge period on the teachings of Pythagoras, one of the world's greatest educators. An Olympic athlete and a vegetarian, he taught the importance of a sound mind in a sound body. Pythagoras also taught that life must be lived according to moral principles. Like Pythagoras, I was building moral standards that were higher than those found in normal society. To some readers, this may sound strange, since we gay men and lesbians are the ones accused of lacking good morals. We are the ones condemned for our morality, and yet, contrary to popular perception, we are often the first to oppose racism, misogyny, and sexism.

Because I had been discriminated against, all forms of discrimination were repugnant to me. And this was also reflected in the fraternity. We were committed to diffusing culture by sharing and learning from our diversity. We were made up of blacks and whites, Arabs and Jews, conservatives and liberals; we even had jocks and nerds, but we all worked together, pulled for each other.

With all these changes happening in the fraternity, it was only natural that some of the brothers would feel that the old ways were better. After all, they had to suffer degrading antics during hell week, so why not these pledges? A few of the brothers tried to undermine my authority and power. Well, I accidentally gave them the opportunity.

As I mentioned, I am an Italian-American, and we are raised hugging and kissing our friends, male and female alike. One day I was in the parking lot of the university saying good-bye to a friend who was transferring to another school out of state. As we said good-bye, I hugged him and gave him a kiss, which he reciprocated. As fate would have it, a sorority girl from one of our sister organizations saw the kiss and started telling everyone that I was gay. She did not bother trying to understand that perhaps it was an innocent kiss between friends.

The rumor got back to me, and I decided to confront it. The issue for me was not whether I was gay but if my behavior had in any way reflected badly on the fraternity. At our next chapter meeting, I stood up and gave a little speech. "Well," I said, "there is a rumor going around that I'm gay. Now I don't recall having sex with any of you guys or even making a pass at any of you." This got a good laugh, because it was true. "So if you don't mind, I will just ask you to stop the spreading of this rumor until I give you cause. But if there is anyone who wants some good sex, then please let me know." Well, this caused more laughter and defused the situation. Mike, the new fraternity president, stood up and defended me and said that any one individual's sexuality was of no concern to anyone else, and he asked everyone to stop any rumors. He said that my behavior was exemplary and the fraternity was no place to make those kinds of judgments anyway. "This fraternity is open to all kinds of people, gay and straight." I was frankly quite impressed by his speech, and in fact it made me feel a little guilty that I had not just come out in the first place.

I graduated a while after that and fell in love. I was proud of my new relationship. About a year later at an alumni function, I was chatting with my old pledge brother Craig. I finally came out to him and told him about my boyfriend, Greg. I was surprised at how angry he became with the news. He was angry with me for not telling him in the first place. He said that after all my teachings about brotherhood and trust, I should have trusted him and told him about my feelings. He said, "Do you really think I would have respected you any less?" I felt like an ass.

All we could do was hug each other and laugh and cry.

I am very thankful for the love and support that my fraternity brothers have shown me over the years. This essay will be my coming out to many of them.

I am no longer afraid. I have learned to love myself and trust my feelings. I am sorry, guys, that I was so closeted that I was never able to share more of myself with you. I hope you can understand and forgive me. I was fighting for a higher principle than just my sexuality. I was fighting for the right for all of us to love each other. My years with you were some of the happiest that I have ever known.

Well, that was almost 20 years ago. I am 45 now. Greg died of AIDS-related complications more than 13 years ago, and I grieved his loss for many years. I have been together with my partner, John, for nine years now, and we have been married for over five years. Yes, we were married by a Catholic priest in the Lutheran church around the corner from our home. The trust that I learned in Sigma Pi I now am able to share with John.

I am still an activist and still a hippie, although my hair has been gone for a long time. Just as I have learned to love and trust myself and others, others have learned to love and trust me. I am way out of the closet now. I hope that this story may help a lonely frat boy somewhere find the courage to tell his big brother he has a secret that he would like to share. And I hope that all you big brothers hold those secrets close to your hearts along with the little brothers who so desperately need you. We all just want to be accepted and loved. We all want to believe in "sibaste pistis."

On Being a Gay Greek Adviser
by "Quentin Vig"

Their positive response set the tone for coming out to other brothers. Sharing allowed our friendship to grow. It felt great to have integrity, honesty, deeper relationships.

Gay Did Not Seem Like an Option

Throughout my high school and college years, I denied my feelings for—and attraction to—men. Being gay in North Dakota in the 1970s did not seem like an option, and I certainly did not relate to the few gays on television news or those in drag marching in parades in San Francisco or New York. I felt very alone, as if there were no one else like me who was attracted to men sexually and emotionally—who wanted more than just friendship. Gays were freaks; I was no freak.

Why Fraternity?

I joined Delta Tau Delta my freshman year over the objections of my parents. They did not want their son to be a "playboy." That was not my motivation. It was not the parties and the girls that attracted me to Delt. I felt like an outsider in high school, and the Delts offered me a home environment with warmer friendships than I experienced in my small town. If you were not a jock or rich, you did not count in the old hometown. The Delts cared more about the content of my character, my intellect, and my ability to be a friend. I felt alive with my friendships for the first time.

The brotherhood developed almost immediately. I invested much time in my new home, volunteering for work and positions of respon-

sibility, talking way into the night about any and all subjects. The bond
was forged, but my sexuality was buried deep within me. I had dates
for social functions but did not date otherwise. I preferred to spend
time with the brothers but did not let myself think of them sexually.
After all, I wanted children, and needed a wife.

Little Brother Bob

After completing my freshmen year pledging, and eventually serving
as president of the chapter, I was appointed to serve as the pledge educator. That fall of 1974 a pledge from western North Dakota picked me
to be his big brother. My "family" in the chapter was one of the largest,
and I was delighted to have another little brother to mentor. Bob was a
strong student, an accounting major, president of his high school student
council, involved in theater, and had a girlfriend for over two years. He
was good Delt material, and I was glad he was my little brother.

Bob and I became good friends, talked frequently, and enjoyed cultural events as well as college and state politics. Bob was a model
pledge. I was proud of him, and we enjoyed each other's company.
Many times his girlfriend would be a part of our visits and activities.

After his initiation and well into his second semester of college, his
relationship with his girlfriend changed. He did not talk much about it,
and I did not pry. During one of our late-night visits, he confessed that
he had been sleeping with men. Hesitantly, I was supportive of him; but
the details of his new life were making me uncomfortable, since I
longed for the same experience but was very afraid to act on the impulse. I was hoping to find understanding of myself by understanding
Bob, but I held back, being both drawn to this subject and afraid of it.

Bob Comes Out! I Stay in the Closet...

Bob came bursting out of the closet near the end of the second semester. Not only was he telling me about his sexual adventures on campus and around town, he was also telling a couple of the other brothers. There was plenty to tell, since he frequently visited the bathrooms
in the student union and in the campus library. I was amazed at how
many men he was having sex with, and I had no idea men were going

to public bathrooms to have sex. I cautioned Bob to be more discreet, but he did not seem to care.

Over the summer of 1975, the fact that Bob was gay was spreading among the brothers. The chapter adviser became very upset and was encouraging the chapter leadership to "take care of the problem." A small group of brothers was ready to bring Bob up for unbecoming conduct and started expulsion proceedings. I became scared for Bob and prepared to defend him at the first meeting of the year.

The tension was thick at the chapter meeting. As the "subject" was about to be brought up, Bob seized the initiative and stated, "There is talk going around that we have a gay brother among us, and we do; that brother is me." One of his pledge brothers said, "Bob, you blow me away—oops poor choice of words." That broke the tension. Bob's roommate, captain of the rugby team, quickly spoke up that Bob had earned his place in Delt and would remain one of his best friends. The tone was set.

Discussion went back and forth about our reputation, ability to attract pledges and women, and the meaning of brotherhood. The final vote was to overwhelmingly defeat the motion and not to proceed with expulsion. I remember closing my eyes and holding back tears of relief. The brothers were far more understanding and supportive than I had dared hope or believe possible. Good for Bob, but what about me?

Coming Out to Myself

During my second senior year, I came out to my little brother Bob, and he acted as my guide and mentor to the gay world that he had discovered on his own. A new world unfolded for me as I discovered friends in other chapters were gay, also. There were several late-night parties with 15 to 25 fraternity men having our own post-party at someone's apartment after the chapter parties were over. The group was composed of intellectual, hardworking, involved people like me. We also shared the fraternity experience, and the "secret interfraternity gathering" was both fun and exciting. I could identify with my new gay friends, unlike the gay images on television and in the print media. I was becoming comfortable with my sexuality and started to feel better about myself and my identity. But would my other friends understand, or would I be an outcast?

My little brother and I continued to have female dates at Greek events. However, as soon as most events were over, our dates were dropped off and we went out into our own world. Our social lives were full. One memorable evening I was double dating with my little brother to the Delta Gamma luau. We joined two other couples. The guys were big and little brothers at the Sigma Alpha Epsilon house—and gay. The eight of us were together all evening: at the pre-party, the luau, and the post-party. Laughter marked the evening, since we were dressed up in Hawaiian garb. We thoroughly enjoyed the irony of being at the party together with our female dates, but the DGs missed our special connections.

Coming Out to Brothers

My little brother Bob was pretty well-accepted in the chapter. Most brothers treated him well, and many friendships were deep. In this environment coming out seemed fairly safe, but I was still nervous. For several weeks I thought about how to come out to my closest friends in the chapter, letting them know that the dating was a cover—a lie—and that I was really attracted to men.

I waited until after graduation to tell anyone, and I traveled to a small town in South Dakota to tell my closest friend, Tom, where he was working that summer as a pilot. We walked in the country and talked of many things. Then I took a deep breath and told him I was gay. He paused and then looked at me and said, "You are still my closest friend, but I don't ever want to hear about this gay stuff again." Hmm. This did not go as I had hoped. I wondered if I should risk telling others or keep the secret to myself.

About three months later I met Tom and his fiancée (my dance partner from college classes and a wonderful friend) at a hockey game in Minneapolis. I brought along a mutual friend and a date, Aric, an SAE. At a time when Tom and I were alone, he asked, "Are you dating Aric?" At that moment I finally knew Tom was becoming more comfortable with my being gay. He was OK with me. Becky, his fiancée, played a large part in Tom's progress, since she was very supportive. For this I was thankful.

Tom has been a close friend for more than 20 years. This relationship is immensely important to me, as is my relationship with Becky. We talk of the joys and disappointments of life, share our concerns and fears, and care about what happens in each other's lives. More of my gay life is shared with Becky than Tom, because she is more interested. The "gay" subject is not avoided, but it is not dwelled on either. It is a comfortable, warm relationship that matured with honesty and integrity. The risk of sharing was worth it.

Coming Out Was Right for Me

Fortunately, the brothers with whom I was close in college remain close. With some I share more of my of my life than with others, depending on their level of comfort and interest. With some, gay issues are what we talk about (gay marriage, gays in the military, news events, etc.), and with others it is my social life and friends. My gay friends have always been welcome in their homes. Spouses have been particularly good in keeping our friendships going, which is true for other fraternal relationships as well.

The brothers have been wonderfully supportive for the most part, and certainly have been very supportive of my continued involvement as an alumni leader in the housing corporation, as an adviser, and as a fund-raiser. I had the advantage of forming a relationship before coming out to the brothers, but they also had the option of discontinuing contact over the years—and have not. There are alumni that I suspect are homophobic, but nothing hurtful has surfaced. Twice I have been recognized with the outstanding alumnus award, and I have been elected president of the housing corporation.

Our Adviser Is Gay

For several years I kept my personal life away from the undergraduates. In many ways this was a carryover from my first days of coming out—keeping my private and professional lives completely separate and compartmentalized. "The less said about my personal life, the better" was my motto. Tell no lies, but do not tell much. "Don't ask, don't tell."

After a time, however, people seem to notice when you do not have a female date at fraternity or other community events. The world seems to be made for couples, and single people draw attention. When brothers asked if I was bringing someone as a date, I was evasive. I did not feel good about being evasive. I had several mental debates about how to answer questions. I was not sure what was the best way, but I knew that I wanted to keep my integrity. That meant telling the truth, continuing to come out of the closet. Risky stuff. What if the brothers reject me?

I first came out to an undergrad brother ten years ago, when Brad asked the question, "How come you don't bring a date to our parties?" Brad and his roommate Scott were very entrepreneurial, and I had enjoyed not only working with them on fraternity matters but also giving them encouragement and advice on getting their sportswear business up and going. When Brad asked the question, I decided to take the risk—to tell the truth.

Brad responded amazingly well. He thought it was no big deal, and he seemed proud that I would share this information with him. Our friendship became stronger, and he sought opportunities to spend more time together. He encouraged me to come out to Scott. He too was very accepting and supportive, and our relationship grew. Their positive response set the tone for my coming out to other brothers. Sharing allowed our friendship to grow. It felt great to have integrity, honesty, and deeper relationships.

Brad and I grew close. This was the first brother with whom I shared my gay friends, went to gay bars, and included in the gay aspects of my life. We vacationed in San Francisco and Europe together, and he met my little brother Bob. Brad is a handsome man who has done some modeling and dancing onstage. He is very popular with and very comfortable around gay men. He will often dance with gay friends at a bar. He has lived for six years now half a continent away. We get together once a year and speak on the phone often. His wife of two years and I have become good friends, and she is every bit as supportive of gays as Brad.

For a decade now I have been open and honest to the undergrads. For the most part, the response has been very positive. There are those few brothers who avoid me, and I cannot say that it is always because I am gay. Maybe it is because I am an authority figure, or perhaps it is just a conflict of personality. But there have been no ugly incidents or harassment. There are some members I do not care for, and I do not seek them out. However, as an adviser, I must be accessible to all, and I am.

Sometimes new members will avoid me. If members do not make eye contact, or position themselves in a room away from me, I give them their space and let them deal with me from a distance. More often than not, time takes care of the avoidance and we begin relating to each other. Many times I am the first openly gay man they have had to be around or deal with, and it pays to let them adjust at their own pace. Luckily, it takes several semesters before some members get to be officers and chairmen, so we have time to work out those issues. By the time they are leaders, we are friends.

For the past five years, I have made the assumption that the brothers tell each other that I am gay. I do not wear my sexual orientation on my sleeve, nor do I hide it. When appropriate, I use gay humor around the guys. I am careful not to flirt with or hit on the guys, even in cases when a brother may be flirting with me. I do not want to jeopardize the comfort, trust, or respect that has been built up.

A Pledge's Antics

In the mid 1980s we had our first pledge who was openly gay. We have a split-level chapter house with windows on the lower-level bedrooms at ground level. Dave was having overnight visitors in his room who entered and left by the window. Chapter leaders became concerned about his behavior and told me after the fact how they approached the situation. Dave was told he would have to have his guests come and go from the front door like anybody else, and he was welcome to bring over anybody he wanted. Surprisingly, the issue was using the window as a door, not who was staying overnight. But Dave's social life got in the way of his academic life, and he did not make good enough grades to go active. He was popular, well-liked, and would have been a member had he done so. This situation opened my eyes about the brothers' attitudes—they were better than I realized.

A Member's Secret

Although I assume members know I am gay, one incident indicates that that assumption is not always accurate. Brian, a communications major and a junior, asked for an interview for a class. He needed to interview a community leader, and we agreed to meet at my home on a Saturday afternoon. After nearly an hour of questions and answers, he paused and asked me why I had not married. I smiled and responded that I had not found the right man yet. He just stared at me for a while, and then turned his face away. Suddenly I wondered how he was going to react. Brian was tall, muscular, and very manly. After processing my answer for a while, he put the writing pad in his lap. He looked at me and stated that his mother was in a lesbian relationship—not the response I was expecting. He had his own secret.

We talked for three more hours, including discussing his feeling that he could not share the information about his mother with anyone in the chapter. We spent many hours talking and sharing our lives. Honesty allowed me to be a better adviser and friend.

AIDS Quilt

I have been continually surprised by how mature and supportive fraternity men can be of gay alumni if given a chance. Two years ago I was on the committee to bring the AIDS quilt to campus, and in a chapter meeting I mentioned that the quilt was coming—an event they should not miss. Several guys volunteered to work on the project—without prodding from me. Four or five guys made two quilt panels to remember two of our 1970s alumni who had died of AIDS-related complications. They called family to get permission and secure all necessary information to make the quilt panels. I was very proud.

Sharing who I am with the brothers has been a positive experience. The honesty has fostered better communication, deeper relationships, respect, and trust. While serving as a chapter adviser, I also serve as an educator, providing new perspectives and insights on gays to people who may not have been around gays much. Pushing gay issues is not my style, but I also do not hide anything.

There have been unsettling moments of fear, doubt, and disappointment. I have felt hurt, anger, and loneliness when brothers were not very attentive or responsive when I have been down. But on balance my alumni and undergraduate brothers have been very supportive and have been brothers in every sense of the word. They are more supportive than my birth family and far more involved in my life. My sexual orientation did not distract from my ability to be a good adviser, or from my fraternity experience. I am a better person because of my fraternity experience and my gay experience and filled with more depth and empathy because of my gayness and my brotherhood. Approaching life with integrity and honesty has added to the fraternal experience for the brothers and for me.

We Are Everywhere!

I have served on two committees at the national level for six years. My sexual orientation is known and is, for the most part, a nonissue. There are homophobic people in key positions, but there are more advocates who are understanding brothers. There are several alumni who are also gay, and our fraternal bond has grown. We look forward to seeing each other at regional and national meetings and set aside time to visit in each other's company.

A recent committee meeting was held in Indianapolis, and another gay alumnus and I went out on the town after the meetings and meals were done. At a strip club we were enjoying the young dancers who were in the audience looking for dollar bills to be placed in their G-strings. One muscular stud was keeping me entertained, and I placed several bills in his pouch. He moved on to my good friend but stopped when he saw my companion's badge. He slipped him the grip, and we discovered a brother from DePauw University. We had a nice visit, and soon the other dancers were giving us much attention. The dancer was from a chapter in Indiana with a very homophobic bigwig. The irony and the attention was too much fun.

The following evening we went to a local college gay bar and discovered two former chapter consultants among the crowd. Both came out after they worked for the national fraternity and were surprised to see us. Our suspicions were confirmed, and a new bond was formed. We truly are everywhere!

Truth Succeeds, Always
by Michael T. McRaith

I was alone, isolated, and afraid. I fought the truth. The truth was confusion, the confusion was pain, and the pain tore from me the appreciation for each moment, each friendship, even my friendship with Brian. The pain consumed me.

Indiana University at Bloomington—a large, state-financed institution. A Greek system with a population of more than 4,000 students. My fraternity had between 75 and 90 live-in members, and I was one of the students in its collection of football players, ex-football players, drug fiends, womanizers, business majors, and those few others who roamed and sampled from all groups. Worked diligently enough as a student to graduate early with a double major. As a sophomore voted to the chapter's executive committee my first semester after initiation. As a junior, in the second election after initiation, voted chapter vice president. As a junior, selected to be one of nine IU fraternity members serving on the prestigious Interfraternity Council's judicial board. As a senior, chosen by other judicial board members to serve as chief justice. As a senior, chosen to be director of the student government's legislative relations department. As a senior, selected to be a member of Blue Key Mortarboard. As a senior, chosen and rewarded by the University administration for being one of four "outstanding Greek males." As a senior, recognized and rewarded for leadership, scholarship, and achievement by the administration of my national fraternity. As a senior, voted chapter "man of the year" by my fraternity brothers.

As a junior and senior, I shared a room with Brian, a childhood friend with whom I attended Catholic grammar school and an all-male Jesuit high school. He was a year younger academically, but Brian and I spent many years forming the bond that time and common experience forge between comrades. Every weekday for two summers, we worked side by side on the grounds crew of our high school. We played tennis after school, on weekends, and after work during the summers, scarcely missing a day. We hit balls back and forth, day after day, sometimes for hours, in rain, cold, or oppressive heat. Brian's mother and my father grew up together as neighbors. Our sisters were best friends. Our families were part of the same small, tightly knit group within our Catholic parish. Although I have two older brothers, my friendship with Brian was a fraternal relationship in ways not then understandable. Brian is not gay.

Despite my having several vague and distorted homosexual experiences during my last two years of high school, life as a gay man was inconceivable to me before and during my college years. As in high school, I maintained sexually intimate relationships with women. I enjoyed the challenge and gratification of a woman's consent and, ultimately, the ecstatic heat of sexual penetration. Occasionally, however, in a state of keg-induced inebriation, a word or hand would slip and my confusion and truth would stand naked before a stunned friend.

In the fraternity system of the mid 1980s, homosexuality remained a concept to be scorned. One brother would deride another with the label "fucking homo" or "fucking faggot." Rumors of homosexuality met with homophobic responses, rejection, and hatred. We did not know anyone who was gay, although we discussed openly the women who *must* have been lesbians. If we wanted to befriend or accept someone known to be gay, then we had to do so in secret, removed from the prospect of association.

At the time, only the "freaks" were openly gay. If we had actually *known* a homosexual, our phobia might have been adjusted. We simply did not have friends who came out. AIDS heightened homophobia because it was thought to afflict only homosexual men.

Objectively, my college years were successful. I did well academically. I earned recognition for leadership and achievement. I was prominent on campus. On a personal level, my girlfriend, Melissa, was intelligent and ravishing. Many people liked me. I had friends from all groups on campus. Yet I was alone, isolated and afraid.

I fought the truth. The truth was confusion, the confusion was pain, and the pain tore from me the appreciation for each moment, each friendship, even my friendship with Brian. The pain consumed me.

Pain sprung from every compliment and every success. These people did not know me. After two years of physical intimacy, Melissa did not know me. Brian knew only that I once confronted him with a foggy proposition for some uncomfortable sexual interaction. I maintained a safe emotional distance from every "friend," especially Brian, because the truth I was so frightened of required that I limit my exposure to vulnerability. I thought and believed that if people knew me, they would not like me. Homosexuality was my affliction.

Although I graduated a semester early in December 1986, I remained on campus until late March. From Bloomington I returned home to Evanston, Ill., where I spent several days prior to departing for a solo journey through Europe. During these several days I came to know that my parents were divorcing after five children and 25 years of marriage. Suddenly "future law student" became my only identity. Every important component of my life was literally a matter of history.

I traveled for two months, alone, on a train, with only a backpack and a journal, in nations where English was not the primary language and few citizens knew of Indiana University. Fewer still knew of my fraternity. All alone, minute after minute, immersed in solitude, I confronted my fear. I was afraid to be gay. But being honest meant admitting I was gay.

I had no choice. Brian—even Brian—would have to know.

I returned to the States and told some brothers with whom I felt a connection. With amazing haste my brothers spread the news that I was a faggot. One brother, who had expressed his heartfelt admiration for me only six months before, broke the news to Melissa in an effort to persuade her to sleep with him. She did.

After I revealed my homosexuality to a selected few, my insecurity and fear drove me away from those friendships that had developed over late-night conversations, road trips, parties, daily meals, team sports, all kinds of activities. When I did see my former friends and brothers, many were hostile, passive-aggressive, or could express only a salutation. Out of fear of rejection, I alienated myself from the brothers. I chose not to return telephone calls, and I declined invitations. Distance and new relationships provided safety for me.

I am now openly gay, proud to be who I am, and proud to be a part of the diverse gay and lesbian community in Chicago. I work hard to succeed as an attorney with a private law firm. I spend time and money in support of the homosexual political movement, primarily so that young men and women do not need to fear the truth, as I felt I did.

Nine years have passed, and I speak with none of my fraternity brothers.

Almost a year ago I telephoned Brian in an effort to engage him in conversation and to reestablish some strand of the friendship that had been so vital a part of my life. Brian did not return my telephone calls for six months. This is not hyperbole. Six months passed from my first phone call to him until I spoke with Brian. I felt like a spurned lover whose disinterested flame has caller ID. Finally, Brian and I met for drinks, and we talked. I explained that I was confused back then, that I was sorry but that I still had the same integrity and the same core that I had before the world came to know that I prefer intimacy with men. Whether he cared, I am uncertain.

My partner, Eric, was killed suddenly and tragically on July 30, 1996, and, prior to the funeral, in a desperate attempt to connect my past and present, I asked one of my younger sisters to call Brian. He did not return her call. Eric, who brought part of my soul to me, was dead at age 30. I lost myself in grief and, to this very moment, I feel Eric's absence as if it were a cold and wet shirt. Eric was dead, and I was and remain alone in the present, supported by my family and the tremendous heart of the gay and lesbian community. The past does not know me and cannot support me. The past did not know Eric, does not know that he died, and does not know that we loved.

I cannot overestimate the respect, appreciation, and love I have for my family and friends. I also cannot overestimate the pain caused by the absence of my fraternity brothers, especially by Brian's absence. Perhaps this pain is a testament to the value of honesty. Without honestly acknowledging our truth, without sharing that truth with our friends and brothers, what is the value of the friendship ? Today, I say, for me, those brothers were not friends. By fearing my truth, I lived with distance, ignorance, weakness, and isolation.

Eric's death and his interminable absence have taught me that truth succeeds. Always.

CAMARADERIE AND BROTHERHOOD

We must learn to live together as brothers
or perish together as fools.

Martin Luther King Jr., Alpha Phi Alpha

Family and the Bond of Brotherhood
by David Anglikowski

I asked myself: Do I want to join an organization that condemns someone who is gay? *I asked our pledge-class president, Chris: "What would it take for the fraternity to kick someone out?" There was only one thing that he could think of. The only reason that someone might be kicked out would be if he was gay. This was the answer that I feared. They would kick out a pledge, Chris told me, but maybe not a brother.*

There was something different about this fraternity that I liked. It was not the *Animal House* organization that I thought it would be. Yes, they drank. Yes, the members partied. So did I. But they had the right image about their partying. Yes, they could throw raging parties with 300 people on the beach, but they could also enjoy a nice Italian dinner with a good bottle of wine. It was this uniqueness that motivated me to pledge.

Only one of my new brothers knew about my dilemma—being gay. I had discussed my situation with Paul before pledging had even started. He was very supportive about everything I was going through, and now he was one of my pledge brothers.

As most know, pledging a fraternity takes up a great deal of time, so as pledging went on, I spent more and more time with my pledge brothers and the active members. This was when I began to notice their attitudes about homosexuality. I had become aware that I was gay, but they did not suspect because I did not give off any of the stereotypical gay signals. I did not talk with a lisp, swish my hips from side to side, or give any sexual glances. This was not because

I was trying to hide anything from them but simply because it was not me. As time went on, I started to notice the little jokes they made about gays. I joke with my gay friends about being gay, but we never cross the line of being offensive to each other. My brothers, unlike my gay friends, did not see this line.

Over the next few weeks, my ears became attuned to the references that were made about gays. Never once did I hear a positive one. The word "fag" came up as a derogatory term in every other sentence with certain brothers. Never once did I hear something that made me want to stand up and say, "Hey, I'm like that—I'm gay." The more comments I heard, the more I did not want to tell anyone. I asked myself: *Do I want to join an organization that condemns someone who is gay?*

I asked our pledge-class president, Chris, a question one night when we were driving over to one of the fraternity's houses. "What would it take for the fraternity to kick someone out?" There was only one thing that he could think of. The only reason that someone might be kicked out would be if he was gay. This was the answer that I feared. They would kick out a pledge, Chris told me, but maybe not a brother. They would only make it so that he would not want to be a member anymore. When I think about it, there are plenty of ways that the fraternity could make a person want to leave. Part of me can understand why. Many of the events that happen are geared for straight couples, thus it would seem out of place at something like a date dash to have two guys there together. Why does that have to be?

I had to think about what my integrity meant to me. Part of me thought that it was none of their business what my sexual preference was. But then another part of me kept thinking that I was being dishonest with them. The fact that I am gay is a part of who I am, and I was not sharing that part with them. I know they would not have accepted me if they knew I was gay when I pledged. Even if some of my brothers did not have a problem with me personally being gay, they might have a problem with having a gay man in their fraternity. The last thing they wanted was to be known as the "gay fraternity." It would kill the house.

During hell week I told the oldest pledge brother, Ray, that I was gay. We were outside at his car when I told him that I might not be at initiation. When he asked why, I told him that there were certain aspects of my life that the fraternity could not accept. Right then and there, he knew that I was gay.

We talked about my situation for a few hours that night. Ray had a totally different view from anyone else. He said, "It doesn't matter one bit. If you had enough self-esteem, then you wouldn't care who knew and who didn't." What meant the most to me was that he said, "I will stick by you if you decide to tell. If the others can't accept you, then they have the problem, not you." Coming from one of my pledge brothers these words meant something special. I had spent eight weeks with my pledge class, and a bond had formed that was very special to me, a bond I did not want to give up.

I ended up going to initiation the next Saturday, mainly because of my talk with Ray, but I have to say that it was not easy. Before the actual initiation they took the pledges into a room and gave a preparation speech. The alumnus who was speaking asked us questions. Questions that I could not answer honestly. Questions like, "Do you swear never to do anything that would intentionally harm the fraternity?" My being gay could definitely harm the fraternity. "Do you know of any reason you should not be initiated into this fraternity?" I am gay.

I did go through with initiation.

Since then I have not told any more of my brothers. Instead I have tried to get their views about the subject first. This is a hard thing to do without sounding like a queer. Gays do not come up much in conversation in a fraternity.

I honestly think that I will tell the fraternity. My fraternity has become my family, in a way. The bond of brotherhood makes us our own family. In any family there are those relatives that we love and cherish, those we are ambivalent toward, and those who we wish were not born into the same family. But in the end we realize that our family is our family and we love them because they are part of our family.

I know that if I do tell my brothers, not only will they know, but the whole school will know. Yes, it is a secretive organization, but secrets do leak. I need to be able to have my being gay become common knowledge before I can tell them.

My friend Megan, who is against fraternities and thinks they are full of narrow-minded, conservative drinking buddies who buy their friends, has advised me against telling my brothers. She is under the impression that I will be beaten up, because she has experienced negative attitudes from fraternities in her role as president of the gay group on campus. I am prepared to face physical violence if that is what it comes down to.

Since this was first written, I have come out to my fraternity. I have not told all of them, but the ones who should know do. The support I have received has been overwhelming. Many of the brothers were shocked at first, but they all seem to accept it. My situation has been awkward at times, but I know that my brothers are doing the best they can to be accommodating. I feel more comfortable around them, and at times I think I was silly to assume that my brothers, my family, would not accept me. The differences among the brothers is what makes a fraternity strong and allows brothers to learn and grow from fraternity experiences. I learned that brotherhood goes beyond gay or straight. If one can truly call the members of one's fraternity his brothers, then coming out should not be a fear. If the experience of coming out to a fraternity is negative, then maybe the brotherhood was never there.

Re: Defining Brotherhood
by Roland Sintos Coloma

I guess I have always been bisexual; I just never knew the correct term. Although I felt that a big burden was lifted off my shoulders when I faced my bisexuality, unfortunately I could not share this self-revelation with anyone. I was not ready to come out publicly, especially not to the fraternity.

I came to the United States right after I turned 13, when my family emigrated from Asia in 1985. Through American films and television programs shown in the Philippines, I thought of the United States as a placed filled with urban European-Americans with extravagant, carefree, and adventurous lifestyles. Since I was an immigrant and a person of color, these images fueled my growing desire to assimilate and to discard my true nature and culture. My arduous attempts to become "American" were manifested through the denial and shame of my ethnic heritage and family, my "native" language and accent, and other characteristics and features that marked me as different from the mainstream. My development as an adolescent was a conscious and painful process of assimilation in order to fit in, gain acceptance, and redefine my image and identity.

Going to college was never a question; it was more a matter of choosing which one to attend. I eventually chose a moderate-size campus in Southern California. It was far away from my family yet accessible enough for me to go home for the holidays. I felt that I had to be away from my family in order to develop and discover myself. I knew that I would be the only one from my high school attending this university, thereby allowing myself an opportunity for a fresh start.

The Quest(ion) for Brotherhood

I had consistently experienced problems in associating and interact-
ing with other men, specifically heterosexual men. There had been occasions when I had felt weird and different around them. It seemed that
my male peers and I hardly had anything in common, and I felt out of
place. I was more drawn to women because I was able to share more of
myself with them. I admired their inner strength, firm conviction, and
style of communication. I relied on them for emotional support. On the
other hand, men tended to focus on terse communication, fierce athletic and intellectual competition, and rigid definitions of status and reputation. There always seemed to be an invisible wall encouraging emotional and physical distance among men.

I thought that joining a fraternity would resolve my predicament in socializing with, relating to, or being in the company of men. The first week
of my freshman year in 1990 coincided with fraternity rush. I hesitantly decided to rush, afraid that I would not pass a certain set of unspoken, rigid
standards. I was very self-conscious and was not sure what I was getting
myself into. Swayed by the images engendered from movies about college
life, such as *Animal House* and *Revenge of the Nerds,* I knew the kind of fraternity house to which I would not want to belong. I sought after a group
that was actively involved on campus and had a respectable reputation, that
promoted leadership and academic values, and that ensured recognition
and easy access to social functions. Joining a prominent house would also
be, I thought, a key factor in my assimilation into the mainstream.

The rush process involved four grueling days of endless introduc-
tions, themed events, and self-marketing. I was thrilled when I was offered the chance to join by my first choice, one of the most popular fraternity houses on campus. My preconceived idea of college life would
not have been complete without fraternities and sororities in the picture.
Greeks seemed to dominate the social activities at that time on this campus as well as others. I wanted to be somebody, and yearned to belong.

The beginning of pledge period was Greek Games, a week of fun activities in which a fraternity house coupled with a sorority house com-
peted against other Greek pairs. Our fraternity was the three-time con-
secutive champion; therefore, my pledge class had big shoes to fill. I
became highly involved in two major events: the pledge pyramid and the

talent show. Since I was a member of the college cheerleading squad at the time, I had a large role in ensuring that my pledge brothers who had no dance, cheer, or stunt experience were properly coached. To prepare for some of the riskier stunts, my pledge brothers would usually practice lifting or throwing me up in the air before using a sorority pledge. The feelings of trust and safety as well as the resulting platonic intimacy that developed between me and members of my pledge class had a positive and enduring impact on my interactions with men.

Since our theme was based on the *Dick Tracy* movie for the talent show, I taught the actives and pledges how to dance to Madonna's "Vogue." Imagine me teaching more than 40 fraternity guys and sorority gals the intricacy and flexibility of voguing. Since I had already performed "Vogue" at a talent competition prior to entering college, I showed them the proper techniques for what they called the "swishy" arm and "limp" wrist movements as well as the mandatory fierce attitude and other accompanying bodily contortions. We watched the music video over and over to perfect our moves. Some of the actives from my fraternity commented on how some of the guys on the video looked like "faggots" and joked about how they felt so "gay" performing the routine. It required what seemed like endless rehearsals. At the end all of the hard work paid off, and we staged a successful show. But this was challenging to me emotionally and psychologically, since I knew that this was the time when questions and rumors regarding my sexuality arose.

I firmly believed that I could not have been "completely" gay. If behavior was the determining factor in sexual identification, then I would have and actually did label myself straight, since I had so far been intimate only with women, and this would remain the case until after I graduated from college. But calling myself heterosexual was a half lie, since it further negated my inherent attraction to people's overall aura and personality, regardless of their sex. I did not feel that I was hiding in the closet, but I could not escape the issue of my sexuality.

I never fully understood what *bisexuality* meant until I came across the anthology *Bi Any Other Name* in 1992. A bisexual identity was defined as the potential, not the requirement, for emotional, romantic and/or physical involvement with more than one gender, in either reality or fantasy. After reading the personal anecdotes in the anthology, I felt affirmed. I finally had found a term for—and other people who un-

derstood—my desires. Since identity had nothing to do with sexual behavior or history, I came out to myself as a bisexual during my sophomore year in college, prior to ever having sex with a man. I guess I have
always been bisexual; I just never knew the correct term. Although I felt
that a big burden was lifted off my shoulders, unfortunately I could not
share this self-revelation with anyone. I was not ready to come out publicly, especially not to the fraternity.

Survival in the Closet

Carefully conforming to a mainstream mode of male behavior, appearance, and language was my strategy of "straightening" up and "e-race-ing"
whatever made me different. I was also able to remain in the closet and
somehow quiet the incessant inquiries regarding my sexuality because my
fraternity brothers were aware of my relationships with women. I did not
feel that I was missing anything, since these relationships had been fulfilling emotionally, intellectually, and sexually. By no means did I intentionally use them to cover up my closely guarded internal struggle regarding my
sexuality. To some degree, my last college girlfriend and I made serious attempts to address my internal struggle. However, I was not and could not
be as honest with others, especially with my brothers in the chapter.

I assumed that most of my fraternity brothers would not understand
me since their attitudes and jokes were tinged with blatant and hurtful
homophobia. I did not have the courage or the words to describe my
feelings or explain bisexuality. I feared that coming out to my chapter
would result in my becoming marked as a social pariah in the Greek
system. I'd spent a long period trying to fit in and be liked; I couldn't
face rejection. I already worked hard to diminish my differences as a
person of color in order to easily assimilate and be accepted. There was
no way that I could consciously allow my sexuality to hinder my
"progress" into the mainstream.

One of my older pledge brothers asked if I was gay in a nonjudgmen-
tal tone. He told me that rumors had been milling around and that he
would rather find out from me since we were pledge brothers. Although
he had been very protective and understanding, I still did not feel safe
coming out to him. He confessed that it did not matter to him either way,
but he warned that there might be more direct queries. Therefore, when

the questions actually came, I was prepared to give a well-rehearsed response. My (bi)sexuality, which might have been discussed in other private circles, remained unspoken publicly within the chapter.

To deflect questions regarding my sexual orientation, I remained very involved in the chapter and on campus. I wanted to ensure that I was seen as an asset, bolstering our fraternity's reputation. As a chapter officer, I wrote an exemplary report to the international headquarters that garnered the fraternity's highest recognition. For my campus leadership and involvement, I received the coveted Greek Service Award and was admitted to an activities honors society. For my contributions, I felt invaluable and respected in my fraternity.

Discovery and Disclosure

Nonetheless, I remained marked. In fraternity pictures and gatherings, I was one of the few Asians and people of color, "brown"-ing the almost lily-white scene. While involved in the fraternity, I became active in ethnic organizations and groups advocating social justice. Through my interactions with other Asian and Pacific Islander student leaders on campus, I was able to understand and connect the historical patterns of discrimination, the current oppressive conditions, and the urgency to mobilize for social change.

Interestingly enough, many of these activists were either openly gay or very open-minded about sexuality. I was inspired by these queers of color who were comfortable with, and saw the link between, their race and sexuality. Our friendship forced me to intricately confront my earlier struggles regarding racial identification and gradually helped me to dismantle the illusion that assimilation would lead to a greater status in society. The painful realization and the empowering articulation of my racial identity were both liberating and challenging. I felt free from the confines of wanting to be "white," to be part of mainstream America, and to change my true nature in order to dissolve into the giant melting pot of American society.

They embodied a struggle for liberation. They juxtaposed the various forms of systematic and interweaving oppression and mandated our collective responsibility to fight on all fronts, since our liberation was similarly connected. Although I had come out to myself as bisexual, I was debating within myself the possible consequences of public revelation. Although I knew that certain friends would be supportive, I was

not courageous enough to lose my fraternity, my initial source of camaraderie, and confront physical risks and other complications.

Right after graduation in 1993, I was offered work at my alma mater
in a full-time student-services staff position. Realizing that I was in a
highly visible role on campus and would have a wide impact on student
life, I decided to come out publicly. I was beginning a career and was
financially and emotionally stable, which gave me the strength to be
honest about my bisexuality. My coming out had a domino effect, and
people found out even before I had told them. In most cases the responses were very supportive and understanding, although some of my
queer friends confessed that they had been suspicious and waiting for
some time. Once my family, coworkers and the friends I cared about
knew and demonstrated reassuring support, I felt a surge of relief, as if
another chain holding me down was broken and I was set free. In my
attempts to be honest with myself and others, to make myself whole and
complete, and to know the real "me" better, I also found out who my
true friends were and who accepted my true self.

I capitalized on this sense of liberty by continuing and expanding my
advocacy work, especially for the lesbian, gay, bisexual, and transgender
community. On campus I became a member and was then selected to be
a cochair of the Chancellor's Advisory Committee on the Status of Lesbians, Gays, Bisexuals, and Transgenders. I also helped begin a discussion group for Asian and Pacific Islander students who identified as lesbian, gay, bisexual, or transgendered or who were questioning their
sexuality. When I was an undergraduate, my friends who found harmo-
ny in their racial and sexual identities were my role models and sources
of support and advice. It was my sincere hope that I could give back to
this queer community of color what they had generously provided to me.

Brothers for Life or by Choice?

I was inspired and continuously aspire to live by my fraternity's three
founding ideals: friendship, sound learning, and moral rectitude. In my
opinion my fraternity exemplified the core values of brotherhood, academic achievement and campus involvement. On campus we presided
over the leadership of the Interfraternity Council and won many prestigious Greek Man of the Year awards. Our involvement crossed nu-

merous boundaries, from student government and intramural sports to community service and campus clubs. I was proud to wear those letters, since they represented honorable principles and significant contributions on campus and in the community at large.

But after my coming out, I consciously made limited interactions with my fraternity. Even though I worked at my alma mater for 3 1/2 years and was interested in working with the chapter, I rarely visited the fraternity house, participated in rush and alumni activities, or talked to new members. I no longer felt that I was welcome as a brother. Averted glances and uncomfortable conversations became the norm in my subsequent interactions with my fraternity brothers on campus. The silence of most of the alumni and active members indicated their discomfort and resistance against the acknowledgment of my sexual orientation, or, worse, my existence. I knew that some wanted to deny my fraternity affiliation. I faced the reality of what I had previously feared and painfully realized that certain kinds of "brotherhood" ran only skin-deep.

To my knowledge, there are other alumni from our chapter who have come out of the closet. I am sure that rumors have proliferated regarding my chapter's homosexual membership. Being tagged as the "faggot fraternity" has been a major source of gay baiting and denial within fraternities on campus. This reputation has been used cruelly and unfairly against our chapter by other houses during rush events. It would have been easy for me to reveal houses whose alumni I have seen and met in gay bars or pride events, but I do not play those games or by those rules. Yet when I was working on campus as an out bisexual of color, I somehow felt this enormous guilt for my chapter's slow decline in pledge numbers and overall status.

Now I remain in contact only with my little brother and a select number of alumni. My supportive little brother never fails to give me a warm brotherly embrace, even in public, and even celebrated his acceptance to law school with me and my male partner over dinner. In a note, I eventually told the truth to the brother who initially asked me if I was gay when we were still pledges. He thanked me for being honest with him and told me that if the chapter has a problem with my (bi)sexuality, then they have to grow up and deal with their own homophobia.

What kind of reaction would I get if I attended a chapter meeting now? What would my brothers think and do if I brought my male partner (who is also bisexual) to a chapter social or an alumni function? Would they expect me to act a certain way so that I would reassimilate, be "just like them" again? Would our conversations remain a nostalgic recollection of what it was like in the "good ol' days" when we were pledges or actives? Would we traverse borders, break the silence, and deal with the unspoken realities? I do not expect mere acknowledgment if that recognition continues to evade the issues of sexuality, race, and gender. I do not want false embraces from so-called brothers who perpetuate rigid rules of who and what types of men should belong in the fraternity. What I want is a sincere commitment to uphold the fraternity's founding ideals of friendship and brotherhood. I want fraternities, in general, to critically evaluate themselves, including their recruitment, selection, and training of pledges; their development of actives as leaders on campus and beyond; and their incorporation of alumni as mentors, advisers, and brothers. Only through this honest examination can fraternities begin to comprehend their crucial role in the development of responsible men.

Fraternities are strong socialization forces in colleges and need to challenge themselves to remain true to the principles set by their founding fathers. They are a part of an educational process that defines manhood and reinforces certain social norms and mores. They have a responsibility to address pertinent issues—especially on race, gender, and sexuality—that affect all students and their surrounding communities, and they must embrace the university's ideals of a diverse educational environment. They need to hold each other accountable and establish an honorable set of standards to measure progress. Fraternities can serve as role models for the campus and community at large. I am a product of the Greek system. My experiences as a pledge and an active member are valuable and, for better or worse, have made me who I am today.

Fraternity life was definitely a valuable experience but could have been better for me had there been more understanding, acceptance, and recognition of differences in sexuality. Going back into the closet is definitely not an option, now or ever. My fraternity brothers' inability to accept and respect me, much less my work with the lesbian, gay, bisexual, and transgender community, is no longer my problem. I have dealt and continuously live with the scars of my painful and internal struggles regarding my race and sexuality. I want to help put an end to the pervasive homophobia, racism, and sexism within the Greek system. But where are my allies? Where are my brothers?

Never the Only One, Never Alone
by Juan Felipe Rincón

Many would be inclined to call Seal and Serpent a "gay" house. To the degree that a gay house is a house where a gay man can feel welcome, comfortable, and proud, I guess Seal and Serpent would be a gay house. For me, Seal and Serpent is more than just a gay house. It is a place where sexuality, religion, and ethnicity are not the defining characteristics of the individual. It is a place where ROTC members and peace-studies majors meet, where atheists and practicing Jews have fun together, where Republicans and Democrats get along, and where gay and straight live together in a spirit of mutual respect and camaraderie.

"Oh, I want to do all these things to you, I'd make you so happy," he whispered in my ear. Alan rarely whispers. Alan is one of the loudest people who lives here.

Yet this was whispering material: "I feel these feelings, and I want to make you feel good."

He had more to drink that one night of homecoming than he had ever had before or anytime since, and he was telling me he loved me. Yet he would never have said that while sober, at least not with his tongue in my ear. Alan would not have tried such a thing. He would not have told me about his wanton glances at the other men in our house; he would not have hit on one of our alumni; he would not have tried to obtain a kiss from me. Sobriety exerted no control over Alan that night.

I am one of the few close gay friends Alan has. I live in the same house. We are brothers of the same fraternity. I am out to everyone. Before that night he was out to a few very close people, myself included. That night he pounded open a window in his closet, through which he now dares to look out. I made ashes of my own closet many years ago and have not had a need or desire to rebuild one. He is trying to understand what he wants; I knew in tenth grade. Regardless of that, Alan that night seemed to need to hear the words that he would not tell himself.

As alumni relations director, I was in charge of all the homecoming events. I could not afford to handle a crisis. I could not afford to have my own pent-up sexual energies aroused while 40 alumni and their spouses vied for my organizational energies. (Sure, I am a selfish fool. I should have my office as cochair of the Cornell Lesbian, Gay, Bisexual, and Transgender Coalition revoked. I should not be considering myself a well-adjusted member of our community if I cannot handle that situation.) A little nagging voice inside me decided that I would set out to talk to him that evening, regardless of his state, regardless of my obligations. *Coming-out crises come first in any set of priorities,* that little voice said.

Alan was getting harder and harder to control. Frederick, an alumnus who was visiting for the weekend with his partner, was fortunately within eyesight. As I sat Alan in the living room, I told him I would return in a couple of minutes as soon as I sorted out two last things downstairs, where the alumni were reminiscing about old times. Frederick looked my way and, with a couple of words exchanged between us, knew what was up and what to do.

I sorted out whatever it was that I went downstairs to sort out and returned to find Frederick sitting in the living room, listening to Alan pouring out years of repressed thoughts and memories. I joined them, hoping that Frederick's presence would make it easier to avoid an unpleasant situation. I should not have worried. If Frederick had not been there, Gregory, one of the brothers who almost joined us downstairs, would have been enough protection, since he sauntered in and sat to behold the spectacle of Alan talking. But I really should not blame Gregory, since two others soon joined him and sat down. I will say this once again and a hundred times more: Unless you go and lock yourself in a closet, having a private conversation is not possible in Seal and Serpent.

Alan said more things about himself and his thoughts, emotional and sexual, than he had ever shared with me or anyone else in the house. Gregory was not really as concerned as many other heterosexual men would have been when Alan mentioned that he was someone who had been lingering in his erotic and suppressed subconscious. Gregory was more worried about Alan's being able to be honest with himself without a dozen drinks.

Finally, two of the brothers had to leave. Frederick joined his boyfriend in their room, and Gregory and I were left to tend to Alan. I decided that the best thing to do would be to take him to where he was sleeping that weekend and make sure he was safe. As I held Alan, Gregory got his sheets and blankets. Alan once again started saying things in my ear, trying to kiss me, wanting me to stay with him. After much pushing and prodding, I managed to help Alan into his spot on Tony's floor, apologized to Tony for the inconvenience, and figured we would talk about this whole situation in the morning.

The events of homecoming 1996 allowed me to reflect on my fraternity membership and how fortunate I was.

I remember the first time I had heard of Seal and Serpent, apart from noticing its odd name on a campus map, was when one of my orientation counselors pointed at the house and said, "That's Seal and Serpent. That's the gay house. But they keep it really neat and clean." I wish I had thought of asking her what she meant by calling it the "gay" house. There did not seem to be anything about it that was particularly gay. It was the usual situation, in which some group, comfortable enough with itself to not care about someone's sexual orientation, is labeled as the "gay" something-or-other.

I did not arrive at Cornell particularly receptive to the idea of fraternities. I did not have any intention of putting myself in a situation in which I would have to be subservient to someone else and in which I would have to endure physical and emotional abuse and humiliation to be a part of some abstract ideal like "brotherhood." I had only abhorrence for the womanizing, homophobic, racist, elitist, bigoted, and exclusionist superficiality that the Greek system symbolized in my mind. I wanted no part in that.

I became involved in queer activism on campus fairly quickly. I had been out since tenth grade and was really looking for that outlet. Some described me as the gay organization's poster boy because I was there all the time, active in everything, loud and chanting and proud as a newly arrived freshman. I participated in support groups, went to rallies, chalked, postered, volunteered. Fraternities were rarely more than something to use when in need of a punch line. I had no intention of participating in rush and remember seeing my roommate coming back from different rush parties in varying states of sobriety, always commenting on what flakes these people he had met were and how much he was not into the whole "frat" thing.

I went back to my parents' home in Costa Rica for the holidays and returned to Cornell the first day I could enter my dorm room, a day that coincided with fraternity rush. I got a call from my friend Don's girlfriend, saying that another friend of hers had told her that they were having this rush thing at his house and that she should come over and bring friends along. I really was not in the mood to go to a frat party. The three I had gone to before were shamelessly dull, with a bunch of freshmen overly excited about standing around, drinking watery beer, and listening to some drunken man's impression of good music. But I did not have an excuse, and I really did not have many other things to do.

As we walked there, I giggled to myself, wondering what their reaction would be if I asked if they had any rules against incest. I opted for prudence rather than wit that night. I would give this place a chance to prove itself.

The first thing that struck me as I walked into my first Seal and Serpent party was that, along with the usual beer, people could choose from Zima and Snapple. I made a note of that. Not many fraternities I knew would think of offering a beer substitute, let alone a case of bottled juices.

I moved along, sat on a bench, and watched as the whole thing unfolded. I recognized a couple of faces, one from a comedy troupe I had enjoyed seeing in the fall and one who was a friend of a friend of a friend, but it seemed like a frat party. My friend's girlfriend introduced me to someone whose parents were Colombian. We talked about soccer, a particularly unappealing subject to me. I did my best to be charming.

Someone else invited me to go on a tour of the house, and I figured I would take a look. It all did seem neat and clean. The guy who was giving us the tour was friendly and unusually nonfratlike. It did not seem much like a "frat" at all.

I knew this place was different two days later when, at an event Don had dragged me to, one of the brothers—who would eventually become my big brother—asked me what I did on campus. I answered quite frankly, "Oh, I'm in the orchestra, I'm in Cornell National Scholars, I do AIDS activism, and I'm also in the gay, lesbian, bisexual, and transgender coalition." He then went on to ask me about the role of Cornell's health services in AIDS awareness campaigns on campus and the role the coalition played politically in light of the conservative backlash last November. We got into an incredibly pleasant conversation about governmental involvement in the creation of AIDS policy, without even a hint of discomfort. He said during the conversation "Some of us are gay, some of us are not. It really is not an issue here." It struck me that he used "us" to describe everyone, that he did not make an effort to disassociate himself as a straight man from the out gay brothers in the house. It made an impact.

A few conversations later I was convinced that there was something different about this place. People were interesting, stimulating, different, accepting. Disagreement kept a degree of cordiality. When they organized events, they tried different things and made sure all had something to be happy about. Their description of their independence, their alumni involvement, their goals, their expectations, and what they wanted to get out of their experience at Seal and Serpent sounded inspiring. I surprised myself when I signed the invitation to join and began pledging a week later. I was not quite sure why I was joining Seal and Serpent. I knew only that I would have an interesting undergraduate experience living in that 70-year-old house

I mentioned to our pledge educator a couple of weeks into pledging that I was concerned because I did not know if I was out to everyone in the house. He told me a number of stories about brothers, about the past ten years in Seal and Serpent, and about the days when more than a third of the active brothers were gay. He never really answered my question on whether they had discussed my sexuality during their rush meetings, but after our conversation I did feel that just casually mentioning it would not be a big problem.

I did not need to worry. I was involved in a protest later that week in which a large group of us activists sat in the Plant Pathology Department's offices. We were protesting a professor's abuse of his position as a faculty member at Cornell to give veracity to his advertising of a "cure" for homosexuality—mostly a collection of pseudo-religious, pseudo-scientific, homophobic rhetoric. The *Cornell Daily Sun* published a cover story on the sit-in the next day, and to my surprise I was shown right in the middle of the picture that went with the headline GAY STUDENTS TAKE OVER OFFICE. That picture saved me 20 individual conversations.

I received hurrahs and encouragement from the brothers. Questions came from many places, but they were all positive, supportive, or simply curious. This was a group of men in which the label attached was not important, in which I could be who I am without leading some sort of double life.

Seal and Serpent's support has been tremendous. I feel I can invite my activist friends over and know they will want to come. I feel I can mention I am in a fraternity with independent-minded people and justify it with truths. I am currently organizing a support and social network for gay, lesbian, and bisexual members of the Greek system. I know that I can count on Seal and Serpent's support.

Out alumni of Seal and Serpent have been instrumental in the establishment of Cornell's Gay and Lesbian Alumni Association. Seal and Serpent's gay alumni live and work in all areas, come back with their partners, and always know they will feel welcome. Alumni from the 1960s who have since come out, have visited our house, have come out to the brotherhood, and have been surprised at how few ripples it caused.

I was one of two out active brothers last year. Coming into this fall, I was the only out active. While Alan was pledging, he let me know that he had received one of my mass e-mail messages announcing a volunteer workshop for our campus homophobia-awareness group, and I understood. His homecoming weekend and the conversation we had the next day put him on the way to coming out as bisexual and feeling that he could be honest about who he was. Alan will not be the last out brother at Seal and Serpent, not if it continues being an open-minded place for all brothers.

Many would be inclined to call Seal and Serpent a "gay" house. To the degree that a gay house is a house in which a gay man can feel welcome, comfortable, and proud, I guess Seal and Serpent would be a gay house.

For me, Seal and Serpent is more than just a gay house. It is a place where sexuality, religion, ethnicity, and nationality are not the defining characteristics of the individual. It is a place where ROTC members and peace-studies majors meet, where atheists and practicing Jews have fun together, where Republicans and Democrats get along, and where gay and straight live together in a spirit of mutual respect and camaraderie.

How did Seal and Serpent get there? I do not know. Our house has gone through every phase in its 92 years of existence. We have been the jock house and the glee-club house, the party house and the house of campus leaders.

There has been a consistent search for the "different" by the members of Seal and Serpent. Alumni from forty and fifty years ago emphasize the same characteristics that we are proud of today: individuality, mutual respect, diversity, closeness. I am thoroughly convinced that it is the manifestation of that diversity that has taken Seal and Serpent to where it is today—where its members speak out about themselves and make their own experiences known. It has been easier for new brothers to come out at Seal and Serpent over the past few years because there has been at least one out brother in the house throughout that time. The impact of that visibility cannot be downplayed in my mind. It determines whether a house is accepting in practice, in theory, or not at all. And it is not restricted to sexuality. The expression of one's identity is essential if he is to be respected and appreciated. Seeing others feel pride in their own identities is a form of empowerment. Individual strength gives a house its power to maintain true diversity and remain strong.

When I thought of Greek life as a freshman, I thought of beer bashes; rampant homophobia; racial, religious, and ethnic homogeneity; institutionalized sexism; and general obnoxiousness. I saw in Seal and Serpent a place where those things did not exist, where diversity was not a buzzword but a reality. I think of Seal and Serpent as something closer to the original ideal of a fraternity—promoting the growth of its members intellectually, socially, culturally, and emotionally. I believe Seal and Serpent is close to accomplishing that goal.

Truth and Brotherhood
by Shane L. Windmeyer

I finally came out and said the words, "Jon, I am gay." Tears ran down my face with those words as I began to cry. If he had not said, "Shane, it's OK," and reached out to give me a hug, I think that in my emotional state I might have considered committing suicide that evening. I truly felt alone and afraid, the most isolated I had ever felt. Jon, by showing his love and support, made that evening a changing point in my life. I had come out, and his response had made all the difference.

My first time over to the Phi Delt house was for a Super Bowl Sunday party. It was during my sophomore year in the spring of 1992 at Emporia State University in Emporia, Kan.

All I remember is that there were 25 guys and a handful of girls sprawled across couches, chairs, pillows, and cushions, drinking beer, eating chili, and watching the football game. All eyes were intently focused on the 23-inch tube, watching whatever team get the tackle, intercept the ball, and make the touchdown. Don't ask me who was playing. I still do not know. The only football player that comes to mind today is Troy Aikman. Go figure.

Commercials were time for an occasional introduction to other guys in the house, refills on beer, and more chili. Halftime entertainment was a female porn flick on the VCR supposedly for all to enjoy and to raise spirits for the last half of the game. At key points in the game, some of the guys would yell and clamor on the edge of their seats while others grunted in idle disgust. And there I was, two touchdowns later, ringing a cowbell and cheering while others hollered from across the room, "Yeah, man…score!"

Memories can be scary things. I had limited knowledge of both football and fraternities that Sunday. But I knew just enough to fit in with the other guys. That Sunday was probably one of the most stereotypically heterosexual, testosterone-driven days to visit the fraternity house. And—believe it or not—I liked it.

I liked it so much that, a bowl of chili later, I found myself signing an interest form listing my GPA, skills, talents, and favorite sports (not football)... and who knew? Before the next tackle and two bites of chili, I was a brother of Phi Delta Theta fraternity.

Not surprisingly, that Super Bowl Sunday represented everything that I knew I was not—and yet what I deeply desired to be. I thought that joining Phi Delta Theta was a way to try to be someone else—a way to deny to myself that I was gay. The last thing I ever wanted to be in life was a faggot, as gays were often referred to in high school. That word was something my mother despised, my friends ridiculed, and I held closely as my personal secret. I felt that fraternity life was the ideal remedy for being gay and the best disguise to fit in among the campus community. I naively thought that by joining the fraternity, learning to like football, and possibly watching more of that halftime entertainment something might change.

And I was pleasantly surprised. Over the next four years, things did change. I learned some more about the game of football, the fraternity, and myself. Most important, I came to value the sense of brotherhood and support that my chapter had to offer. We shared so much together—nicknames, pepperoni pizzas, shaved heads, and the occasional compact disc that somehow never got returned. I vividly remember the late-night "jock jogs" to the sorority houses (optional, of course), the early-morning "bangin' pots and pans" sausage-and-biscuit breakfasts at the house, and the never-ending road trips to anywhere but Emporia, Kan. One of my favorite annual fraternity events was a philanthropy for the local battered women's shelter where we sat atop a ten-foot pole for more than 32 hours and gathered financial donations from passing motorists on the street below. Sounds crazy, huh? Times like these created fond memories and forged close bonds among the brothers. Of course, we also enjoyed the pleasure of late-night partying at the local bar, Bruffs. But it was also not unusual to find brothers studying and helping one another with difficult classwork or providing occasional emotional support when a brother's family member passed away. In all respects, we were a family. As such, I learned to care deeply and to be proud of my brothers, and in return they also taught me to care for and be proud of myself. I believe that it was through this brotherhood that I finally learned and accepted that I was indeed gay.

Coming out is not easy for anyone. I was just as afraid as the next person of the possible rejection from my family, friends, and, in this case, my fraternity. Even though I was vice president of the chapter, had held numerous chapter leadership positions, and had recently won an award for leadership from our international fraternity headquarters, I remained fearful that somehow the brothers would not accept me after being told the truth—that I was gay. The practice of immersing myself in campus leadership activities and winning awards had become one way of proving my worth as a "good" person. I thought if I could do one more activity or win another award, somehow that would prove that I was "OK," and it would be easier coming out to my parents, friends, and the fraternity. I was tired of lying to my family, my friends and especially my brothers. I felt guilty, a hypocrite, for not telling my brothers that I was gay and for not relying on the unconditional support and brotherhood that I had come to know. I was petrified that the brotherhood I held so high would fail to live up to the challenge of my coming out. I feared that everything I had worked so hard to accomplish in the chapter would be forgotten if they knew I was gay.

The pressure to come out increased when I learned that I was selected for an academic internship in Washington, D.C., the following semester. I knew that I had to tell my brothers the truth and put my faith in brotherhood. Luckily, I had many brothers who supported me and stood by my side during this difficult time. I came out to each brother individually, one after another. They had similar and yet unique reactions. One said, "I thought you might be. That's cool. Don't worry, you are still and will always be my brother, Shane. I love you, man." Another brother said it a little differently: "I am sorry. Is everything OK? I want to be here for you. You are a brother, no matter what anyone tells you. Always remember that." Probably the most difficult person to come out to was Jon. He was the first person (and the first brother) I had ever come out to. Jon and I had spent a lot of time together the past year, and I was one of the brothers who got him to consider joining the fraternity. We hit it off right away, and I was extremely committed to our friendship. He was everything I ever wanted in a brother growing up. He was carefree, thoughtful, strong-willed, intelligent, and an all-around great guy to have as a friend. I felt that if he rejected me for being gay, no one else, including my family, would accept me either. Thinking back on this moment, I feel very fortunate to have had Jon as my brother. After rambling about how I value his friendship for what seemed like forever, I finally came out and said the words "Jon, I'm gay." Tears ran down my face with those words as I began to cry. If he had not said. "Shane, it's OK," and reached out to give me a hug, I think that in my emotional state I might have considered committing suicide that evening. I truly felt alone and afraid, the most isolated I had ever felt. Jon, by showing his love and support, made that evening a changing point in my life. I had come out, and his response had made all the difference. A few weeks later I made the announcement that I was gay in front of the entire fraternity during a chapter meeting. The brotherhood endured. My brothers stood by my side then and continue to stand by my side today.

My friendships with the brothers continued to grow the following year after I had come out. Many of the brothers with whom I lived in the chapter house would ask questions and would even joke with me about gay and straight stuff. One brother would joke, "Why did you join a fraternity? To get a date?" I would smile and simply reply, "If that were the case, I would have joined another chapter on campus." Such jibing would be followed by laughs and another sly reply. I realize now that for some of these brothers, the bantering humor was their way to express their feelings and show support for me.

I specifically remember one night when several brothers were going out to a "gentlemen's club" (a female strip bar) and failed to invite me. I asked if I could come along, and some brothers looked oddly at me and said, "Sure, why not?" To my surprise, I was the first guy approached that night to receive the so-called pleasure of a table dance. Of course, I felt obliged to tip the woman. So I wrapped my dollar bill in an inconspicuous spot around one of her few choices of straps and left it at that. She continued doing her stuff on the table and moved on. All of us got a big kick out of it and really enjoyed the irony of the situation. I think after that night, several brothers, including myself, realized that being gay or straight does not really matter when it comes to brotherhood and having a good time.

A month later, on a Saturday night, a few brothers even decided to accompany me to a gay bar called the Cabaret in Kansas City. Trying to live up to my "straight-acting" performance at the female strip bar, one of my straight brothers placed a dollar bill into the G-string of a male dancer who was previously dressed for a very short time as a policeman. Definitely a law enforcement moment I will never forget. As a joke I sent that brother for his graduation gift a card with a dollar bill for the next time we go out. He laughed and said, "Sure, why not?"

My fraternity experience was very positive, and I think it truly reflects the brotherhood's reaction to my coming out. To them, I do not believe that it was a big deal having a gay member in the chapter. We all shared an understanding of the meaning of brotherhood and would never think of hurting another brother for any reason. Such an atmosphere was safe for gay and straight brothers alike and fostered a strong diversity of opinions and ideas within the chapter. As a result, another active brother came out to the entire chapter shortly thereafter. We even rushed someone who was gay the following semester. Immediately after coming out, I continued to discover gay members in Phi Delta Theta and other fraternities on the ESU campus as well as other campuses. Suddenly we were everywhere! Gay men in every house on campus, actives and alumni. You would have thought gays were among the founding fathers of every fraternity. I would not be surprised if that were the case.

Phi Delta Theta taught me many lessons about myself over the course of four years, and I continue to learn more as I reflect on my fraternity experience. I once thought that if I could learn to like football, then I could learn to be straight too. Since then I have watched an occasional Super Bowl and a few games on *Monday Night Football*. I have even run for a touchdown and thrown my underwear on a goalpost at 3 A.M. But no matter how much I try to learn to like football, I still cannot change who I am. Phi Delta Theta showed me how to be proud of who I am, and my fraternity brothers have proved that truth and brotherhood can prevail over homophobia.

I'm In, I'm Out!
by Wil Forrest

I proceeded to playfully jump in the closet and then out again, repeatedly chanting the words "I'm in...I'm out." It finally clicked for him, and he promptly embraced me. He told me he was happy to hear that I was gay, because he was too.

I love being a gay Greek man, but it was not always that way. As I look back now, I realize that being both gay and Greek was more challenging and rewarding than being either of the two separately. Being both has frightened me; being both has comforted me; and being both has helped me to define who I am to myself and others. When I was in college, though, I had a hard time comfortably incorporating these two aspects of my life.

When I think about my experiences of being a gay Greek man, a couple of images instantly come to me: first, the fear and uncertainty of coming out to my brothers, and second, the stress and relief I felt as I attempted to reconcile these aspects of myself.

In the spring of 1991, as a sophomore, I joined Pi Kappa Phi fraternity after loyally rushing for two semesters. Beyond the invitation to become a member, I was not sure what I sought by rushing. Maybe I wanted the opportunity for companionship, leadership, and scholarship. Maybe I wanted to appear straight to an unaccepting world. Maybe Greek life was the last undergraduate frontier I had not yet conquered. I was not quite sure of my motivation. I just knew I had to become a Pi Kapp, and so I did.

Soon after accepting my invitation to become a Pi Kapp, I sought leadership positions within my chapter, and I quickly found myself on the executive board as the secretary. Being an executive board member in the chapter, I felt that I had commanded respect and had become invaluable to the fraternity. To avoid difficult topics and situations, I kept my relationships with many of my brothers business-oriented. I do remember that on some level I was always afraid to be completely myself with my brothers.

That spring two close female friends asked me to live with them the following summer. However, they thought that before I accepted their invitation, I ought to know that they were a lesbian couple. This was an excellent opportunity to finally tell others about my hidden sexual orientation, and so I did. I uttered the words, "I never thought I would tell anyone this, but I am gay." They were not as shocked to hear me utter these words as I was.

Coming out was liberating! Soon thereafter I came out to some other gay friends. I was still apprehensive about coming out to many of my straight friends, including my fraternity brothers. Would straight people understand? Because of the pressure in my chapter to conform and be straight, I felt I had to form a strong support network among my non-Greek friends before I could reveal my true feelings to my fraternity brothers.

Eventually I came out to virtually everyone except my brothers. To find ongoing support and to hide from my unsuspecting brothers, I accepted my lesbian friends' invitation and moved into an apartment that summer with them and my boyfriend. Each week was carefully divided between being social with my fraternity brothers and my gay sisters. Still, I was afraid of being both Greek and gay; I felt safe and confident being just one or the other but not both. Something had to change.

With my new living situation and my many new gay friends, I knew that my best friend in the fraternity, Chili, would be suspicious. I had to tell him I was gay. Because of prior conversations, I had a feeling that he also had homosexual tendencies. One day Chili stopped over as I was hanging up some shirts in my small walk-in closet. He inquired about why I had wanted to talk with him. I said that I needed to tell him something, and I proceeded to playfully jump in the closet and then out again, repeatedly chanting the words "I'm in...I'm out."

It finally clicked for him, and he promptly embraced me. He told me he was happy to hear that I was gay, because he was too. We were both relieved and comforted by the understanding and compassion we shared. As a result, we became even better friends as we became more out, but we still opted not to tell other brothers about being gay. We hid the secret from our brothers for as long as we could, partially to give ourselves time to develop strong support systems in case we lost our friends in the chapter and also to avoid the probable misunderstanding and persecution from unaccepting brothers. We knew we could not hide forever.

Later that summer I was confronted by one of my dearest fraternity brothers, with whom I used to live in the residence halls and who was as straight as an arrow. He said he heard that Chili and I were at "one of those gay parties held in town." Next he asked me the question, the one I dreaded since I first stepped in my fraternity house: "Are you gay?"

I remember pausing and pondering my response. I knew that if I were truthful, my fraternity life could be ruined. I knew if I were dishonest, one of the most important relationships I had in college would be forever tainted. I looked him in the eyes and came out.

"Yes, it's true," I said. "I was at some gay parties…and I'm gay." He quickly replied, "I'm sorry." Confused by this remark, I asked him why he was sorry. He went on to say that he was sorry if he had ever said or done anything that made me feel uncomfortable when we had lived together. At first I was shocked by his selflessness and his emotional focus on my feelings, then I was relieved by his caring and supportive words. We continued to have an honest and comforting conversation. He told me that he knew other gay Greeks and that he was supportive of them, as he wanted to be for me. He agreed that it might not be easy to come out to the chapter, but he pledged to be by my side. My brother opened a door to a new world, one where I could be completely myself.

Gradually over the next semester, both Chili and I came out to brothers individually and in small groups. Many told other brothers before I did, but no one was rude or overtly unaccepting. I was never insulted or intimidated by any of my brothers. In fact, many inquired about being gay. They asked me about myths and stereotypes that they had heard and other assorted questions. Most incorrectly assumed that Chili and I were a couple because we were both gay and had spent time together. This was a wonderful educational opportunity. I could explain that gay people can be friends without being sexually involved. Furthermore, several of my brothers told me about bisexual experiences or tendencies. A few more brothers even came out to me personally or the entire chapter.

My brothers' unconditional acceptance and support helped me move from being afraid of my brothers to being at peace with their companionship. It was important that I was self-confident about being gay and not covert and apologetic. Consequently, my brothers saw that I had no problem with being gay, so they had no problem with it. It also helped immensely to have a brother like Chili with whom to share the coming-out process. We relied on one another, and we demonstrated to the chapter that chapter leaders and ordinary brothers could be gay and it was OK!

Fully reconciling being both gay and Greek was difficult to achieve, though. I knew when I started dating a Greek man from the fraternity next door that some of my brothers would not be quite ready for this. We attended several fraternity parties at not only my fraternity house but also my boyfriend's. We were both quite nervous, but we met with indifference from our brothers. Since neither my boyfriend nor I were into public displays of affection, many brothers did not even make the connection that we were together, and the ones who did never said a mean word. The chapter was entering a new level of understanding, of unconditional brotherhood.

My brothers amazed me. I often feel bad about my original stereotyping of them as closed-minded "frat boys," when in reality they were rather mature men who saw me as a friend and a brother. My caring and supportive relationships with many fraternity brothers have outlasted the relationships I had with anyone I dated in college. These fraternal relationships have weathered many rough storms and offered me unconditional love and support. Even though I have tested my brothers' definition of being a Pi Kapp, I am confident that during their struggle to understand what it means to be gay and be Greek, they have learned something, and so have I—brotherhood.

A STRAIGHT BROTHER'S PERSPECTIVE

Being Straight Did Not Help
by Thom D. Chesney

Sadly, it has taken me ten years to realize how much I regret not reaching out to a brother who shared his most personal secret with me, hoping that I might help him find a way to do the same with our entire chapter.

I left the generally quiet and conservative environment of Sioux Falls, S.D., in the fall of 1984 to begin my freshman year at Washington University in St. Louis. I had few aspirations of either widening my horizons very quickly or joining a fraternity my first semester in college. The former position was shattered on day one.

I arrived at my dorm; met my Indian roommate, whose parents lived in Libya; witnessed a woman wearing only a towel give my parents directions to the resident assistants' suite; and discovered grits were as likely to be a side dish with dinner as they were a main course for breakfast. On the other hand, while my RA, Aaron, turned out to be a fraternity member, he did little to impress upon any of the male residents a need to rush or join a Greek fraternity. I liked that and became fast friends with him.

In those first few weeks, I realized almost immediately that the world was not only not all white but also not all American, Christian, or Republican. It is not difficult from here to gather the rest of my previously narrow view. Fortunately, my parents had raised me to welcome change, new experiences, and others' opinions. My roommate, Ram, and I became good friends, often staying up until first light talking about our families, debating politics, bashing the "less bright" students who had chosen to study the humanities instead of engineering, and coercing the pizza-delivery people into believing they were late and that our pizza should be free or come at a discount.

On a few occasions Aaron invited me to join him for lunch, an evening cocktail mixer, or an after-hours bash at the Sigma Chi house. I rarely turned him down. My father was a Sig Chi, but I did not want to make instant "friends" by playing the legacy card and getting a bid to join just because it was in my blood already. And so I kept the connection a secret, socialized, danced, and drank as hard as any of the serious rushees. But I bowed out of the competition when asked whether I was actively seeking fraternity membership.

When rush ended I remained an independent by choice, not by force. I told Rich and several other Sigma Chi brothers that I would keep them in mind for next fall. I was hoping they would do the same for me.

That August I returned a week earlier than most students in order to start cross-country practice. Ram and I took over the suite, so to speak, residing in the two single rooms and continuing to hold court in the living room on occasion. I had survived my first year with only a few dents in my armor and realized that I had managed my time well enough that I could probably join a fraternity in the fall of 1985, if one would have me.

I chose Sigma Chi, not so much because I knew my father would be proud but because the mix of college majors and financial backgrounds appealed to me a great deal. To be sure, racial diversity was all but nonexistent, as it was at nearly every house on campus. What the chapter lacked in melting-pot qualities, though, it made up for in camaraderie.

Our small class of only eight brothers (two of whom were ethnic minorities) became close very quickly. My dual pledge fathers, Aaron and Charlie, helped me get to know the active brothers and their idiosyncrasies, while our pledge trainer, Brady, schooled us on the history and tradition that has made Sigma Chi internationally well-known and, for the most part, a highly respected Greek organization. At no time did anyone mention the issues of race, color, religion, economic background, or sexual orientation. Brothers were brothers all and living under the same Sigma Chi standard and creed. I took these principles at face value—almost too literally at times—and, as humans will, often failed to live up to these high ideals.

Sadly, it has taken me ten years to realize how much I regret not reaching out to a brother who shared his most personal secret with me, hoping that I might help him find a way to do the same with our entire chapter. In the end the distance between us went from infinitesimal to cavernous in a matter of moments. I walked away, while he silenced himself, his secret, and the smile that had many times drawn men and women alike into his circle of discussion, dancing, or deliberation.

Looking back, I am certain that few, if any, of my brothers besides myself knew that Trev was gay. Much like the other 60 or so brothers, we were both very active, always participating in social events, accepting elected offices, and playing intramural sports. In the midst of all this, Trev spent as much time with me as did any of my original pledge brothers—both before and after our initiation. We sometimes went for hourlong walks around campus and the surrounding area, discussing our classes, our instructors, and our plans for the future. I complained a lot, and he listened patiently. There was no question that I could turn to him at any time as a sounding board and source of comfort.

What is bothersome to me, though, is how that feeling was all too limited to just the two of us. At the time I felt as if that warm, all-inclusive, much larger group of 18- to 22-year-olds nonetheless possessed enough narrow-mindedness and homophobia to potentially make the remainder of Trev's undergraduate life uncomfortable or even miserable. My being straight did not help, but the night Trev came out to me is an important moment in my life for two reasons. Of all the times someone has placed his trust and confidence in me, none has been more life-altering, and while I have matured as a person in the months and years that followed, I still see that event as an unnecessary personal failure, despite my growth since.

On a Friday night in February 1987, Trev and I spent the better part of six hours with three sorority women at their off-campus apartment. I would hardly have defined myself as outgoing at the time and would never have thought of going on such an excursion if invited alone. Trev was the one they had asked, and as had so often occurred in the past, I came along as his shy and sensible sidekick. The punk and alternative rock flowed as smoothly as the vodka shooters and Budweiser. At one point, Trev and I cleared off a coffee table and danced for the Pi Phis on our makeshift stage. But more than the music and alcohol, it was the intimacy of our group's conversation and interaction that brought me out of my shell that evening and left its mark on similar evenings to come. I was growing comfortable with myself and my surroundings, and that included strangers and friends alike.

By 2 o'clock in the morning, Trev and I took our hosts' yawns as a cue for us to find our way back to our own homes, and so we bundled ourselves into our jackets, scarves, and hats and kissed and hugged our friends farewell at the door. Neither of us able to drive, we chose to walk the two miles back toward campus, handing back and forth the beer-can, plastic-cup, and paper-plate trophy the women had construct-ed and awarded me earlier for being "Mr. Pi Phi." The frigid air seemed just a little warmer as we walked along Delmar.

"Chesney, you've outdone yourself tonight," Trev said and smacked me on the back. "Mr. Pi Phi. You're going to get a lot of dates out of this one. Those three will talk, their sisters will talk. You'll be swimming in it."

I heard him but said nothing. I was probably glowing or doing a mental inventory of who I hoped would call and how soon.

"You know, it wasn't so long ago that I would have envied you. But I'm over that now."

I was still counting names and clutching the trophy under my arm, scuff-ing my hiking boots on the pavement to stir up the circulation in my feet.

"Did you hear me? I said. 'I'm over that now.'" Trev was irritated.

"Over what?" I said.

"I'm over the whole woman thing."

"Yeah, well I gave them up for Lent last spring," I replied. "Nearly cost me a formal date. When I realized that formal was on the Saturday before Palm Sunday, and I kind of panicked. I thought maybe the word was out, that I wouldn't get a date. Talk about paranoia." I looked up at his blank face. "So how long are you planning to boycott them?"

"Forever."

"Yeah, I said that too. You won't make it, you know. Especially you. You're too popular, too good-looking, too—"

"Jesus, stop it!"

I stopped talking and walking at the same time. We were over a block from London and Son's, but I swear I could still smell their chicken wings and barbecue in the frozen air. "Stop what?"

"I'm not talking about Lent, Thom. I'm talking about life."

I stuck a woolen finger in his chest. "You're not talking. It's the booze talking." We walked two more blocks without a word.

"We spend a lot of time together, so you can understand where I'm coming from, can't you?" Trev asked. I had no idea what the topic had changed to. Trev was carrying the trophy now, and it seemed destined to disintegrate each time he waved his hands.

"Coming from on what?"

"On this whole situation. Women, men—I think you get the picture."

The light that was supposed to come on over my head had not. We crossed Skinker at the light and continued up into University City. "Are you trying to tell me that you're going the celibate route?" I asked. "Have you really thought this through?" We stopped in front of a record store with a recessed doorway and moved out of the wind for a moment. "Look, I got a lot of seminary stuff during high school when our youth priest planted the bug in someone's ear about me. I said, 'No way. I want to have kids and be a dad someday.' They left me alone after that." Trev was staring blankly at me. "You see? You'd better think about this. You want to be a dad? You want to have kids? You think not now, but wait a couple of years."

"You are so damn self-centered sometimes!" Trev answered. "How did this get to be about you? I'm the one who is reaching out to you to listen to me for a minute, and you keep coming back at me with another anecdote about how you know what I'm going through, have been there, are OK with it now. Are you going to let me talk or not?"

His initial assertion was still ringing in my ears. No one had ever called me that. "Talk away, buddy. And I'm not self-centered."

Trev walked out of the alcove and jogged up the street away from me, shouting, "Sixty seconds! Damn, 60 seconds. Can you shut up and listen for 60 seconds?"

I was glad it was cold and late enough that no one was hanging around outside the bars to see this drunken episode. I quickly chased him down, steered him into the side street that led toward our respective apartment buildings, and dragged him to a stop. There, with my gloved hands planted firmly on his shoulders and less than three feet of steamy breath separating us, I promised him I would shut up for a full minute and listen to whatever it was he had to tell me.

"What is it, Trev? Has your mind finally cleared on this one? I told you it would."

There was no drama, no crying, not even a trace of the sentimentality that at that point in my life I would have expected to accompany his next words.

"Thom, I'm gay. I thought I should tell you, thought I could tell you, am telling you."

I squinted at him and shook my head. "Here, take the trophy. Get some rest, man. You're a mess. You'll sleep this off in no time."

He stared back at me without flinching—seeing into me—and still no drama. I broke his gaze, slung my shoulder around him, and walked the final block to his place. My feet were cold again. I was cold. Trev spoke only once more, in the entryway to his building.

"There's more to this, you know. You need to understand that and understand me. I need to know nothing has changed between us."

"Sure," I said. "Nothing has changed. You're gay, I'm not. We're both drunk, and by tomorrow I won't remember being Mr. Pi Phi, and you won't even remember being gay for a night." The big metal door hissed to a close between us, and I walked home alone, scuffing my boots, kicking at snow, and blowing out steam.

Trev and I were never again as close as we had been before that night. He graduated that spring and even attended our formal with one of the women who had given me the trophy. I have done a lot of scuffing and kicking and blowing off steam since that time and think often how my own self-centeredness cost me a friend and an opportunity to under-stand something as new to my world as Ram had been nearly three years earlier. The trophy is long gone, but the door between us remains locked. I have not talked to Trev in over ten years. Whether he just want-ed to tell someone or was turning to me for support in the same way that I had so often turned to him, I still do not know. True friends know these things implicitly, I suppose, but I failed to recognize this at the time.

Today, I teach literature and writing on a college campus. I have many gay and lesbian friends and students from all walks of life, and the time we spend together continuously informs and reshapes my reading, my writing, and my thinking. Ten years ago I would have never considered writing an essay such as this, but in the process of drafting it I have shared my story with dozens of people—my way, at this late date, of encouraging other straight brothers who find themselves in my shoes to be much more supportive and much less secretive. With my straight and gay friends alike, I share as many similarities as I do dif-ferences; as such, in our awkward moments I am reminded of the most awkward ever and find myself again. So much has changed, yet in the case of Trev, nothing has changed between us: my loss, my fraternity brothers' loss, and very little drama. It does not have to be that way.

Straight From the Heart
by B. Kurisky

I believe that being gay does not make anyone less of a brother. All brothers must realize that every day they interact with individuals who are homosexuals. Coming out to someone is not an easy experience. The atmosphere that the brothers create in the fraternity should be one that is supportive of everyone's decisions. The chapter should be a place where brothers support and respect each other.

Why was Darius unable to tell me directly that he was gay, instead of my finding out from a third source?

This question is probably one of the main reasons I am writing this story. Darius was one of my best friends and the person who got me interested in joining a fraternity. Before then I had never really thought of myself as a fraternity man. I remember when we both first met at the student organization fair called Main Street. And before I knew it, I was rushing a fraternity and, of course, Darius was my big brother.

Darius always made sure that I was not getting overly involved in fraternity functions and tried to look out for my best interests. That spring I was selected to do an internship at the national headquarters. After I had completed the internship and arrived back on campus, the chapter was hesitant about working with me because I had worked at the national office; however, Darius treated me just the same as before.

In the spring of 1994, I graduated with my second degree. At the party held for the graduating seniors in the chapter, Darius took me aside and gave me a gift. When I opened it I found a picture of us at one of our annual cookout parties. I had totally forgotten about the picture. Of all of the gifts I received for my graduation, I treasured this one the most. It came from the heart.

I accepted a position at a university in the Southwest to teach communications while getting my master's degree. While I was out there, Darius and I talked a few times. He said that he had cut back on his class load to only two classes a semester, so he would not be graduating for another two years. Because of the great distance between us (around 1500 miles), it was hard for me to visit or remain in close contact with my brothers who were still at college.

In March of 1996 I had some time off from my graduate work and decided to head back to my alma mater and visit some of my friends, including Darius. The night I arrived I went out with my old roommate to one of the bars close to campus. I arrived to find one of the guys I pledged with there at the bar. After getting a drink, I sat down and started talking with Jay about what was happening in his life.

After talking for about 25 minutes, he asked if I had talked with or heard from Darius lately. I said that I had not really talked with him in the past three months, and the last time we talked it was brief because I was late for a meeting. Jay asked what we had talked about, and I said that basically, our conversations were just superficial, everyday conversations to catch up on what was happening in our lives. Jay then asked if I had talked with Darius since I arrived in town. I said that I had not yet contacted him.

I knew Jay wanted to tell me something, so I flat out asked him what he was getting at. He informed me that Darius had announced he was gay and had even shown up at a brother's wedding the previous month with his partner. I originally thought he was joking so I started laughing, but Jay did not return the laughter. That was when I knew he was serious.

After I had time to process this information, I began to reflect on everything that had happened between Darius and me. I began to wonder whether there were any sexual motives behind anything that had transpired between us while I was an undergraduate. I left the bar with a lot of questions in my mind. When I got back to the apartment, I called a friend in the Southwest who simply stated that I was being heterosexist. How did I know that I was Darius's type? I was flattering myself into thinking that he wanted something more. We talked more, and it helped allay some of my fears. However, one constant question kept being repeated in my mind: *Why was Darius unable to tell me directly that he was gay, instead of my finding out from a third source?*

I have tried to answer this question many times. Since we had been not only brothers but also best friends, why could he not talk to me about this?

As I think more about the question, I guess I can see why he felt as if he could not approach me and tell me. Even though I never made remarks to degrade homosexuality, many of my brothers did make such homophobic comments on a continual basis. I did nothing about it for fear that I would be thought of as a homosexual. I also think my upbringing may have been a reason for why he may have felt uneasy talking to me. I will admit that I am a Republican; however, I am a moderate who believes that what goes on behind closed doors between consenting adults is no one else's business.

While I was an undergraduate, I never expressed these beliefs to anyone around me. I was raised in an extremely conservative family and attended a private school where issues such as homosexuality were discussed only in the negative sense. My entire fraternity knew not only that I attended a conservative private school but also that I was a religious person who attended church regularly; therefore, I was classified as a religious conservative on many issues. I can only think that a combination of all of these factors made Darius uneasy about approaching me.

I am not hurt that Darius is gay. I am hurt that Darius did not feel that he could talk to me about his decision to come out. To me, Darius is no different than he was the day we met. I shared a lot with Darius throughout my undergraduate years; however, I realize that the sharing of information was basically one-way. He was constantly helping me in both my decisions and my life, but I was not there to aid him in his decisions or his life. If I had been a good brother, I would have seen that he wanted to tell me something. I should have talked with him about it, attempting to help him in any way I could.

I believe that being gay does not make anyone less of a brother. All brothers must realize that every day they interact with individuals who are homosexuals. Coming out to someone is not an easy experience. The atmosphere that the brothers create in the fraternity should be one that is supportive of everyone's decisions. By looking beyond whom one loves, the chapter will benefit by allowing for a greater diversity of opinions. Such actions also will show brothers that one is not judged in terms of what he does in private but the work he does for the community and the chapter. The chapter should be a place where brothers support and respect each other.

I can only imagine how difficult it was for Darius to come to his decision to come out. I have attempted to think about how a brother who is gay can come out to other brothers. I would suggest that he approach a brother with whom he feels comfortable discussing the subject. If a person is truly a brother, he should support a fellow brother no matter what he decides to do. After talking with this brother, the individual could then come out to others and eventually the entire chapter. I would also suggest that he answer honestly and openly the questions that will inevitably be raised by various brothers. The brotherhood then can begin to understand that he is still the same brother as before he came out.

I look forward to a time when acceptance and understanding of brothers who are different from the majority will be commonplace in fraternities. Only then will gay brothers feel safe coming out to their straight brothers.

I have not talked to Darius since I found out from Jay that he is gay. I am still working through my feelings concerning his not telling me. If I were to talk to Darius, I would let him know my feelings toward him have not changed. In fact, my admiration and love for him have only increased with his decision to come out.

CONCLUSION

A Closer Look Out on Fraternity Row
by Shane L. Windmeyer and Pamela W. Freeman

Simply by sharing the stories of gay fraternity brothers, we have shown that they are not alone and have taken an important step toward breaking the cycle of invisibility. The often silenced voices of gay fraternity men are now being heard, and we have begun to learn about homophobia and how it can jeopardize the goals of brotherhood and the fraternity experience.

The initial goal of this anthology was to heighten visibility, but the impact of the stories has gone beyond that. The stories provide a qualitative description of being gay in a college fraternity and provide an educational tool for the Greek community and for colleges and universities. In his introduction, Douglas N. Case identified themes that emerged from his research and from the stories in this book. By our examining the stories, revelations about the fraternity system became evident. We have attempted to identify a few of these revelations and to discuss the changes necessary to move the Greek system forward regarding sexual-orientation issues.

One revelation is that the existence of homophobia in the fraternity system hurts everyone, irrespective of sexual orientation. Homophobia creates a hostile environment which obstructs the development of male friendship and brotherhood. As noted by Arthur W. Chickering and Linda Reisser in the second edition of *Education and Identity*, "Homophobia discourages closeness between males. Men are more likely than women to equate warmth and closeness with sex and look for an erotic component when a strong emotional connection exists."[1] As such, men distance themselves from expressing affection or emotions with other men and act out the role of hating gays to prove they are not homosexual.[2,3] Homophobia also creates an environment in which there is an increased likelihood of rape-prone attitudes toward women as a result of men needing to prove their heterosexual masculinity.[4] In the stories the consequences of homophobia are related to the excessive use of alcohol. Fraternity brothers, straight and gay alike, use alcohol as a guise to express their emotions as they grapple with their identity development. Such negative effects associated with homophobia are highlighted as common occurrences throughout the stories.

Another revelation is that chapters with a well-developed sense of brotherhood are more prepared to provide support and acceptance of gay brothers than are those who do not have an understanding of brotherhood. Several writers found that coming out while active was an extremely rewarding experience that would not have been possible in the absence of the strong brotherhood within their fraternities. The brotherhood provided for a nurturing environment in which individual members could grow through their coming-out process. The stories suggest a meaning of true brotherhood that evolves from their shared experiences and reflect common values that are congruent with respecting individual diversity. Brotherhood is defined as a family devotion to other men who share a common bond, friendship, and love for their fraternity and welfare of their brothers; a willingness to help or aid a brother in time of need; and shared common values of loyalty, honesty, understanding, and respect.

If fraternities exist to foster brotherhood, then that brotherhood must not be denied to any brother. Such a definition of brotherhood provides a shared meaning for brothers to understand more fully and builds on the philosophy of the college fraternity.

The stories further reveal that change is a constant process. Fraternities must seek significant change when it comes to fostering a brotherhood that is free from homophobia. In fact, change is occurring over time, as shown through the comparison of stories from different generations. But this change remains limited in its ability to alter organizational culture and is usually reactionary to a brother coming out to a particular chapter or individual(s). In the book *Deep Change*, Robert E. Quinn, a business faculty member at the University of Michigan, speaks of the constant demand for "deep change" in today's diverse global environment. He notes that "deep change requires new ways of thinking and behaving. It is change that is major in scope, discontinuous with the past, and generally irreversible. Deep change effort distorts existing patterns of action and involves taking risks."[5] These three revelations provide a perspective for the Greek community to move toward deep change and to address sexual-orientation issues as they relate to the college fraternity.

Indeed, when describing the value of fraternities at the turn of the 21st century, we must emphasize the significance of brotherhood and the need for deep change. The following statement from *Baird's Manual of American College Fraternities* describes the purpose of fraternities and provides an accurate summary of the reasons given by our writers for joining a fraternity.

> Let it be said that fraternities are about what matters most: enduring friendships founded on shared principles and personal affinities; living out good lives, not just having good times; cordial laughter, delightful gaiety, robust merriment; the lively pleasures of good companions; the sustaining loyalty of old comrades through whatever fortune or adversity may appear; the settled conviction that lives are lived to the best effect when firmly secured by mutual bonds of deep affection, administration, and respect. In freedom, if wisely chosen, there is fraternity, and in fraternity, if rightly used, there is joy.[6]

Unfortunately, researchers have found that fraternities have certain maladies that lead one to question their ability to live up to these ideals. National studies have documented the excessive use of alcohol as a normal part of fraternity life, the negative impact on gains made by first-year students who pledge fraternities in measures of openness to diversity, and the questionable advantage to students who join fraternities in terms of leadership development.[7] With such challenges being made on a national level about the value of fraternities, there is need now more than ever before to undergo "deep change" within the college fraternity system.

But this change cannot be based on the model of the past. The 21st century Greek system must acknowledge and discuss certain truths, including homophobia. Actions to change the Greek community must recognize that gay members exist in the fraternity brotherhood and that these brothers make significant contributions to Greek life. Homophobia must be addressed not only to strengthen the brotherhood but also to create more positive environments for the identity development of both gay and straight men.

As Quinn notes, we must discuss the "undiscussable issues" within our organizations in order to move toward deep change. Many times an undiscussable issue is one that is viewed as an enormous threat to the group's structure and that stimulates feelings of fear, anxiety, stress, tension, embarrassment, and pain among members.[8] Homophobia is one of these undiscussable issues in the college fraternity. A survey of fraternity and sorority national headquarters personnel indicated a lack of interest or willingness at an organizational level to deal with issues related to the sexual orientation of their members.[9] The stories also reveal that this is the case among individuals at the local chapter level as well.

Today, a few national fraternities have taken steps toward recognizing the needs of gay brothers and fostering a stronger environment for brotherhood. But we should expect more. The stories reveal that men, straight and gay alike, need environments that assist their male identity development and their ability to form healthy friendships with other men. Homosexuality should not be viewed as a threat to the college fraternity. Instead the presence of a gay brother dispels myths and destroys the fear that perpetuates homophobia. Elimination of homophobia breaks down the barriers that keep men from expressing affection and emotions in male friendship. There exists no better place to do this than the college fraternity, the locus of brotherhood.

Given the small though not insignificant improvements that have occurred in the fraternity system with regard to homophobia, fraternities should be urged not only to discuss but also to enact policies and practices that support gay brothers and educate members about homophobia. The collective harm of homophobia must be addressed at all levels by individual chapters, national headquarters, national fraternity associations, and colleges and universities. Educating members about homophobia and including language pertaining to sexual orientation in a fraternity nondiscrimination statement should be common practice, not a rare occurrence. Such an approach may surprisingly help the entire Greek system move toward deep change.

A significant void still remains in formal research related to the needs of gay, lesbian, and bisexual college students, especially in Greek-letter social organizations. National studies mention that fraternities tend to be more homogeneous than the student body in terms of sexual orientation.[10] While such an observation may be true on the surface, the stories tend to reflect that gay fraternity brothers are often closeted during their undergraduate experience and are at least as present in the college fraternity as they are on campus in general. Until more formal research is conducted on gay college students, it is not possible to generalize these numbers accurately. Current research studies about college students need to begin asking questions to identify gay students and to inquire about their college experience in order to fill this void.

While the research remains limited, this book begins to shed light on the needs and experiences of gay men and the underlying issues of male identity development within the college fraternity. The stories recall different experiences, raise many questions, and present a dialogue from which we all can grow. In an effort to facilitate this process, we have included suggested educational interventions and resources to assist local chapters, international organizations, national fraternity associations, and colleges and universities.

We believe that many of the accounts in this book are representative of all fraternities and are generally more positive than the reality of Greek life for gay fraternity men. Much like the editors, the writers believe in the goals of the college fraternity system and have a vested interest in the topic. Nonetheless, the stories share a much-needed perspective on Greek life and bring heightened attention to breaking the cycle of invisibility.

For too long the invisibility and silence have kept us from recognizing gay brothers and addressing issues such as homophobia in the college fraternity. We place the burden on others, but seldom do we recognize our role in producing the change. Most of the writers use their real names in showing that gay fraternity brothers do exist and are not alone. In our individual roles we also must come out of the Greek closet—whether it be as a gay Greeks or straight allies. Such visibility will only help our gay students realize that they do have positive role models and that they are not alone. Now that we have taken a closer look out on fraternity row, let us create the change necessary to foster stronger Greek communities that are free from homophobia.

Notes

[1] Arthur W. Chickering and Linda Reisser, *Education and Identity,* Second Edition (San Francisco: Jossey-Bass, 1993): 170.

[2] Donald F. Sabo, "The Politics of Homophobia in Sport," in *Sex, Violence, and Power in Sports: Rethinking Masculinity,* Michael A. Messner and Donald F. Sabo, eds.(Freedom, Calif: Crossing Press, 1994): 101-112.

[3] Warren J. Blumenfeld, *Homophobia: How We All Pay the Price* (Boston: Beacon Press, 1992): 24-37.

[4] Peggy Reeves Sanday, *Fraternity Gang Rape: Sex, Brotherhood, and Privilege on Campus* (New York: New York University Press, 1990): 122.

[5] Robert E. Quinn, *Deep Change* (San Francisco: Jossey-Bass, 1996): 3.

[6] Jack L. Anson and Robert F. Marchesani Jr., eds., *Baird's Manual of American College Fraternities,* 20th Edition (Indianapolis, Ind.: Baird's Manual Foundation, 1991): 1-7.

[7] George D. Kuh, Ernest T. Pascarella, and Henry Wechsler, "The Questionable Value of Fraternities," in *Chronicle of Higher Education,* 19 April 1996, Opinion section.

[8] Quinn, *Deep Change,* 189-191.

[9] Michael J. Hughes, "Addressing Gay, Lesbian, and Bisexual Issues in Fraternities and Sororities," in *Beyond Tolerance: Gays, Lesbians, and Bisexuals on Campus,* Nancy J. Evans and Vernon A. Wall, eds., (Alexandria, Va.: American College Personnel Association, 1991): 104-107.

[10] Kuh, Pascarella, and Wechsler, *The Chronicle of Higher Education,* Opinion section.

EDUCATIONAL
INTERVENTIONS

How to Use Stories as Educational Tools

Whether you're planning workshops for new-member education or preparing to teach a class of college freshmen, finding materials that are relevant and effective can be challenging to even the most accomplished of presenters. The stories in *Out on Fraternity Row* provide a wealth of real-life experiences to which students can relate. Two ways that the stories can be used in part or in full by presenters or instructors are by summarizing them into case studies or pulling quotes from them for "read-arounds." Having authentic information for such activities can greatly increase their impact, especially when the information is presented in a nonthreatening atmosphere in which participants can feel free to discuss openly their feelings and opinions.

Case Studies

Before you select stories to convert into case studies, consider the purpose of the presentation being planned, as well as the roles of persons who will attend. For example, new-member education or a diversity course for undergraduate students may have as a goal increasing understanding about homophobia, while staff training may be focused on the responsibilities of staff in providing a supportive environment for all students. Therefore, in order for case studies to be effective, they must be written clearly and they must fit both the purpose and audience of the presentation or class.

How the case studies will be presented also must be carefully planned. Simply having participants read and discuss a case study might be informative. However, preparing participants to consider specific questions that are matched to the planned outcomes of the session can help them to extend the information to practical use as they carry out their roles as students, staff, or whatever the case may be.

To demonstrate how the stories in this anthology can be used in presentations, two of them have been converted to case studies. The first, Carl Einhaus's "I Love You, Man" is presented as a thought-pro-voking story that could be used to challenge the executive leadership of a fraternity to consider whether their chapter is accepting of brothers who dare to be honest about being gay or whether the chapter is intolerant to the point of forcing gay brothers to remain closeted or to leave. The second, Thom D. Chesney's "Being Straight Did Not Help," provides the reflections of a fraternity member who had an opportunity to support a brother during his coming-out process. This story could be used with new members during orientation as a way to show how people's responses to gay brothers can affect the quality of brotherhood for all members. Possible issues and questions for discussion are listed following the cases and are designed to stretch the thinking of participants.

Case Study 1
"I Love You, Man"

One of Carl's main reasons for pledging a fraternity was to "experience the most out of college life." He quickly learned that the influential members of the house were the executive board members. While he viewed them as positive role models who influenced the chapter's volunteer activities and general level of accomplishment on campus, Carl also saw them as the instigators of many negative messages, such as "to be a man, you must party like a rock star, have sex with women to gain status, and never show signs of weaknesses or feelings."

Carl tried to fit in by assuming leadership positions, playing sports, and drinking alcohol. Part of the camaraderie in the house was developed through drinking together and making fun of brothers who became emotional when drinking. Drinking also helped Carl, who was gay, to have occasional sexual experiences with women in order to have stories to share with his brothers. Without such stories members were subject to ridicule or were suspected of being gay. Carl was sure that he would be rejected by his fraternity if it were learned that he was gay.

He observed that the fear of rejection and the need for acceptance were driving forces in motivating the behavior of many of his brothers.

To be accepted and to show that they were not gay, brothers frequently made vivid and violent comments about gay men's sexual acts and, in return, were guaranteed laughs and a sense of shared hatred of homosexuals. When rumors spread through the membership about a brother, Ed, having hit on a guy and tried to get him into bed, Carl observed that Ed was no longer seen around the house. Carl worried about the mental anguish that Ed, a dependable and helpful person, must have gone through during this time in the fraternity. Carl viewed this "squeezing out" of Ed as a clear message to every closeted brother in the fraternity—stay closeted or be pushed out of the chapter.

Carl remained closeted until a year after his graduation. He referred to his coming out as "the best choice I ever made." For Carl, it was important to have the choice of when to come out. For him, it was best to wait until he was no longer an undergraduate, especially given the lack of support for being gay in his fraternity chapter.

Possible Issues and Questions for Discussion

Possible issues might include heterosexism, homophobia, the need to conform in fraternities, that use and abuse of alcohol, and objectification of women. Questions which could be used to stimulate discussion about these issues are as follows:

1. What messages exist in your chapter that communicate the criteria for being acceptable as brothers? Are there similarities between Carl's fraternity and yours?

2. What steps could have been taken by the leaders of Carl's fraternity to provide a supportive environment for a gay brother to come out? Why do you think Carl waited to come out? How do you think that made him feel?

3. Why are the pressures to have only heterosexual members so great in fraternities? What are some of the subtle—as well as blatant—pressures that are placed on members in your fraternity to influence conformity?

4. What can you do as a leader to discourage homophobia and encourage a climate of acceptance in your fraternity? On your campus?

5. As a leader, what sources of support exist on your campus for educating members about homophobia?

6. What ideas do you have for fostering brotherhood that would not involve the abuse of alcohol, objectification of women, and denial of members' feelings?

7. If rumors were being spread through your house, such as those about Ed, what would you do as a leader?

8. If heterosexual brothers were not accepted in the chapter and the expectation was for all brothers to at least appear to be homosexual, how would you feel? What would need to change to make both homosexuals and heterosexuals feel fully integrated into the brotherhood?

Case Study 2
"Being Straight Did Not Help"

Searching for camaraderie among a group of guys with a variety of college majors and backgrounds, Thom pledged his fraternity at the beginning of his sophomore year. His relatively small pledge class of eight members quickly became friends, studied and learned the standard and creed, and developed a sense of brotherhood among the 60 members of the chapter. One of Thom's pledge brothers, Trev, was very close to Thom and was always there to provide a listening ear and source of comfort, when needed. Trev, unfortunately, was also the subject of Thom's greatest regret as a brother.

On a cold winter night, Thom and Trev were socializing at the off-campus apartment of three sorority women. Trev had received the initial invitation and had brought his shy friend, Thom, along to the gathering. After an evening of beer and laughter, Thom and Trev walked back to campus, knowing that driving in their state of inebriation would have been ill advised. As Thom recapped the evening's events, anticipating future dates galore because of his success in impressing the women, Trev announced that he was "over that now." Confused about the meaning of Trev's words, Thom asked him to clarify. Trev responded, "I'm over the whole woman thing." Not believing Trev to be serious, Thom joked, "Yeah, well, I gave them up for Lent last spring. Nearly cost me a formal date." Thom refused to take seriously the message Trev was trying to convey—that he was gay. Trev remained silent. Thom ended the conversation by saying, "Nothing has changed. You're gay; I'm not. We're both drunk, and by tomorrow, you won't even remember being gay for a night."

Even though Thom and Trev had been very close prior to their conversation that evening, the closeness of their friendship was never the same afterward. Trev soon graduated, and Thom regretted that his self-centeredness had cost him a friend and an opportunity to learn about something unfamiliar to his world.

Ten years after the night that Trev tried to come out to him, Thom reminisced that "of all the times someone has placed his trust and confidence in me, none has been more life-altering; and while I have matured as a person in the months and years that followed, I still see that event as an unnecessary personal failure, despite my growth since."

Possible Issues and Questions for Discussion

Issues might include the ability of men to communicate emotions, factors influencing alcohol use and abuse, the effects of alcohol use and abuse, the extent to which a lack of openness about sexual orientation affects the brotherhood, and the use of women as tools for proving masculinity. The following questions might be useful in stimulating discussion about issues:

1. What feelings do you think Thom was having when Trev came out to him that night?

2. What feelings do you think Trev was having when he came out to Thom?

3. What do you believe would be common reactions to a surprise coming out of a friend that you, as a heterosexual, thought you knew well?

4. Do you believe that most brothers would be prepared to respond in a supportive manner when faced with a friend who was coming out? Why or why not?

5. Can you think of ways that brothers could become prepared for such an event?

6. Do you believe that alcohol was a factor in Trev's coming out? In Thom's response? Would the scenario have been different with no alcohol involved?

7. To what extent are you willing to be helpful to a friend who wishes to come out? What are some ways you could show your willingness to be helpful?

8. What options are available to gay brothers when no one is likely to be supportive if it is learned that he is gay?

9. Can you think of behaviors or comments that are typically made in your chapter that would either encourage or discourage a gay member from feeling safe to come out?

Read-Arounds

"Read-arounds" is one title given to an activity in which participants are given slips of paper with quotes or statements on them to be read aloud to the whole group.[1] Information in the statements is intended to raise awareness about a certain topic or to create a particular mood during the session. The facilitator could then number the statements and call on a particular number of a statement that would be especially timely during the presentation.

As in the case studies, the stories in *Out on Fraternity Row* contain quotable material that can be readily adapted to read-arounds that are based on real-life experiences in fraternities and can be, therefore, especially meaningful. Hearing peers read the actual comments of fraternity members can be a powerful way to raise awareness about what fraternity life is like for gay brothers. Following are a few examples of quotes from the stories, which would lend themselves to a read-around and discussion.

Over the next few weeks, my ears became attuned to the references that were made about gays. Never once did I hear a positive one. The word "fag" came up as a derogatory term in every other sentence with certain brothers. Never once did I hear something that made me want to stand up and say, "Hey, I'm like that. I'm gay." The more comments I heard, the more I did not want to tell anyone.

(David Anglikowski, "Family and the Bond of Brotherhood")

After I revealed my homosexuality to a selected few, my insecurity and fear drove me away from those friendships that had developed over late-night conversations, road trips, parties, daily meals, team sports, all kinds of activities. When I did see my "friends and brothers," many were hostile, passive-aggressive, or could express only a salutation. Out of fear of rejection, I alienated myself from the brothers. I chose not to return telephone calls, and I declined invitations. Distance and new relationships provided safety for me.

(Mike T. McGraith, "Truth Succeeds, Always")

Coming out was liberating! Soon thereafter, I came out to some other gay friends. I was still apprehensive to come out to many of my straight friends, including my fraternity brothers. Would straight people understand? Because of the pressure in my chapter to conform and to be straight, I felt that I had to form a strong support network among my non-Greek friends before I could reveal my true feelings to my fraternity brothers.

(Wil Forrest, "I'm In, I'm Out!")

I did not voice my feelings. Instead I joined the other guys in making fag jokes sometimes. Drawing a good laugh from my brothers made me feel included and appreciated. In my naïveté, I saw common targets as common bonds. At many times during my college days, I felt my sexuality clawing to emerge from me, but I kept it at bay with a big straight act and a lot of hoping. I hoped I was wrong about my feelings. I hoped a great woman would come around and change me. And I hoped none of the men on campus would notice I was drooling over them in the meantime.

(Mike Pecen, "Tattooed")

I am not hurt that Darius is gay. I am hurt that Darius did not feel that he could talk to me about his decision to come out. To me, Darius is no different than he was the day we met. I shared a lot with Darius throughout my undergraduate years; however, I realize that the sharing of information was basically one-way. He was constantly helping me in both my decisions and my life, but I was not there to aid him in his decisions or his life.

(Brian Kurisky, "Straight from the Heart")

There have been unsettling moments of fear, doubt, and disappointment. I have felt hurt, anger, and loneliness when brothers were not very attentive or responsive when I have been down. But on balance my alumni and undergraduate brothers have been very supportive, and have been brothers in every sense of the word. They are more supportive than my birth family and far more involved in my life. My sexual orientation did not distract from my ability to be a good adviser or from my fraternity experience. I am a better person because of my fraternity experience and my gay experience and filled with more depth and empathy because of my gayness and my brotherhood. Approaching life with integrity and honesty has added to the fraternal experience for the brothers and for me.

("Quentin Vig," "On Being a Gay Greek Adviser")

These activities can be effective in classes, staff training, workshops, or other presentations designed for students within and outside of Greek-letter organizations as well as staff, faculty, and administrators in the broader campus community. While it is acknowledged that designing educational programs on topics related to diversity can be extremely challenging, findings in a national study on student learning provide evidence that the efforts are worthwhile. It was found that participating in a single awareness workshop can have a positive effect on a student's openness to diversity.[2] Presenters and instructors are urged to be persistent in the search for effective strategies and are invited to adapt the information in this book for educational purposes.

Source: Shane L. Windmeyer and Pamela W. Freeman, Lambda 10 Project.

Notes

[1] Daniel Watts and Tammy Lou Maltzan, "Some of My Best Friends...Lesbian, Gay, and Bisexual Awareness for Greek Letter Organizations" (training materials presented at the joint conference of the National Association of Student Personnel Administrators and the American College Personnel Association, Chicago, Ill., March 1997).

[2] Ernest Pascarella, "Evidence on Student Development from the National Study on Student Learning" (research report presented at the 15th Annual Spring Symposium of the Campus Life Division at Indiana University, Bloomington, Ind., May 1997).

Meaning of Brotherhood Concentric Circle Exercise

Brotherhood remains at the heart of any college fraternity. Often the meaning and practice of brotherhood is based on the individual fraternity. These meanings may be communicated by the interpretation of fraternity ritual or by the actions of older brothers. Fraternity men may not have an opportunity to discuss or to agree on what the meaning of brotherhood is for their chapter. The practice of having a dialogue about the meaning of brotherhood enables all brothers to have a shared experience defining their fraternity brotherhood.

This activity is designed to give all participants the chance to interact on a one-to-one level to define the nature of brotherhood for their chapter. When a fraternity brother comes out, those chapters that share an understanding of brotherhood are more likely to respond in a supportive manner to the gay brother. The phrases and questions listed below create a dialogue on the meaning of brotherhood and assist in setting a foundation to more readily accept diversity. Such an exercise may be used as a warm up activity prior to a leadership retreat or in combination with other chapter functions in discussing the meaning of brotherhood and the value of a college fraternity.

Purpose

- To foster a dialogue on the meaning of brotherhood.
- To define or redefine brotherhood based on the shared experience of members.
- To create a personal commitment in the meaning of brotherhood among brothers and to encourage the practice of that brotherhood among the chapter.

Instructions

1. Instruct the brothers to find a partner.
2. Have the brothers face each other and join with other pairs so that the entire group has formed two concentric circles (an inner and an outer circle).
3. Read aloud the following:
   a) I will give you a question to discuss with your partner. First, one of you will speak for 30 seconds, and then the other one will get a chance to talk about the question. Respond to the question with whatever comes to mind and with what you are willing to share about the question.
   b) When I signal, the brothers in the inner circle will move one person to their right to find their new partner.
   c) I will give you another question, and you will discuss the question as before. We will continue in this way for about ten to 15 minutes.
4. After completing the concentric-circle dialogue, ask all brothers to sit in one large circle and use this dialogue among the brothers to define or redefine the meaning of brotherhood for their chapter. Other issues may arise for future educational sessions, so keep a notepad handy to write down comments. Encourage the brothers to publicly read their meaning of brotherhood on occasion to remind one another throughout the year.

Possible Discussion Questions

1. How does one be a good brother?
2. What did you learn about brotherhood prior to joining a fraternity? From your family and friends?
3. What words do people use to describe a brother?
4. What words do people use to describe a fraternity?
5. What are some of the stereotypes about a fraternity?
6. What traits or characteristics are unique about our brotherhood?
7. How do you show your brotherhood on a daily basis?
8. What values do you expect from another brother?
9. Why would somebody be excluded or kicked out of the fraternity?

10. In what ways can a brother show he cares for another brother? Is he willing to help or aid brothers in time of need?
11. What qualities create a healthy, strong brotherhood?
12. How do you show support for another brother?
13. Why do you think fraternities may have a negative public image or are stereotyped?

Sample Definition of Brotherhood

A family devotion to other men who share a common bond, friendship, and love for their fraternity and welfare of their brothers; a willingness to help or aid a brother in time of need; and shared common values of loyalty, honesty, understanding, and respect.

Source: Shane L. Windmeyer and Pamela W. Freeman, Lambda 10 Project.

What Do You Do When You Learn a Brother Is Gay?

Most fraternity nondiscrimination policies and educational efforts neglect to discuss or mention sexual-orientation issues. As a result, many fraternity brothers may never have encountered someone who is gay or may not know what to do when they learn a brother is gay. Such practices jeopardize brotherhood for both gay and straight fraternity brothers by perpetuating the ignorance and fear surrounding homosexuality. This list provides some suggested ideas to keep in mind when a fraternity brother learns that another brother is gay.

A Fraternity Brother Comes Out to You
What to do?

- Listen to what your brother has to say and try to keep an open mind.
- Understand the personal risk he took in telling you, and if you are confused, be honest about your feelings. Realize the trust he has placed in you.
- Realize that your brother has not changed. You may be shocked, but remember that he is still the same person as before he came out to you.
- Respect his choice to tell you by letting him know that you will not tell anyone that he is gay. Realize that he has to come out to the fraternity chapter when he is ready.
- Feel free to ask questions to better understand your brother, such as:
  How long have you known that you were gay?
  Do other brothers or friends know that you are gay?
  Has it been hard for you to carry around this secret?
  How can I be most supportive of you?

• Actions speak louder than words so offer your support and willingness to help him through his coming-out process. He may really need a brother to count on right now.
• Communicate support to your brother. He may feel isolated, as if he is the only one.
• Know what you are talking about by using resources on the college campus. Try to educate yourself and, if comfortable, be an ally on the issue.
• Most important, remember the meaning of brotherhood and be a brother.

A Fraternity Brother Is Outed to the Chapter
What to do?

• Approach the brother in private (if possible) and let him know you are willing to listen and be a brother.
• Calm the brother if he is upset by the outing and allow him to take the lead or speak about his feelings.
• Stand up for your brother as you would for any other brother.
• Attempt to resolve any conflict among other brothers who may not understand by asking them to give the brother some time to process his feelings.
• Seek expertise from campus officials or national headquarters if you are concerned about the chapter's response and need assistance processing the experience.
• Let the brother know that you value him as a brother and as a person, no matter what.

A Fraternity Brother Is Suspected or Perceived to Be Gay
What to do?

• Try not to assume anything about your brother's sexual orientation.
• Remember that your brother may be gay, but he may not be ready to acknowledge this to himself or others. He needs to come out when he is ready.
• Be supportive of your brother, possibly bringing up gay topics to

communicate that you would be a person with whom he can talk.
- Understand that your brother may not be gay.

Your Brother Is Gay
What not *to do?*

- Do not think it is just a phase and that you can help your brother find the "right" woman.
- Do not be afraid to ask questions about being gay or about his coming-out process.
- Do not assume that your fraternity brother finds you attractive.
- Do not try to change your brother. Do accept him as being gay.
- Do not ignore your brother or treat him differently after he has come out. Still invite him to go along when you go out and, most importantly, do not change who you are.
- Do not be ashamed or fail to defend a brother who is gay if otherwise he is a good brother.
- Do not be be afraid to use the word "gay" and do not ignore him when he brings up gay topics.
- Do not try to restrict the brother's freedom to share being gay or to be a public role model. The Greek system and the campus at large need more out student leaders to identify with—do not be surprised if more Greeks start to come out of the closet.
- Do not be worried about what other chapters think or about the reputation of the chapter. Lead by example and remember that there are gay men in every house. Some are simply less fortunate and do not have the open-minded environment for brothers to come out.
- Do not assume that all his guests are his dates and do not make a big deal if he brings a date to the house or a fraternity function.
- Treat him with respect as you would any other person.
- Do not kick your brother out of the fraternity for being gay. Such an action may be in violation of university policy and definitely contradicts the ideals of brotherhood.
- Do not be afraid to approach a gay brother if you think his actions are inappropriate. Hold a gay brother to the same standards as all other brothers.
- Do not treat the brother as if he is a public relations disaster for the

chapter since he has come out. Support your brother's openness and work together to communicate similar messages. He will always speak as a member of the fraternity. Trust that your brother is going to proudly represent your fraternity wherever he goes, as always.

- Do not feel let down if the brother decides to leave the house because of other members' actions or behavior. Be supportive and still be his friend.

Source: Shane L. Windmeyer and Pamela W. Freeman, Lambda 10 Project.

How Homophobia Hurts the College Fraternity

Homophobia is defined as the fear and hatred of people who love and who are sexually attracted to those of the same sex, and it includes the prejudice and acts of discrimination resulting from that fear and hatred. Derived from the Greek *homos*, meaning *same*, and *phobikos*, meaning *having a fear of and/or aversion for*, the term *homophobia* was coined by George Weinberg in 1972 in his book *Society and the Healthy Homosexual.*[1]

Like other forms of oppression, homophobia not only oppresses members of the target or minority groups (gays, lesbians, bisexuals, and transgendered people) but also, on many levels, hurts members of the agent or dominant group (heterosexuals). As a result, everyone eventually loses, and, more specifically, the negative effect of homophobia on fraternities is enormous.

Fraternities increasingly are coming under intense scrutiny by college and university administrators to guard against acts of discrimination and harassment in all their forms. Many times societal homophobia as well as sexism and other forms of prejudice compounded by peer pressure results in many of the negative actions associated with fraternity life, including, for example, substance abuse (alcohol, drugs, etc.), date or acquaintance rape, and other forms of harassment and violence.

Therefore, homophobic beliefs and actions not only pose potential harm to individuals of all sexual orientations but also jeopardize the very existence of the fraternity itself. Despite this, most Greek educational efforts either fail to address homophobia altogether or raise it simply as an isolated side issue unrelated to other issues and concerns. In actuality, homophobia harms all brothers and the goals of the college fraternity.

The following list adapts the theory Warren J. Blumenfeld devised in his book *Homophobia: How We All Pay the Price* to the college fraternity and the male experience.[2] This information may be useful to foster an educational dialogue about how homophobia hurts the college fraternity and to heighten awareness on issues of sexual orientation.

1. Homophobia jeopardizes brotherhood by inhibiting close, intimate friendships among fraternity men and their ability to show affection toward other men for fear of being perceived as gay.

2. Homophobia locks fraternity men into rigid gender-based roles that inhibit self expression and exploration of male identity. Men tend to foster anger toward homosexuality and gender roles because of their inability to settle their identity conflict and the impacts of social conditioning. Such practices restrict the development of a positive male identity, straight or gay.

3. Homophobia creates a negative environment for brotherhood by compromising the integrity of heterosexual fraternity men, enabling them to treat gay people badly. As such, homophobia is used as a tool for men to prove their heterosexuality by acting in the role of "gay hater."

4. Homophobia creates an environment in which fraternity men are expected to channel their feelings of affection or express emotions in potentially destructive ways. For example, fraternity men construct often dangerous and humiliating hazing rituals and consume excessive amounts of alcohol and drugs in order to allow men to touch or hug the skin of other men and/or to openly express their emotions with other fraternity brothers.

5. Homophobia can be used to stigmatize, silence, and target people who are perceived to be gay or labeled by others as gay. Such an environment may be hostile to these brothers and lead to harm.

6. Homophobia creates an environment in which fraternity brothers are sometimes pressured to "get laid" in order to establish their virility as heterosexual males and "real men." Men who do not "get laid" may risk being viewed as less than men or homosexual. Such environments lead to higher likelihood of rape and the use of women as objects of sexual conquest.

7. Homophobia is one cause for premature sexual involvement, which increases the chances of pregnancy and sexually transmitted diseases such as HIV. Fraternity men often may be pressured to

prove their heterosexuality and "normalcy" by becoming sexually active. Such a perspective impairs educational efforts on safer sex and sexuality awareness in the college fraternity.

8. Homophobia restricts communication among fraternity brothers and diminishes the possibility of creating a true sense of brotherhood and community, especially when the fraternity learns that another brother is gay.

9. Homophobia prevents fraternity chapters from receiving the benefits of friendship and leadership offered by gay fraternity brothers. Fraternity chapters may blackball or kick out members who are suspected to be gay. At other times, the gay brother may leave the fraternity because of harassment and/or fear of violence.

10. Homophobia remains the highest cause of suicide among youth.

11. Homophobia compromises the entire learning environment on a college campus for all students.

12. Homophobia inhibits the appreciation of diversity in a campus community and adds to the harassment and violence toward all minority groups. Such an environment impairs the progress of educational efforts on multiculturalism and diversity by not recognizing gay students in the campus dialogue.

13. Homophobia saps energy from more constructive fraternity projects. The time and energy could be better spent doing brotherhood activities or philanthropy.

Source: Shane L. Windmeyer and Pamela W. Freeman, Lambda 10 Project.

Notes

[1] George Weinberg, *Society and the Healthy Homosexual* (New York: St. Martin's Press, 1972).

[2] Warren J. Blumenfeld, *Homophobia: How We All Pay the Price* (Boston: Beacon Press, 1992).

Creating a Diversity Peer Education Program in the Greek System
by Matthew L. Supple

Close your eyes for a moment and think of the people you trust the most and whose opinions you value the highest. Think of the toughest decisions you have had to make and whom you sought out to help make those decisions. Chances are, the people you thought of included your parents and family members; significant people in your life, such as teachers and coaches; and your peers. Each of us can think of innumerable times when we have learned from and often right along with our peers—and I emphasize *with* because often our peers do not know the correct answers to the questions we ask. Rather, they know the correct questions to ask to help us uncover what we ourselves never knew or have known all along but have been unable to verbalize or articulate.

The self-discovery that occurs through peer interaction is the basis for many educational endeavors on college and university campuses nationwide. The concept is simple: We learn more about ourselves with the help of friends and peers who informally facilitate discussion and guide our conversations than we could on our own or through lectures or presentations. After all, our values and principles are often reinforced and influenced (if not based on) the values and principles of our friends. These concepts are the basis for peer education.

Peer education is the backbone of college life! Not a day goes by between the ages of 18 and 22 that students do not seek the advice of their friends. To this day, most of us consult our closest friends before we make a final determination about a major life decision. Greek-letter organizations provide the structure to meet and make friends with people who share many of the same values and beliefs. Fraternity and sorority chapters provide young adults with a place to gather to answer the questions of adulthood. Within these chapters—on college and university campuses across the nation—students meet as peers to find the support and answers they cannot get from their parents, their professors, their advisers, or adults in general. Students congregate to perform the age-old ceremony of shaping and forming personality traits and opinions that will often go unchallenged for a lifetime.

The Purpose of a Diversity Peer Education Program

Safe places are rare for many college students and often rarer for students who are gay, lesbian, or bisexual. Leaving the security of home and high school is a frightening experience for many. The challenge of feeling comfortable enough to talk about your darkest fears and your biggest dreams in a new environment clearly exists and requires enormous trust. Fraternities and sororities are where many find sanctuary, including gay, lesbian, and bisexual students.

Some might argue that true peer education does not exist in most fraternities and sororities, but in essence it occurs day in and day out. Simply put, fraternities and sororities exist because they provide a safe place for people with shared values and principles to come together and interact. Unfortunately, most peer education occurring within chapters is not geared toward raising awareness regarding issues of diversity, including being gay. Instead it is based on perpetuating existing stereotypes. The challenge, therefore, is to intentionally create an atmosphere that facilitates dialogue focusing on issues of diversity.

Certainly there is a need for diversity in all of its interpretations within fraternities and sororities, yet rarely is it present. That is why the Greek experience can be enhanced so greatly by a diversity peer education program. Being part of a diversity peer education program, a gay, lesbian, or bisexual student—whether closeted or out—has the opportunity to educate members of the community on important issues surrounding being gay, lesbian, or bisexual. Many closeted gay Greeks may not join a gay student organization for fear of being harassed or even outed. They may, on the other hand, join a diversity peer education program that deals with multiple issues of diversity. Diversity peer education programs provide gay, lesbian, and bisexual students with the means to confront and educate their friends and/or brothers and sisters on insensitive or hurtful comments or behavior without jeopardizing their secret. For out students, diversity peer education programs provide the opportunity to help educate members on all issues of diversity.

Not all conversations will be positive, however. Diversity issues are often controversial and almost always deeply rooted and sensitive. Both peer educators and other participants may need to seek extra support from an adviser or counselor. Diversity peer education programs are created to combat such issues as homophobia, racism, sexism, and other forms of oppression and discrimination. The purpose of a diversity peer education program is simple: to identify and train members of an already established community who will then educate the other members of the community through active and passive interventions.

Creating a Diversity Peer Education Program

Response to peer education programs on many campuses has been overwhelming. Groups and organizations such as resident assistants, academic tutors, and others have been very successful in supplementing a student's learning through peer education. An example of a peer education program probably exists on every campus in the country right now—perhaps not within the Greek community but certainly somewhere on campus.

Creating a diversity peer education program on campus simply requires educating members of established communities on how to facilitate open discussions among peers about difficult and often controversial issues. For a peer education program to succeed, there must first exist a safe environment in which conversation can thrive. There must also exist a need and purpose for peer education. An example may prove helpful. Fraternities are often accused of being bastions of homophobia. If a chapter has members who have been trained as peer educators through a diversity peer education program, those peer educators could do a number of things to introduce the topic of homosexuality into conversations. Once the topic has been introduced, participants in the conversation are forced to examine and confront their beliefs and opinions regarding homosexuality, sometimes for the first time. For closeted gay, lesbian, or bisexual members, participating in or observing such conversations could provide them with the opportunity to learn more about who they are, talk to others about the issue, or even find support. At the same time, it allows them to remain closeted until they are willing to come out with the support of other members.

To create a diversity peer education program, one must begin by drawing together a core group of students who share a common interest in promoting diversity awareness within the community and empowering them to act. This group's first order of business should be to assess the specific needs of the students, the programs already in existence, and the campus climate in general to determine what issues and challenges students face. Creating the program mission, goals, and objectives are also instrumental in establishing an effective program and should be identified through student discussion. Ideally, creating a diversity peer education program should be a proactive endeavor. It could, however, be used as a creative sanction under the appropriate circumstances.

The structure of the Greek community facilitates the process of forming a peer education program. Education through peer discussion allows individuals to ask questions and dispel stereotypes within a safe environment. It can be hypothesized that chapter members rely heavily on their peers within the chapter for guidance and support. Greek communities have long been accused of being homogeneous in both thought and behavior. Ironically, the most effective diversity peer education programs begin within the chapter. When accepted and trusted members of an internal community foster discussion of controversial issues, the community is more receptive to new ideas.

Any diversity peer education program must contain certain fundamental attributes in order to be successful. When you set up a model for diversity peer education within the Greek community on your campus, several questions will undoubtedly arise and need to be answered:

1. Who advises the group?
2. Who funds the group?
3. How is the program implemented?
4. How are the governing bodies of the fraternities and sororities involved?
5. How are peer educators identified?
6. How many peer educators are required to form a successful group?
7. How are peer educators trained?
8. What issues are included in training?

9. Do peer educators set up diversity programming for the entire Greek community or just their own chapter?
10. What campus resources exist?
11. What does a typical workshop look like?

Examples of Diversity Peer Education Programs

Although the specifics of each diversity peer education program will be unique on each campus, an example of a diversity peer education program exists within the Greek community at Indiana University at Bloomington. In 1992 a pilot program called Fraternal Implementation Regarding Strategic Training: Starting to Educate Peer Presenters (FIRST STEPP) was created in response to the growing need for change and action. Contributing to the need for a diversity peer education program were the changing demographics of students, an increased emphasis on awareness of issues of diversity on campus, public scrutiny of the Greek community, students' increased responsibility to be educators, an increase in the number of minority Greek-letter organizations, and an intensive look at the product that chapters were marketing to prospective members. The FIRST STEPP program, modeled after the DELTA program at the University of Arizona, was founded to increase the level of awareness among Greeks concerning issues of racism, sexism, sexual orientation, gender differences, and other issues of diversity. It was not founded as a reaction to a hostile climate but was a proactive effort to address a growing need. The program was also founded to create leadership opportunities for Greek members. The basic description is provided as a reference (see FIRST STEPP model below).

FIRST STEPP
Fraternal Implementation Regarding Strategic Training
Starting to Educate Peer Presenters

Outcome

To have a group of student leaders willing and prepared to facilitate diversity education programs and workshops on such issues as racism, gender roles, and sexual orientation within the Indiana University Greek system.

Goals

To have two representatives from between four to eight chapters who are committed to enhancing diversity education within their chapters. To experience and learn specific facilitation techniques. To identify and appreciate the unique characteristics of program participants with attention to meeting the diverse needs of individuals and groups within chapters. To develop an informal network among participants across chapters. To increase participants' skills and confidence level in workshop facilitation. To discuss fears participants have about facilitating workshops. To get chapters to begin to think and talk about such issues as racism, sexism, ableism, and sexual orientation.

Assumptions

Participants understand the importance of chapter programming and its impact on community development. Participants have reasonably good communication skills. Participants possess the willingness and ability to follow through with an ongoing time commitment. Participants will be in a chapter for the upcoming academic school year and must be willing to maintain this commitment during this time period. Participants have at least a basic knowledge of group dynamics and issues of diversity education. Facilitation skills can be learned. One of the primary blocks to our willingness to facilitate is fear.

Advantages

- Recognition from Inter/National Chapter.
- Increases chapter community.
- Personal reward and experience.
- Participants will be among the leaders not only on campus but also across the country in diversity among Greek chapters.

Peer presenters, the driving force behind the program, are student facilitators who live and work within their chapters to increase awareness of issues of diversity. They use workshops, one-on-one conversations, posters, videos, speakers, panels, and other avenues to spark discussion among members. The greatest strength of the program lies in the fact that it has a guaranteed impact: By drawing attention to issues such as homophobia, peer presenters allow students to confront their own fears, stereotypes, and prejudices in nonthreatening ways. Although not every student may gain an appreciation or understanding of different communities, many will. In essence, there is no failure.

Training peer presenters can consist of many elements. The Indiana University program consists of a two-day retreat focusing on teaching facilitation skills and providing the opportunity for presenters to practice those skills. A diversity education resource guide is also created in a collaborative effort by campus administrators to inform presenters of the many resources available to them. Peer presenters are then required to attend two workshops as participants before presenting on their own. It is important for peer presenters to understand that their role is not that of "expert" on the issues. Rather, their purpose is simply to engage others in dialogue and to get them to think.

The Benefits of a Diversity Peer Education Program

The benefits of a diversity peer education program are enormous when the program is implemented correctly. Providing a safe environment for members of groups to communicate and grow is essential to development and education. Allowing members of a population to become actively involved at a low level of risk can be incredibly empowering. I believe that providing an avenue for peers to help guide and focus discussion on issues of diversity within this safe environment produces the greatest laboratory for personality development possible.

Regardless of how much input, advice, and support an individual receives concerning a specific issue, however, the ultimate decision is the student's. Therefore, an individual must first be willing to take an objective look at his or her identity—the stereotypes, prejudices, and generalizations—before truly learning how to overcome them. Greek communities across the country have the opportunity—and the responsibility—to educate their members on issues of diversity, including sexual orientation. Peer education on homophobia and other diversity issues can create more positive, inclusive Greek communities. A formalized approach such as this recommended diversity peer education program is necessary to promote and facilitate discussion within the Greek community. Such a program will also provide students with leadership opportunities. The ultimate goal is to create an atmosphere that facilitates open dialogue focusing on issues of diversity. The outcome will be a supportive, inclusive, and caring community for all, including gay, lesbian, and bisexual students within the Greek community and on campus.

Matthew L. Supple has been the fraternity adviser at the University of Maryland since 1994. He is an initiate of Phi Kappa Psi fraternity (Indiana Alpha, DePauw University, 1991) and founded the diversity peer education program FIRST STEPP at Indiana University at Bloomington. He earned his master's degree from Indiana University in 1994, where he also received the Commission on Multicultural Understanding Award for outstanding diversity programming for his program, FIRST STEPP.

Creating a System to Report Harassment Directed Toward GLB Students

Everyone knows the adage, "An ounce of prevention is worth a pound of cure," and most of us probably agree with its wisdom. Ideally, with adequate resources and appropriate educational efforts, students should know to respect one another and harassment should not exist on college campuses. In truth, however, even those campuses where considerable attention is given to education about social issues are marked by incidents of harassment. In fact, the National Coalition of Anti-Violence Programs found when data were collected on antilesbian and antigay violence in 1995 that an increase in media attention, often owing to political action around gay issues, was accompanied by an increase in the number of reported incidents of violence targeting gays and lesbians, including harassment. The reported incidents were fewer or stayed the same as the previous year, when there was little public attention given to gay issues.[1] Sexual orientation is often what causes a person to become the target of harassment. Whether the harassment is intentional or inadvertent, its negative effects can interrupt the ability of the victim to attend classes, engage in social activities, study, and lead a generally comfortable student life.

Following a model that had been established for responding to racially motivated incidents at Indiana University, the Gay, Lesbian, Bisexual Anti-harassment Team (GLBAT) was formed in 1990 in direct response to requests from students. This team provides a recourse for all students when they are faced with harassment based on sexual orientation. The team also reports data several times each year for use in monitoring the campus climate on issues surrounding sexual orientation. With a lack of civil rights legislation to mandate the compilation of statistics on these data, the voluntary documentation of harassment based on sexual orientation that is occurring on campuses can provide extremely useful information for educational interventions and policy development.

About the Team

Consisting of fewer than ten staff members, faculty, and graduate students from various departments on campus, team members are appointed by the vice-chancellor for student affairs. Each member has expertise in diversity issues and conflict resolution. The team meets weekly to review reports and consider strategies for carrying out its two basic purposes, which are to (1) assist and support students who report an incident of discrimination based on sexual orientation in finding a resolution and (2) document information about these incidents in order to combat discrimination more effectively.

All cases are kept confidential, and students who report are assured that they will be consulted before any action is taken in their cases. In this way, reporting to the team can be an empowering experience for the victims, in contrast to the sense of helplessness most victims have experienced during the harassment.

What Kinds of Incidents Can Be Reported to the Team?

Several of the stories submitted for *Out on Fraternity Row* include descriptions of harassing behaviors or fears of brothers who believed that they would be harassed if their sexual orientation were to be discovered. For example, a banner is hung outside a fraternity house to announce that a brother in a rival house is gay. Or the most commonly used slur when brothers become angry with one another is "faggot." Or a brother withdraws from school when his room is vandalized after it is learned that he is gay.

Indeed, in the years that the GLBAT has existed, there have been reports about harassing behaviors in fraternities from both fraternity members and the campus at large. Having a confidential, safe mechanism for reporting, members who have experienced harassment because of being gay or being perceived to be gay have been able to consider alternative ways of addressing the harassment.

What Happens When an Incident is Reported to the Team?

When a report is received by the team, there are three possible outcomes: (1) The report is kept for data only, and no action is taken. (2) The case is referred to an existing office or agency that functions on campus or in the community. (3) A direct intervention is carried out by a member or members of the GLBAT. All reports are listed and periodically publicized on campus and in the community but with no identifying information included in the summary. This list serves as an educational tool to help the community learn about homophobia and harassment and to help eradicate denial that such incidents really do occur in our midst. Often students prefer this outcome because they know that their report can contribute to greater understanding on campus, even though they may not feel comfortable having a direct intervention by a team member. Sometimes cases are referred to outside agencies, such as to national fraternity headquarters if the case involves chapter policy. When a direct team intervention is desired, the chapter officers on the local level sometimes are asked to assume a leadership role in bringing brothers together to process the incident. One common result of such processing is an increased attention to educating chapter members about sexual orientation, homophobia, and harassment. If the victim wants only minimal contact with the chapter, dialogue can occur in written form or a team member can meet with persons within the chapter in the absence of the person filing the report. In some cases the victim has requested direct team action but with anonymity of the reporter. At the heart of the process is the decision-making role of the victim. No action is taken without the full approval of the victim. The following flow chart summarizes the process followed by the GLBAT.

Process Followed by the Gay, Lesbian, and Bisexual Anti-harassment Team

An incident is brought to the attention of the team.
Options for action are discussed, and a team member contacts
the individual who filed the report.

Team members and the person who is reporting the
incident discuss what kind of response is most desired. This person,
not the team, will make the decision.

▼   ▼

A team member follows the case
to advise/assist the person who
reported the incident.

Offices external to the team
are contacted:

• Department where the
alleged offense occurred

• Campus judicial system
(if alleged offender is a student)

• Affirmative action office
(if the alleged offender is a faculty or
staff member or a student)

• Academic complaint procedure
(if the alleged offender is a faculty
member or administrator)

• Legal procedure
(Campus or community police, attorneys,
or the Human Rights Commission
may be contacted.)

A decision is reached
about what kind of
result is desired.

The team takes appropriate action:

An action plan is developed between
the team and the person who
reported the incident. The plan
addresses the following possible
responses:

• Meditation

• Educational intervention

• Other actions

If no action is deemed necessary,
a report is filed for informational
purposes only.

An intervention is made.

▼   ▼

Results are discussed by the team and evaluated. The file is
closed, with follow-up options continued with the person who
reported the incident.

A report is filed with end-of-the-year statistics.

Note: All steps are discussed at team meetings while a case is active.
Follow-up discussions also occur at team meetings.

What Is the Benefit of Having a Team?

As more support is shown on campuses for gay, lesbian, and bisexual students and more students consider whether to reveal their sexual orientation, it is important for students to know where they can seek assistance if they are harassed. Knowing that an administrative response mechanism is in place can be a positive influence in supporting a student's decision to come out. By having the GLBAT as a central student-affairs function, fraternities do not need to feel that they are being highlighted as the area in most need of such a team on campus. Also, if a student is afraid to report to other chapter members, there may be some comfort in knowing that the team is not affiliated with any one organization, thereby encouraging the student to file a report.

One of the most valuable by-products of having had a team in place on our campus for seven years has been the documentation that has resulted from students filing reports. The documentation and resulting data have proven that harassment motivated by homophobia is real, that students need a place to report the incidents, and that further education is always important. Four years after we created the GLBAT at Indiana University, a student movement to secure funding for a gay, lesbian, and bisexual student support services office was successful. The success of the students' effort was attributed in large measure to having documentation about harassment and the prevalence of ignorance about sexual-orientation issues.

Campuses wishing to form a response team are advised to follow these guidelines:

1. Secure administrative endorsement prior to starting the team.
2. Select team members who are respected on campus for their sensitivity, their understanding of sexual-orientation issues, and their skill at handling conflict in a constructive manner.
3. Solicit support from student leaders prior to forming the team.
4. Communicate clearly that confidentiality will be protected.
5. Have a method for compiling and publishing data in place, and be sure that public relations staff understand the intent of publishing such data.

When an institution cares enough about gay students to establish a team for responding to harassment, a strong message is communicated to the general community. This message is that harassment will not be tolerated and that, accordingly, gay students are valued. Such a message, combined with efforts to stop harassment can go a long way toward creating a safer campus climate for gay students.

Source: Shane L. Windmeyer and Pamela W. Freeman, Lambda 10 Project.

Notes

[1]National Coalition of Anti-Violence Programs, *Anti-Lesbian/Gay Violence in 1995* (New York, 1996), 1.

Checklist for a Climate of Acceptance

Diversity educators advocate setting a standard of acceptance and appreciation as a normal part of an institution's daily activities. This approach to fostering inclusiveness and respect calls for attention to diversity in all aspects of an organization's routine. One or two token diversity programs each year will not fulfill the need for education. Building a climate of acceptance in fraternities requires a commitment at all levels, ranging from individual members to the group's headquarters and including the university administration. The following checklist is suggested as a guide for creating a climate of acceptance in fraternities—a climate in which a brother who is gay may feel a sense of safety and support among his brothers.

Individual Members

_____ 1. Refrain from ridiculing persons on the basis of sexual orientation, such as through jokes, name-calling, and display of demeaning images or messages.

_____ 2. Confront others who may ridicule or harass persons on the basis of sexual orientation.

_____ 3. Be committed to learning about sexual orientation, as shown through participation in educational programs and personal study.

_____ 4. Assume responsibility for learning how to respond to a brother who is gay and wants or needs to talk.

_____ 5. Insist that leaders of the chapter state their commitment to diversity, including that pertaining to sexual orientation.

Chapters

_____ 1. Include expectations for appreciating diversity in training for pledges and actives.

_____ 2. Create a diversity statement, either from national headquarters or locally developed, that promotes respect for all people, regardless of sexual orientation.

_____ 3. Display prominently the diversity statement in the house and/or in printed materials about the chapter.

_____ 4. Develop a procedure for addressing harassing behaviors, including those directed at persons on the basis of their sexual orientation.

_____ 5. Contribute to the education of other chapters on campus by modeling acceptance and appreciation of diverse memberships.

_____ 6. Support individual members who wish to state publicly their support for persons who are gay, lesbian, bisexual, or transgendered.

_____ 7. Sponsor and support events that contribute to understanding of sexual orientation issues.

_____ 8. Encourage brothers to be honest with each other by creating an atmosphere of support for differences. Remember: This leads to a stronger sense of brotherhood.

_____ 9. Have policies that apply to guests and alumni, making it clear that it is not acceptable to use demeaning language or harass members on the basis of sexual orientation.

_____ 10. Periodically review traditions, such as songs and events, to be sure that language and actions are not demeaning to people who are gay, lesbian, bisexual, or transgendered.

National Headquarters and Professional Fraternity Associations

_____ 1. Promote understanding about sexual-orientation issues through educational materials that have been prepared at the national level and made readily available through publicity to chapters.

_____ 2. Publicize a strong statement about appreciation for diversity and respect that includes sexual orientation.

_____ 3. Provide resources to assist chapters with educational initiatives that are designed to increase understanding about sexual orientation. National chapter consultants who travel to various college campuses should be prepared to address problems and questions about sexual-orientation issues.

_____ 4. State an expectation of zero tolerance for harassment of any kind toward people on the basis of sexual orientation.

_____ 5. Establish procedures for holding chapters accountable if they condone or tolerate harassment based on sexual orientation.

_____ 6. Highlight the accomplishments of gay brothers in national publications.

_____ 7. Review periodically any publications, rituals, and traditional events that include text or behaviors that ridicule or demean people on the basis of sexual orientation and take steps to ensure that such text and behaviors will be discontinued.

_____ 8. Communicate with university personnel the commitment of the fraternity to fostering an environment of inclusiveness, respect, and appreciation for diversity and offer to work with university personnel in responding to any incidents that may occur in the fraternity that would contradict this commitment.

_____ 9. Provide strong leadership in working with other national headquarters toward encouraging a climate of respect and inclusiveness.

University Personnel

_____ 1. Communicate university standards and expectations in regard to diversity to all student organizations, including fraternities.

_____ 2. Make sure you are available to fraternity leaders to assist with planning educational efforts to increase understanding about diversity, including sexual orientation (i.e., develop a diversity peer education program).

_____ 3. Develop a procedure for responding to incidents of harassment based on sexual orientation and communicate to fraternity members that such procedures are available.

_____ 4. Assert a position in support of diversity and individual rights when faced with political pressure to exclude gays, lesbians, bisexuals, and transgendered persons from regular university life, including jobs and benefits.

_____ 5. Provide educational sessions for house directors and housing-corporation boards to explain the university's standards and expectations in support of diversity.

_____ 6. Review periodically all institutional publications and policies to ensure that language that ridicules, demeans, or excludes people because of sexual orientation is eliminated.

_____ 7. Support establishment of a Delta Lambda Phi (a national fraternity for gay and progressive men) chapter on your campus.

_____ 8. Inform faculty and staff who present educational programs in fraternities about human sexuality, sexually transmitted diseases, and related topics not to be heterosexist and assume all members of fraternities and sororities are heterosexual.

_____ 9. Ensure that staff in campus resource offices, such as counselors, health professionals, and advisers, are trained about sexual-orientation issues.

_____ 10. Provide leadership for creating supportive campus environments for other institutions and policy makers.

Source: Shane L. Windmeyer and Pamela W. Freeman, Lambda 10 Project.

Policy Statements and Resolutions Affirming Diversity

Sample policies and resolutions pertaining to sexual orientation are highlighted to affirm diversity on a college campus. Each represents possible models for implementation by chapters, national fraternity headquarters, national fraternity associations, and institutions of higher education.

Our Fraternity's Chapter Diversity Statement

Our Fraternity is an all-inclusive society of brothers. It values differences in people and diversity within our organization, the campus community, and society at large. It recognizes the different perspectives and contributions an all-inclusive people can make toward improving the brotherhood of the fraternity and humanity.

Our Fraternity policy is to welcome and reach out to people of different ages, nationalities, ethnic groups, physical abilities and qualities, sexual orientations, health status, religions, backgrounds, and educational experiences as well as to any others who may experience discrimination or abuse.

Our Fraternity does not discriminate against any group or individual. In fact, the fraternity will actively oppose any and all forms of discrimination.

Our Fraternity also desires to help the Greek community and society at large to develop similar policies and practices that support diversity and assist in making the world a better place for all to live.

Shane L. Windmeyer and Pamela W. Freeman, Lambda 10 Project.

Source: Adapted from the diversity policy of the National Society of Performance and Instruction.

National Fraternity Headquarters

Policy Statement on Sexual Orientation

The following is based on the Zeta Beta Tau Statement on Sexual Orientation, as stated in the Fraternity Code of Ethics, Section III. The italics indicate omissions or changes from the original policy.

National Fraternity does not judge its brothers on the basis of sexual orientation or preference. Thus, if a brother declares that he is "gay," we recognize *this* to be his personal right, free of censure or coercion. Of course, no chapter is required to offer membership to anyone, but it should not use "orientation or preference" as a reason not to offer membership. It may not expel any brother on the basis of "orientation or preference."

Aside from the fact of "orientation," a brother's lifestyle, if it is a gay lifestyle, may be unattractive to other brothers, *just as a straight lifestyle may be unattractive to some brothers. This does not categorize either brother as "right" or "wrong" so long as they are respectful.*

National Fraternity does follow an ethical code when it comes to sexual conduct. Sexual conduct must always be consensual, nonexploitative or coercive, and between equals. *Regardless of an individual's sexual orientation,* we encourage our chapters to process sexual ethical issues on both an informal and formal basis

National Fraternity does believe that brotherhood is incompatible with sexual conduct between members. and we encourage the chapter to have a respectful conversation *about this belief.*

The fraternity's position is brief, simple, and clear. Behavior, not sexual orientation, is the basis for evaluating the worth of a brother.

For those who disagree or who are concerned, the fraternity's policy makes it clear that concerns, objections, even disagreement with the policy does not classify such a person as "right" or "wrong." Our policy states, however, that such concerns or disagreements do not empower a person to deny membership to other persons because their beliefs or *sexual orientations* are different or to remove a person from membership for similar reasons.

Our policy respects *all sexual orientations as well as the individuals who may disagree.* It urges that chapters, with the assistance of professionals, talk about their feelings and concerns.

Source: Shane L. Windmeyer and Pamela W. Freeman, Lambda 10 Project.

Western Regional Greek Conference

Resolution on Heterosexism
Within the Campus Greek Community

Whereas, the Greek community is a vital part of undergraduate campus life and seeks to promote and to engage students in an ongoing process of personal and group development and to provide an understanding and appreciation of the diversity of the peoples on the campus; and

Whereas, heterosexism, behavior that makes individuals the target of oppression, harassment, or discrimination based on their homosexual or bisexual orientation, is directly counter to the ideals of the educational experience and shall not be tolerated or permitted; and

Whereas, the Western Regional Greek Conference has addressed these issues in its 1991 programming; therefore

Be it resolved, that the Western Regional Greek Conference member campuses, through their Interfraternity and Panhellenic councils, be strongly encouraged to challenge all behaviors and attitudes that are heterosexist in nature; and

Be it further resolved, that Western Regional Greek Conference member campuses, through their Interfraternity and Panhellenic councils, discourage and seek to ban from their campuses all activities, competitions, social events and themes, membership recruitment attractions, and other practices that are heterosexist in nature; and

Be it further resolved, that the Western Regional Greek Conference strongly encourages its member campuses to develop and implement ongoing sexual-orientation awareness, education, and sensitivity programs for the Greek communities; and

Be it further resolved, that the Western Regional Greek Conference member campuses be made aware of this resolution through the WRGC newsletter.

Source: Adopted at the 1991 Western Regional Greek Conference.

Association of Fraternity Advisors

Resolution on Heterosexism Within the Greek Community

Whereas, an understanding and appreciation of the diversity of peoples of the campus and world community is one of the goals of the student development cocurriculum on the college campus; and

Whereas, the Greek community is a vital part of the student development cocurriculum and is maintained to promote and engage students in an ongoing process of personal and group development; and

Whereas, heterosexism, defined as behavior that makes individuals the target of oppression, harassment, or discrimination based on their homosexual or bisexual orientation, is directly counter to the ideals of the educational experience and must not be tolerated or permitted; now therefore

Be it resolved, that the Association of Fraternity Advisors strongly encourages the campus Greek affairs professional to implement sexual-orientation awareness, education, and sensitivity programs for the Greek community; and

Be it further resolved, that the campus Greek affairs professional or the appropriate authority be strongly encouraged to challenge Greek chapter or member behaviors or attitudes that are heterosexist in nature; and,

Be it further resolved, that each men's and women's fraternity and sorority be strongly encouraged to implement sexual-orientation awareness, education, and sensitivity programs on all membership levels and to develop appropriate responses to heterosexist behaviors; and

Be it further resolved, that all Association members and an executive officer of general fraternity and sorority be made aware of this resolution.

Source: Adopted December 1, 1990, at the Annual Business Meeting, Association of Fraternity Advisors.

University Statement on Affirming Diversity

The [University] is committed to celebrating the rich diversity of people in the campus community to include all students, faculty, staff, alumni, and guests of the university. We believe that our educational environments must foster freedom of thought and opinion in the spirit of mutual respect. All of our programs, activities, and interactions are enriched by accepting each other as we are and by celebrating our uniquenesses as well as our commonalities.

The diversity of the campus community takes many forms. It includes differences related to race, ethnicity, national origin, gender, sexual orientation, religion, age, and ability. We believe that any attempt to oppress any individual or group is a threat to everyone in the community. We are guided by the principle that celebrating diversity enriches and empowers the lives of all people.

Therefore, everyone who chooses this university must understand that we will not tolerate any form of bigotry, harassment, intimidation, threat, or abuse, whether verbal or written, physical or psychological, direct or implied. Alcohol or substance abuse, ignorance, or "it was just a joke" will not be accepted as an excuse. Such behavior will be dealt with appropriately through the disciplinary process.

Our campus community is a rich, alive, and dynamic academic environment that is designed to enable all individuals to stretch and grow to their full potential. Only by understanding and celebrating our diversities can we create a safe learning environment in which innovation, individuality, and creativity are maintained. We pledge ourselves to this end.

Source: Shane L. Windmeyer and Pamela W. Freeman, Lambda 10 Project. Adapted from the Statement on Diversity from the Indiana University Department of Residence Life, Campus Life Division.

Indiana University Code of Student Rights, Responsibilities, and Conduct

Non-Discrimination and Harassment Based on Sexual Orientation Policies

Under this policy, the university will not exclude any person from participation in its programs or activities on the basis of arbitrary considerations of such characteristics as age, color, disability, ethnicity, gender, marital status, national origin, race, religion, sexual orientation, or veteran status.

Harassment Based on Sexual Orientation

a. Students are responsible to respect each other's personal dignity regardless of sexual orientation.
b. A student has the right to be free from harassment based on sexual orientation.
   (1) A student has the right to be free from harassment based on sexual orientation in any building or at any location on any university property.
   (2) A student has the right to be free from harassment based on sexual orientation that occurs in a building or on property that is not university property if the harassment arises from university activities that are being conducted off the university campus, or if the harassment compromises the security of the university community or the integrity of the educational process.
c. Harassment includes any behavior, physical or verbal, that victimizes or stigmatizes an individual on the basis of sexual orientation and involves any of the following:

(1) The use of physical force or violence to restrict the freedom of action or movement of another person or to endanger the health or safety of another person;

(2) Physical or verbal behavior that involves an express or implied threat to interfere with an individual's personal safety, academic efforts, employment, or participation in university sponsored extracurricular activities and causes the person to have a reasonable apprehension that such harm is about to occur;

(3) Physical behavior that has the purpose or reasonably foreseeable effect of interfering with an individual's personal safety academic efforts, employment, or participation in university-sponsored extracurricular activities and causes the person to have a reasonable apprehension that such harm is about to occur.

(4) The conduct has the effect of unreasonably interfering with an individual's work or academic performance or creating an intimidating, hostile, or offensive working or learning environment.

e. Indiana University administrators are responsible for publicizing and implementing the university's harassment policy in their respective jurisdictions.

f. Students who believe that they are victims of harassment based on sexual orientation may obtain information concerning the university's policy and complaint procedures at the office of the campus Affirmative Action Officer or the Dean of Students.

Source: Indiana University, *Code of Student Rights, Responsibilities, and Conduct,* "Part I: Student Rights and Responsibilities," 1997.

RESOURCES

Visibility comes in many forms and with varying degrees of acceptance. These resources are meant to provide personal support, educational materials, and links to professional organizations. This information does not represent an exhaustive resource listing. Instead the organizations appearing in this section are resources that have educational goals similar to the Lambda 10 Project and that correspond to the subject matter of this anthology. Current updates, educational links, and other relevant resources also will be provided on the Lambda 10 Project's Web site, located at http://www.indiana.edu/~lambda10.

Association of Fraternity Advisors

AFA is the professional association of campus fraternity and sorority advisers, existing to enhance the positive influence of the fraternity and sorority experience. The association has a committee that proactively works on diversity issues, including matters pertaining to sexual orientation.

3901 West 86th St., Suite 390
Indianapolis, IN 46268-1702
(317) 876-4691
fax (317) 872-1134

National Interfraternity Conference

NIC serves to advocate the needs of its member fraternities through the enrichment of the fraternity experience, advancement and growth of the fraternity community, and enhancement of the educational mission of the host institution. The NIC provides information services, educational resources, staff training, and presentations to its member fraternities. The NIC consists of 62 national and interna-

*tional general fraternities and helps to lead the fraternity movement
across the country.*

    3901 W. 86th St., Suite 390

    Indianapolis, IN 46268-1791

    (317) 872-1112

    fax (317) 872-1134

National Pan Hellenic Council

*NPHC represents the association of the eight historically African-
American fraternities and sororities. Each organization works together to foster the growth and future of the African-American fraternity system. NPHC may be contacted through any member
fraternal organization.*

Delta Lambda Phi Fraternity's National Headquarters

*Delta Lambda Phi is a national social fraternity for gay, bisexu-
al and progressive men and has 21 chapters across the United States.
Organized around the experience of collegiate Greek societies, the fraternity works to enhance the quality of life among progressive men,
irrespective of sexual orientation, by providing dignified and pur-
poseful social and recreational activities.*

    c/o: Lou Camera

    1008 10th St., Suite 374

    Sacramento, CA 95814

    (800) 587-3728

Parents, Families, and Friends of Lesbians and Gays

*PFLAG promotes the health and well-being of gay, lesbian, and
bisexual people, their families, and friends through support, education, and advocacy. PFLAG offers several resources on issues surrounding sexual orientation and has more than 400 affiliates in
local communities worldwide.*

    1101 14th St. NW, Suite 1030

    Washington, DC 20005

    (202) 638-4200

    fax (202) 638-0243

    http://www.pflag.org

Human Rights Campaign

HRC is the largest national lesbian and gay political organization seeking to create an America in which lesbian and gay people are ensured of their basic equal rights. HRC actively participates in every stage of the legislative process as well as sponsors specific on-going educational programs such as the National Coming Out Project.

> 1101 14th St. NW
> Washington, DC 20005
> (202) 628-4160
> fax (202) 347-5323
> http://www.hrcusa.org

National Gay and Lesbian Task Force

NGLTF serves as the national resource center for grassroots lesbian, gay, bisexual, and transgender organizations. NGLTF helps to strengthen the gay and lesbian movement at the state and local level while connecting these activities to a national vision of change.

> 2320 17th St. NW
> Washington, DC 20009-2702
> (202) 332-6483
> fax (202) 332-0207
> http://www.ngltf.org

Lambda Legal Defense and Education Fund

Lambda is a national organization committed to achieving full recognition of the civil rights of lesbians, gay men, and people with HIV through impact litigation, education, and public-policy work. The organization has national and regional expertise in all aspects of sexual-orientation and HIV-related policy and law.

> 120 Wall St.
> New York, NY 10005
> (212) 809-8585
> fax (212) 809-0055
> http://www.gaysource.com/gs/ht/oct95/lambda.html

Campaign to End Homophobia

The Campaign to End Homophobia strives to create educational resources and produces several teaching materials for leading introductory homophobia workshops.

Box 819
Cambridge, MA 02139
(617) 868-8280

National Association of Student Personnel Administrators

NASPA serves as a professional association for higher-education and student-affairs administrators. Included within NASPA are two formal networks titled the Fraternity and Sorority Network and the Gay, Lesbian, and Bisexual Concerns Network. Each provide dialogue on issues related to the network and encourage activities to provide professional development.

1875 Connecticut Ave. NW, Suite 418
Washington, DC 20009-5728
(202) 265-7500
fax (202) 797-1157
http://www.naspa.org

American College Personnel Association (ACPA)

ACPA provides leadership for student-affairs professionals in addressing issues and trends in higher education and serves to enhance and develop their abilities to contribute to student learning. ACPA has created a Standing Committee on Lesbian, Gay, and Bisexual Awareness. The standing committee has been involved in several campus projects and collaborations with other national organizations.

One Dupont Circle NW, Suite 300
Washington, DC 20036-1110
(202) 835-2272
fax (202) 296-3286
http://www.acpa.nche.edu

Association of College Unions International (ACUI)

ACUI is a professional association that is dedicated to enhancing campus life through programs, services, and publications, its common goal being to unify the college union and student-activities field. Within ACUI, the Gay, Lesbian, Bisexual Concerns Committee produces resources for college campuses to be more aware of issues surrounding sexual orientation.

One City Centre, Suite 200
120 W. Seventh St.
Bloomington, IN 47404-3925
(812) 855-8550
fax (812) 855-0162
http://www.indiana.edu/~acui

Lesbian, Bisexual, Gay Centers and Programs

Lesbian, Bisexual, Gay Centers and Programs are growing on college campuses across the United States. As such, the professionals working in these offices have a wealth of information pertaining to the lesbian, bisexual, gay, and transgendered college student experience. Information for these centers and programs may be found on the World Wide Web.

http://www.uic.edu/orgs/lgbt/index.html or
http://www.indiana.edu/~glbserv

Lambda 10 Project

The Lambda 10 Project works to heighten the visibility of gay, lesbian and bisexual members of college fraternities by serving as a clearinghouse for resources and educational materials related to sexual orientation and the fraternity and sorority experience. The Lambda 10 Project pledges to provide educational resources on issues of sexual orientation within the Greek system as well as to maintain a Web site that lists updates, provides educational materials, and encourages dialogue on being gay in a college fraternity.

Indiana University Bloomington
705 East Seventh St.
Bloomington, IN 47405-3809
(812) 855-4463
fax (812) 855-4465
E-mail lambda10@indiana.edu
http://www.indiana.edu/~lambda10

It's All Greek to Me
Definitions of commonly used Greek terminology

active: a fully initiated member of a sorority or fraternity

alumnus/alumna: an initiated member who is no longer an undergraduate

bid: a formal invitation to join a sorority or fraternity

blackball: to deny a bid to a rushee or terminate the membership of an active or pledge

chapter: a local group of a national or international fraternal organization

formal rush: the period set aside for structured rushing

hell week: slang term used by some Greek members to describe activities during the week leading up to initiation

initiation: the formal ceremony or traditional ritual that brings the pledge, or associate, into full membership of a sorority or fraternity

interfraternity council: the programming body of collegiate fraternities

legacy: a rushee who is a granddaughter or grandson, daughter or son, or sister or brother of a member of a particular sorority or fraternity

line: the new members of a National Pan-Hellenic Council sorority or fraternity

National Pan-Hellenic Council or Black Greek Council: the governing body of collegiate sororities and fraternities that are historically African-American

Panhellenic Association: the central programming body of collegiate sororities

pledge (also *associate*): a new member who has not been initiated

pledgeship: the time when new members learn the history, traditions, and goals of the sorority or fraternity

rush: the social activity in which mutual choice and selection occurs to seek and determine new sorority or fraternity membership

rushee: person interested in becoming a member of a sorority or fraternity

Source: Adapted from "It's All Greek to Me..." Compiled by Jane S. Campaigne, Administrative Coordinator for Greek Life & Assistant Director for Russell Union at Georgia Southern University. Interfraternity Institute. 1998.